PHILOSOPHY AND HIP-HOP

Philosophy and Hip-Hop

Ruminations on Postmodern Cultural Form

Julius Bailey

PHILOSOPHY AND HIP-HOP
Copyright © Julius Bailey, 2014.

Softcover reprint of the hardcover 1st edition 2014 978-1-137-42993-3

First published in 2014 by
PALGRAVE MACMILLAN®
in the United States—a division of St. Martin's Press LLC,
175 Fifth Avenue, New York, NY 10010.

Where this book is distributed in the UK, Europe and the rest of the world,
this is by Palgrave Macmillan, a division of Macmillan Publishers Limited,
registered in England, company number 785998, of Houndmills,
Basingstoke, Hampshire RG21 6XS.

Palgrave Macmillan is the global academic imprint of the above companies
and has companies and representatives throughout the world.

Palgrave® and Macmillan® are registered trademarks in the United States,
the United Kingdom, Europe and other countries.

ISBN 978-1-349-49199-5   ISBN 978-1-137-42994-0 (eBook)
DOI 10.1057/9781137429940

Library of Congress Cataloging-in-Publication Data

Bailey, Julius, 1970–
    Philosophy and Hip-Hop : ruminations on postmodern cultural form /
Julius Bailey, PhD.
        pages cm

    1. Rap (Music)—Philosophy. 2. Rap (Music)—History and criticism.
I. Title.
ML3531.B367 2014
782.421649—dc23   2013049346

A catalogue record of the book is available from the British Library.

Design by Newgen Knowledge Works (P) Ltd., Chennai, India.

First edition: June 2014

10 9 8 7 6 5 4 3 2 1

To all Philosophers, and those in preparation, who dare to expand our discipline

Contents

Foreword

Starting from the Bottom: The Meta-Philosophy of Hip-Hop Set against the Moral Condemnation of This Art Form Masquerading as Thinking

Tommy J. Curry

Hip-hop suffers, and like the melaninated voices that sing its songs, like the dark bodies that dance its rhythms, their Black pains are often unheard in the academy. The dominant mode of hip-hop scholarship is not in itself *critical*, but elevated to the level of a *critique*, because, as a polemic, it participates in a moral and political condemnation of the symbols, language, and prose Black folk use to express their lives. Largely framed by the implicit moral imperative to recognize the intersections of race, class, and gender, much of the work on hip-hop acts as if simply uttering these intersectional categories, even without any empirical account of how racism, sexual exploitation, and poverty concretely effect and determine the messages that reflect the conditions of urban oppression communicated by the lyrics and videos of many hip-hop artists, gives their account of Blackness moral authority/superiority. It is as if the liberal utopias that are asserted by ubiquitous discourses of equality, feminism, progressivism, and democracy matter more than the ghetto/dystopia that Black language is submerged within. There is a plethora of scholarship that objectifies the language and culture surrounding hip-hop as decadent, misogynistic, materialistic, and immature, and it is in the identification of these pathologies within Black folk and the aesthetics they perform that academic currency, and disciplinary recognition of these writings on hip-hop are deemed insightful and viable as academic scholarship.

The dominant schema of America's liberal democratic order suggests that history be read and time be gauged by the falling away of the organized oppressive structures of the past, where the present is known by the remnants of the last-fading vestiges of racism. The future will be identified by the absence of the barriers and attitudes of both past and present filled with only enlightened white folks who are antiracist, anticlassist, and ever progressive despite America's Puritan sexual hang-ups. Hip-hop scholarship has been no less aggrandized among the bastard postcolonial enlightenments suckling at the bosoms of white disciplines for a taste of their paradigmatic elixirs, where marrying the disdain of Black music with discourses of power, the rhetorical tools of deconstruction, and the pathology of sexism and misogyny allow entrance into the academy. As axiom, academic education determines for us what figures and categories are synonymous with knowledge; it is the bourgeois right of seeking to be "educated." So too is the ethical barometer placed on writings about hip-hop; the slow chipping away, the endless deconstruction of hip-hop should make it not what it "is," but what we, the academic elites, the moral intelligentsia, think (want) it to be.

It is within this constraint of writing about hip-hop generally in the academy, and specifically in philosophy that I met Julius Bailey and encountered his project, *Philosophy and Hip-Hop: Ruminations on a Postmodern Cultural Form.* Hip-hop, as a genre of expression commenting on the postindustrial failings of the America through the manipulation of alternative musical forms, lyrical styles, and technology, is well known, but how to study these expressions beyond objectifying them and encapsulating them within the epidermalized spectacles of Blackness remains a mystery. A mystery, that is, until Bailey decided to engage in a philosophical project that thinks through hip-hop as both a location within the Black community, and one that expands well beyond these origins in the Black community. Hip-hop is a reflective global cultural community that inspires as well as questions the validity of its cultural symbols and messages. Instead of fixating hip-hop upon the historical and material culture of Blackness, Bailey engages in a conceptual project that asks if we can think of hip-hop as the medium through which we understand the postindustrial matrices of capitalist failure and the solidification of racial politics the world over. In arguing that hip-hop must be understood as both art form and community, Bailey has provided an aesthetic context to look forward in the postmodern, hyper-capitalist crisis of intellectual and material commodification that subjects knowledge and product to profit-based valuation. Bailey has suggested an alternative to fixating on the already somewhat-given-racialized-assumption that the Black community is coextensive with the hip-hop nation as articulated in Jared Ball's *I Mix What I Like,* which is motivated by an internal colonialization model of Black existence. Instead, Bailey contends there is a reason to consider—to believe even— that hip-hop can be viewed as a dislocated location that pushes both participants and observers to consider the phenomenological boundaries of their social/cultural/economic location in history.

It is from here that hip-hop retains the historical consciousness of the racialized community that suffers under the neocolonial, hyper-modern commodification of both person and product. At the same time, it strives to overturn the need for teleological accounts that routinely accompany its claims about community, especially when the hip-hop community so frequently finds itself in opposition to the calamitous, oppressive failures of modernity. In being an aesthetic of the existential/political/social/cultural/economic crisis of white supremacy, the music, the dance, the various expressions of Blackness that expresses hip-hop need not be confined to the driving ideologies of the sociohistorical locations from which it is produced. The performance of hip-hop is not simply the imitation of the trends that are now "hip-hop." Rather, the act of performing, the corporeal manipulation of dance and the lyrical contouring of soulful language, is the result of the process of thinking about one's location and place in an ever-changing community that needs, as a function of its dynamism, new messages, concepts, and representations daily. As Bailey says in his introduction to this work,

> The idea of the community at stake departs from modernity's *sensus communis.* Understanding this community as a manifestation of the postmodern or post-historical presents both a challenge and an opportunity. Before jumping into unsettled waters, a simple diagram of community must be traced, touching upon a series of pivotal knots in postmodern institutionalized bodies. These include transgression and excess, immanence and transcendence, art and creativity, reconciliation and the construction of a postmodern community. This diagram will prove to be a supportive underpinning for the philosophical dialogue that will follow.

These pivotal points are, however, not meant to impose a specific order or hierarchy. They are simply the connecting dots of a figure that can be seen as completed by the mind, but which needs to be traced actually in order for a concrete image to emerge.

The postmodern, postcolonial, and rhizomatic formulations of a cosmopolitan community that is communal, but not homogeneous, are but idle abstract idealism until such endeavors take into account the ever-changing dynamics of Blackness as a human reality that, in its contact with, resistance to, and rejection of white supremacism as a valid model for the thinking through of difference, maintains diversity and variety as tools with which the community can overcome the homogenizing ethos of racist neocolonial imperialism they have so frequently encountered in America and indeed, around the world. The negotiation of human existence with the world is not simply a retreat from the world, from the failures of that world, or its tragedy; rather, this negotiation is the fundamental expression of life, the living, the contradictions of human suffering that point out that philosophy must be an existentially rooted endeavoring to make life meaningful. Sometimes, if we are lucky, we get hip-hop as the product and grammar of this particular existence.

Bailey's *Philosophy and Hip-Hop* is a rich collection of powerful personal and existentially motivated reflections on teaching, thinking, and the meanings behind the production of hip-hop and hip-hop scholarship. The failure of modernity does not give one an already prepackaged alternative; one must work tirelessly, think adamantly, and speak freely about the world and community you wish to create. When white, capitalist knowledge fails, then these visceral, organic mediums of thought must rise, but rise up without reproducing the ills of the regime they were crafted to respond to. The overarching ideology (universal-Western knowledge) that seeks to reinscribe itself as a success by simply admitting its failure—the discontent in the poverty, violence, collapse of democracy, racism, and multiple forms of exploitation under capitalism—has no actual copyright on human knowledge or creativity. Throughout this book, Bailey wages a meta-philosophical war on the ways that critical theorists, the theory dedicated to getting one's philosophical tools dirty in the chaos of the real world, fear being stained by Blackness, and continue to turn a blind eye to the aesthetic and philosophical resources hip-hop offers. This phenomenon in the academic enterprise known as philosophy is no doubt due to the mistaken racialized history of hip-hop that still takes the art and the Black people who created it to be objects of study, rather than creators of thought, but in pointing out the failure of white thought/critical theory/philosophy to seriously think "itself," Bailey points out that how one does—or claims to do—philosophy is suspect, not because of the need to constantly be introspective, but because the philosophy as it exists now is a victim to the ontologization of its own existence, trapped within the confines of its imaginary disciplinary history, and blind to the potential of hip-hop to point out the pitfalls of a postmodernism, which strives for postcolonial alternatives in a maddening neocolonial acceleration of state imperialism and market commodification, but continues to fail.

The racist history of Black experience under modernity, as well as the racialized representation of hip-hop is inescapable, but does this mean that the historical particularity, its existential specificity, is still not human, and generalizable to the difficulties of the catastrophes found throughout humanity? For the philosopher, the earnest person thinking about the consequences of human existence, life and death are the two extremities of one's intellectual endeavor. Bailey argues quite convincingly that hip-hop is the fracturing of our conceptualization of communities as decadent and reactionary. His project instills a sense of possibility in a world in which the repetition of pragmatic platitudes and continental concoctions that recycle terms like "power," "discourse," "knowledge," and "history" grows tiring. If philosophy is honest about its continued relevance, then it must resist its historical temperament to simply regard those who disagree with its mode of inquiry as ignorant. In order to deal with the calamities of the real world, it must understand and reflect the aesthetic, political, and cultural alternatives of real people, actual people, yes, even some Black people, who are engaged in addressing the ruptures created by the failure of Western thought. The Occidentalism of old no longer signifies civilization; it only points to decadence, and it is in the ruins of this collapse of the values that justified indifference to or hatred of the poor, the Black, the worker, the woman, the Black-man-not, the Other-ed that whiteness/modernity/capitalism thrived. This is no longer the case. Hip-hop offers the participants and observers a lens to question and see not only how specific groups of people are asserting themselves, their lives, their creations against the machination of dehumanization, but also how people think themselves free from their environment, not only by transcendence, but by negotiation and engagement as well.

Julius Bailey does not claim to take knowledge back to the streets; rather, he dares you to hear the philosopher taught by the streets. This is a groundbreaking text and the first full-length manuscript in philosophy that tackles hip-hop as both a cultural resource and a postmodern form. It is my hope that the reader will embrace the insights of this text, the radicality of Bailey's thought that does not pretend its radicalism is held in the moral condemnation of the art produced, but the condemnation of the mechanisms have created the wretched conditions that necessitated such artistic rebellion to begin with. Julius Bailey's analysis is honest, fierce, and will take courage to fully comprehend—but believe me, the possibilities held within are certainly worth the effort.

Prologue

I am a teacher and I endeavor to be attentive to the craft of pedagogy. This project began with ruminations of the kind common to teachers struggling to make the ideas they impart relevant to students. My teaching journey began as an undergraduate student at Howard University where, after a return from a University of London Exchange Program, I was asked to serve as a teaching assistant in the Department of Philosophy. Later I earned my own set of classes while working on my master's degree. During short stints at Milton Academy in Massachusetts and Harvard University I honed my teaching skills and this prepared me for my first full-time teaching job at Millikin University.

At Millikin I taught Philosophy of Literature with the kind of verve typical of a young scholar. I tried to challenge the rules of academia while simultaneously attempting to fit in with the established faculty. Thus I used a common-folk approach to enter into discussions on popular culture and philosophy in ways that upset traditional academic sensibilities. The courses I developed ranged from "Reflections of Thug-Life in America" to "Evil and the Modern Drama." These included lectures on "Anton Chekhov and [rapper] Mystikal", "Sacrificial Love: Memory and the Haunting Presence of H.E.R. Toni Morrison and [rapper] Common." These were popular with students but received with skeptical attention by my fellow faculty members. I remember planning, in 2000, a public lecture, that I called an "open-classroom day" in which I invited my colleagues and students to get to know me. I prepared for two weeks. Like a DJ in the crates, I dug through piles of class notes, lectures, and records of discussions with Cornel West, bell hooks, Toni Morrison, Michael Sandel, Tricia Rose, Ras Baraka (son of the late legendary poet/activist Amiri Baraka), and Farah Griffin.

This mixed research was accompanied by repetitive listening to the music of Mystikal and DMX. Eventually I developed a lecture I called "Radical Democracy, Re-claiming the Self...the Quest of a No Limit Soldier in a World of Structural Limitations." From that day on, I knew that my pedagogy, and ultimately what would make me or break me in the higher education game, would depend on my ability to remix what the academic canon demands, what love and justice call for, and the life experiences of my students who invariably came to class with their music blaring. I had learned to always ask them, "What are you plugged into TODAY?"

After the publication in 2011 of my edited volume on Jay-Z, sitting with my chief research assistant, Dalitso Ruwe, I embarked on an intellectual journey to bring to the public what is vibrant about my philosophy and my approach to teaching in the classroom. There was a time in academia that I felt like Prometheus, the lone tragic professor bearing the burden of light with wit and compassion for the reality of the marginalized. My use of music, video, and dance as a tool to construct identity and foster solidarity and a democratized community within the classroom were, I thought, bold moves. A close read of this book will give a glimpse into my own existentialism and how I bring my students into intellectual union with me as I wrestle with the angst of life, love, and individual liberty. I hope that you will not only find the fluidity of this book riveting but also understand my approach to classroom teaching as a facilitator for the generation of ideas, and the courage to delve into depths often unconventional or unchartered.

What I am offering in this book are ruminations that allow one to peep into the mind of a public philosopher who has been influenced by music and its meaning all his life. It reflects what I think of when I navigate the waters of the academy while simultaneously living among family and associates outside the academy for whom the language is much simpler than that used in academia. Before I was a professional philosopher, I was a hood-philosopher from the "wild-wild 100s" aka the far south side of Chicago. The nascent path that would begin my life's work was truly a *Philosophy Born of Struggle*, learning that the intensity of inner-city life, and the authenticity of hip-hop, creates a more lived, a more robust philosophy for those seeking urban pragmatic wisdom.

If one must philosophize, then one must philosophize; and if one must not philosophize, then one must philosophize; in any case, therefore, one must philosophize. For if one must, then given that Philosophy exists, we are in every way obliged to philosophize. And if one must not, in this case too we are obliged to inquire how it is possible for there to be no philosophy; and in inquiring we philosophize, for inquiry is the cause of Philosophy (Aristotle in Bowen)[1]

It is my intention that this be an accessible philosophy book written to engage in a theoretical exegesis of semiotics using the cultural tapestry of hip-hop and popular culture in general. This book also provides an insight into the synthesis of philosophy, literature, rhetoric, and history. I propose to academics, and the greater hip-hop community, that hip-hop artists are just that—artists and in some ways unknowable, in its truest sense, as people, but at the same time, they can be intelligible as representations or as *images*.

As an existentialist, my deep concerns are about the emptying out of human souls, under postmodern conditions that evolve from growing levels of alienation, isolation, and marginality. This stance served as the prenatal launching pad for this book. Hip-hop reveals and alleviates this angst. The consideration of the importance of hip-hop runs against the pedagogical fixation on Deleuze, Foucault, Lacan, Heidegger, and other postmodern icons as monopolizing understanding of postmodernism. These writers along with Imani Perry, Jean Baudrillard, Tricia Rose, and Marshall McLuhan are placed in the background in my discussion of hip-hop as philosophical phenomenology or, as Simone de Beauvoir would call it, a philosophy of lived experience or phenomenology.

Phenomenology, a unique way of thinking about the world that appears in European philosophy in the wake of Immanuel Kant who said that we can never know the world as it "really" is because we must necessarily experience it through our senses and models of understanding which are unreliable. Since Kant's continental philosophy understands the realm of humans as separate from "the world" itself, it is argued that we are incapable of understanding the world fully and truly. Philosophy is sought in order to understand the *phenomena* that humans experience, those aspects of the world that are present and available and understandable to us as humans—thus "phenomenology." Unlike those who pursue irreducible philosophical Truths *apriori*, I see credibility in the rich phenomenological contributions of W. E. B. Dubois, Franz Fanon, Chuck D, Tupac, and Queen Latifa as well as Edmund Husserl, Jean-Paul Sartre, and Richard Wright.

In walking on a college campus, in any location, rural or urban, Predominantly White Institutions (PWI) or Historically Black Colleges or Universities (HBCU), it is impossible to avoid the sounds a Kanye West, a Macklemore, Katy Perry or a 2 Chainz blaring through the iPods, radio-speakers, and earphones of students. Before, during, and after they wrestle with their academic schedule, they are being inspired, motivated, and challenged by a lyrical imposition of rap in their favorite music. My colleague and friend Emery Petchauer conceptualizes the "hip-hop collegian" and defines them in his book, *Hip-Hop Culture n College Students' Lives*, as "college students who make their active participation in hip-hop relevant to their education interests, motivations, practices, and mindsets."[2] While looking in their closets they are grappling with ways to turn their "swag on"[3] with the latest fashions often commercialized, sometimes designed by hip-hop culture. For many students early evenings are spent watching videos on YouTube and on television on *106 and Park* and MTV as they attempt to peer at hip-hop's representatives, and develop strategies for emulating them and resonating deeply with the artists so as to enable a kind of self-creation in which their own space merges with that of the hip-hop artists.

Thus I use various forms of popular culture. This is what my classroom calls for. This is what hip-hop also calls for and the only way toward a democratic (classroom) community that does not marginalize, is to amplify those whispered voices so that all be heard through a loving and committed group of persons of like and kindred spirit. Much time is spent in my *Philosophy and Hip-Hop* course wrestling with associated questions like—How do we establish what experience has validity? How do we sift through our experience to something like a theory to explain or organize it into a meaningful expression? These prove interesting in the eyes of students of various races, nationalities, sexual orientations, and genders. In some respect in order for some of my students to get to the courage to say *I Am Hip–Hop,* they have to reject some of the culture's rather exclusionary tones, spaces, and lanes but just watch and listen to a hip-hop cipher, participate in a Dee Jay Battle or a dance-show, and see what music, dance, fashion, and art do for hip-hop. Hip-hop binds people together. I am, in no small part, because hip-hop is!

These are my philosophical ruminations of hip-hop.

Acknowledgments

This project began with a vision I had in 1995 when I professed that one day I will write a philosophical encyclopedia of hip-hop. It was a quixotic affirmation, one that I am sure my mentor at that time, Dr. Cornel West, internally laughed at but externally supported. Though this book is far from that feat, it is, nevertheless, a major step toward that dream. As such, I thank him for 20 years of love and support.

To omit those who sparked my appreciation of hip-hop would be penitent so I give mad love to Ras Baraka, Toni Blackman, Jon Caramonica, Dr. Tricia Rose, and April Silver for academically pursuing this culture since the early 1990s and showing me its deeper recesses "back in the day."

To Dalitso Ruwe and Adam Schueler, thank you. As the founding members of "Degreed Money Entertainment," we continue to promote and support each other in our endeavors as a real family should. To Sha'Dawn Battle and A.D. Carson, our newest members, daily I grow more proud of your journey. I am looking forward to years of thoughtful analysis and creative pedagogy from you all.

To my daughter Heather, and my family who patiently and lovingly sacrificed time away from so that I could offer this project, I love you much.

To Bryan Szabo, who calmly endured my ranting, my frustrations, my joys, and my pains—your helpful support and collegiality seem never-ending.

To my fine university family who supported me: The kind words of encouragement from President Laurie Joyner and husband Jay, Provost Chris ("the Right Reverend") Duncan, board members David Boyle and Wesley Bates; the project grant from the Faculty Development Fund Board; the many student comments and engagements both in and out of class; Drs. Nancy McHugh and Don Reed, my philosophy colleagues who allowed me to become something of a recluse during pressure-filled periods of this project; and, finally, to Dr. Carmiele Wilkerson, always a balm through the aches and pains of this experience.

Very special thanks go to the following colleagues, students, and friends who served vital roles in this project (in alphabetical order): Toni Blackman, Dr. Regina Bradley, Grant Dempsey, Dr. Darlene Brooks-Hedstrom, Dr. Sheryl Cunningham, Dr. Tommy Curry, Grant Dempsey, Dr. David Evans, Laura Harrison, Dr. Kamasi Hill, Dr. John Jennings, Dr. David J. Leonard, Dr. Bettina Love, Martin Lukk, Nicolas Mangialardi, Dr. Michael Mattison, Jonathon McFarlane, Dr. Monica N. Miller, Rev. Dr. Charles Montgomery, Caleb Murray, Katrina Oko-Odoi, Dr. Emery Petchauer, Dr. Christophe Ringer, Dr. Geoffrey Skoll, Dr. Stephany Spaulding, Samuel Tettner, Dr. Daniel Vargas, Rev. Reggie Williams, and Tachelle Wilkes.

To the three high school deans, from all three of my high schools, who didn't believe my life wouldn't amount to much...*look at me now*! To the mentors whose unwavering belief in me saved my life: (the late) Fr. John Collins, Dr. Angela Durante, (the late) Fletcher Henderson, (the late) Rev. Emanuel Hoskins, (the late) Mrs. Curtestine Miller, Fr. Michael Pfleger, and Dr. Cornel West.

Also, my warmest thanks to the students in every hip-hop course I have taught from 1998 to 2013—nearly 1,000 creative and energetic minds in over five colleges: Millikin University, Lewis University, Fresno State University, Central State University, and Wittenberg University. Last, heartfelt appreciation is extended to Palgrave Macmillan and to Burke Gerstenschlager and Caroline Kracunas who entrusted this project to its publishing house.

Introduction

As a philosophical approach this text does not rest—at least not comfortably—with the existing body of historical or sociological studies of hip-hop. Neither does it rest well within the diffuse body of exegetic interpretations of hip-hop lyrics. Such ground has been well travelled; my aim is to open up the philosophical life force that informs the construction of hip-hop—to turn the gaze of the philosopher upon those blind spots that exist within existing hip-hop scholarship.

Hip-Hop and Philosophy, a volume of hip-hop scholarship edited by Derrick Darby and Tommy Shelby, brought a wide range of hip-hop scholars together in order to highlight the many ways in which hip-hop and philosophy intersect. This book is the unofficial sequel to that volume. Darby and Shelby's book contains a number of productive and meaningful talking points focused on the metaphysics and ethics at the heart of rap lyrics. I give Darby and Shelby "props," but, with this book, I will delve a little deeper into the philosophical analysis of hip-hop. By showing how pregnant with philosophical meaning the textual and graphic elements of hip-hop are, I hope to inaugurate the enshrining of hip-hop into the philosophic canon. The academy is increasingly embracing hip-hop into classes that examine American history, sociology, or literature. This book will, I hope, take the examination of hip-hop to a profound enough level to merit its broad inclusion in the philosophy classroom as well. Furthermore, the ethos of the project is to seek official membership into the hip-hop community as a philosopher.

The idea of the community at stake departs from modernity's *sensus communis*. Understanding this community as a manifestation of the postmodern or the post-historical presents both a challenge and an opportunity. Before jumping into unsettled waters, a simple diagram of community must be traced, touching upon a series of pivotal knots in postmodern institutionalized bodies. These include transgression and excess, immanence and transcendence, art and creativity, reconciliation and the construction of a postmodern community. This diagram will prove to be a supportive underpinning for the philosophical dialogue that will follow. These pivotal points are, however, not meant to impose a specific order or hierarchy. They are the simply the connecting dots of a figure that can be seen as completed by the mind, but that needs to actually be traced in order for a concrete image to emerge. Toward this end, it is my humble hope that those artistic, intellectual, organizational, and spiritual giants of hip-hop *receive my little book in all charity*,[1] and welcome me, and my discipline, into "The Imagined Community,"[2] that is, hip-hop.

Where Do Philosophy and Hip-Hop Intersect?

"Philosophy" combines the Greek words for love (*philo*) and wisdom (*sophia*). It is, as Bertrand Russell says, "something intermediate between theology and science."[3] Thus, in its search for truth, it seeks a middle ground between the empirical and the dogmatical. Though it has often been used as a tool to examine both the external and the spiritual world, it is more at home among the categories of thought: mind, matter, reason, proof, truth, and so on. A philosophical engagement with disciplines such as history or science does not seek to solve historical or scientific questions so much as it examines the stuff of thought that structures our understanding of the world; it seeks—and often dismantles—our foundations and our presuppositions. It constantly makes us reevaluate what we know and how we can know it. Only once a practice has become self-conscious can it be considered philosophical. The boundary between such second-order reflection and ways of practicing the first-order discipline itself is not always apparent.[4]

Attitude toward certain disciplines is one of the factors that sets direction of thought and leads to divergent answers to two key questions that were present throughout the history of philosophy.

1. What should philosophy investigate?
2. What are the tools for such an investigation?

The first question addresses the issue of the subject of philosophy and the second one deals with the methodology. Different answers to these questions were the main points of divergence among philosophical schools or movements, and this diversity fueled the progress of philosophy from its beginnings in the West in the fifth century BCE in Greece.

Plato's approach to art did not call for separation of art, metaphysics, ethics, or politics; rather, he proposed an integration of these aspects of life with the drive to discover an ethical and metaphysical order in the world that would, he thought, lead to personal insights. The role of art was to represent this order in such a way that humans could align themselves with it.[5] Ethics was one of the three original sciences of philosophy in ancient Greece.[6] Immanuel Kant concurred with this, asserting that no action could have value without a goodwill, which represented a jewel at the base of human action. If goodwill was present, it could "shine by its own light, as a thing which has its whole value in itself."[7]

Applying a philosophical stance toward hip-hop entails questions about the ontology of the form. That is, does it have a reality worthy of investigation, or does it exist? How should one try to grasp its being? Several modern philosophical schools may be adduced to these questions. Although there is no rigid dividing line between these schools, stating some of the general characteristics of each school may prove useful. The school of analytic philosophy dominated much of philosophy in the first part of the twentieth century. This was a radical move away from the Idealism previously accepted and taught, thanks to the wide acceptance of the Germans. The basic tenet of the analytic movement was that philosophical problems could be solved (or dissolved) by logically analyzing key terms; analytic arguments are primarily concerned with what, precisely, terms and propositions mean for the philosopher and what is the meaning itself. Bertrand Russell, a leading proponent of the analytic tradition, believed grammar to be misleading; the only way to dispel the illusion of language is to express propositions in the formal language of symbolic logic. Gottlob Frege tried to make a foundation of mathematics exclusively on logical grounds and Ludwig Wittgenstein in his early work claimed that our language, our thoughts, and the world all share the same logical form. Analytic philosophy is, therefore, characterized by clarity, precision, and rigor that rely on logic, mathematics, and

science. It asks the question—what is there to know and how can
we know it?

Analytic philosophy later found itself opposed by the phenomenology of Husserl, and its offspring Existentialism (Sartre,
Camus, et al.) and to "Continental" or "Postmodern" philosophy
(Heidegger, Foucault, Derrida). Heidegger urged a break from the
dominion of logic, turning his energies in a new direction more
reminiscent of *fin de siècle* Romanticism.

Rather than relying on science and logic, continental philosophy is more intuitive; its main concern is to understand the human
condition. Profound truths do not lend themselves easily to simple language; continental philosophers, thus, examine poetry,
literature, visual and plastic arts, and modes of nonverbal expression that are able to communicate deep truths about the human
condition in a way that is above the level of simple, descriptive
language.

As such, in the second half of the twentieth century, a new
wave of philosophers and theorists began to examine, tentatively at
first, the products of popular ("low") art/culture in ways that had
hitherto been reserved for avant-garde ("high") art/culture. As
the boundaries of the canon became fluid and negotiable, popular
music, fiction, cinema, advertisements, and a host of other materials that had been largely ignored, before Adorno and Horkeimer
sounded the alarm,[8] became fodder for impassioned debates surrounding the ways in which first-world audiences were consuming
ideology-stamped products in an uncritical way.

The explosion of various subcultures in the 1960s made this
model less tenable. Audiences and cultural productions alike were
fracturing into ever-shrinking categories and subcategories, each
representative of niche markets and tastes. As Simon During notes
in his introduction to the *Cultural Studies Reader*, theorists began
to take notice of these "multiple audiences"; the focus began to
shift from an audience imagined en bloc to those "communities
who, in various combinations, vote, buy records, watch television
and films, etc, without ever fitting the 'popular,' 'ordinary,' or
'normal.'"[9] Identification with subcultures increasingly became a
form of identity shaping, influencing both interior and exterior
elements of the self; what one displayed to the world through consumer purchases was an obvious badge of identification, but one's
religious beliefs (or lack thereof), one's politics, one's ethics were

often inspired as well by the small or large community identity forge.[10]

University classrooms soon began to see an influx of popular culture and subcultures. This reflected a pending shift in classroom values away from the normative and the canonical toward "less restricted (more "other," counter-normative) ways of living."[11] "The Great Tradition"[12] was giving way to a plurality of voices that had been kept at arm's length from educational institutions. Black voices, female voices, the voices of countless marginalized and little-appreciated subcultures began to make their presence felt, and, for students and educators alike, this change was a welcome one. Says bell hooks:

> The call for a recognition of cultural diversity, a rethinking of ways of knowing, a deconstruction of old epistemologies, and the concomitant demand that there be a transformation in our classrooms, in how we teach and what we teach, has been a necessary revolution—one that seeks to restore life to a corrupt and dying academy.[13]

The values and realities of the postmodern world are, in many cases, utterly divorced from the texts and their producers that are the fuel that educators attempt to use to stoke the fires of learning. There is, no doubt, immense value in the search for the universal in the themes of the canonical literature; there are, no doubt, absolutes in terms of the human condition that will ever keep Shakespeare, George Elliot, Tolstoy, Milton, and Dostoevsky relevant for interested readers. During notes the following:

> More and more students are entering post-compulsory institutions without having, or wishing for, traditional European elite taste preferences and without the desire to form themselves ethically through their consumption or knowledge of canons. Their own everyday-life culture is increasingly that of popular culture or niches within it—this is their starting point for exploring the past, for instance. Many students from so-called "minority" communities, often the first members of their family ever to attend university, wish to affirm and learn about their own neglected or repressed cultural heritages.[14]

In America, these attitudes have led to a surge in the use of hip-hop in academic forums. The lived experiences of its poets so closely resemble those of the students from "minority" communities that its relevance in the inner-city classroom is impossible to dismiss. Beneath the ivied bulwarks, acceptance of hip-hop has been slower in coming, but it *is* coming. Hip-hop gurus like KRS-One, Nas, Bun B, 9th Wonder, Common and Afrika Bambaataa, have partnered with academics like Cornel West, Angela Davis, Marcyliena Morgan (Harvard Hip Hop Archive), Michael Eric Dyson, Tricia Rose, Dawn-Elissa Fischer, Mark Anthony Neal and myself introducing hip-hop into an ever-widening range of discussions and debates.

Hip-hop itself has made the study of its poetics and its message more fruitful by constantly expanding into new territories and reinventing itself in sophisticated ways that make its transition into discussions—such as the ones that will follow—all the easier. It is perhaps the most protean of musical forms. What began as an expression of an almost exclusively male feeling, a brutally honest expression of the poverty, oppression, and racism prevalent in inner-city America, developed, with the help of groundbreaking innovators, into a platform for a much broader range of topics and opinions on those topics than hip-hop addressed in its infancy. Female MCs carved out a space for themselves in a (still) largely male-dominated arena. Some (think Foxy Brown and Lil' Kim) played the same hyper-sexualized roles that women had long played in rap lyrics and videos—albeit with a newfound agency in such roles. Others (think Queen Latifah, Lauryn Hill, and Jean Grae) constructed their femininity around images of the untouchable, the autonomous, and the divine goddess.

Hip-hop has also become home to a range of social, political, and religious beliefs. Among rappers there are professed Muslims (Lupe Fiasco, Mos Def, Q-Tip), Christians (DV Alias Khrist, Lord Have Mercy), and Jews (Beastie Boys, Drake, Matisyahu), and this is just a small sampling. There are Scientologists and Buddhists as well. Some advocate Machiavellian street-politics, others speak of togetherness and communal transcendence. Paeans of material wealth exist *cheek by jowl* with manifestos of communalism.

None of this is contradictory. Though, hip-hop moves and speaks according to implicit rules that link different contents to repeatable enactments, it can be rarely conservative. In its tone and in its message, it is revolutionary, demanding quantifiable change within and without the communities it addresses. It eschews the metaphorical for the concrete, pointedly addressing the issues facing this country in a way so direct as to be impossible to ignore. Its refusal to adhere to regulated discourses makes it the art form with, perhaps, the greatest postmodern potential. To take a postmodern position is to accept a blurring of boundaries across disciplines and social relations, in favor of revealing the structures that give rise to systems of knowledge and meaning making. In *The Postmodern Condition*, Lyotard uses the concept of untrustworthiness to describe the essential core of postmodern thought; this excludes the possibility that those of the new school can legitimize the grand meta-narratives of the modern era.[15] Postmodernism is not a style or a historical period (i.e., a condition); it is much more of an "attitude." The freedom of expression and eclecticism that we find in hip-hop reflect this attitude, which is, in essence, a reaction *contra* the rigidly limiting aesthetic of modernism. It rejects conventional moral wisdom and eschews political correctness in favor of the straight dope. Thus, its creators share with postmodernists the tendency to revere subversives. It transforms morally ambiguous antiheroes, crooks, dealers, and pimps into the Robin Hoods of the postmodern age.

At its best, hip-hop as a postmodern form deconstructs, delimits, and resituates discourses that concern us as Black Americans, as political pawns or agents, as autonomous individuals and members of thriving or struggling communities. Hip-hop has elbowed out a well-deserved space for itself in the academy, and, as a philosopher, as an educator, and as a Black man, I'm welcoming it with open arms.

Are We Philosophers, Or Are We Littérateurs?

The use of literature in general—and hip-hop poetics in particular—places the philosopher on a narrow ridge between literary criticism and philosophy. Philosophy purists, ever the antagonists to cross-disciplinary inquiry, tend to identify lyrical exegesis as an attempt at critical literary analysis, which lacks a clear direction in the realm of critical philosophy.

The affinity between literary criticism and philosophy is only increasing as departments devoted to the study of literature are increasingly making use of philosophical texts and theories to get to the heart of what texts means independent of their authors. Since the 1980s, when courses in literary theory—a mash up of postmodern philosophy and textual criticism—emerged as the avant-garde field of literary study, philosophy and literary criticism have been bedfellows. However, they have not yet fused into a single body. Literary criticism is primarily concerned with what texts say and how they say it; philosophy is primarily concerned with what language says, how it builds and uncovers meaning, how it represents our ideas and our tangible world.

The analysis of rap lyrics without a full development into, and appreciation for, the foundational theories upon which these lyrics operate would be a futile philosophical endeavor. Rather than focusing merely on the superficial verbal content of hip-hop's poetry, this project attempts to examine hip-hop as a corpus in which language plays only a part. The philosophy of hip-hop is, after all, not merely textual; it is reflected in the body of dancers, in the visual art of the graffiti artist, in the reshaping of existing music into new sounds through the art of the turntable. Thought and knowledge inform lyrics, but they inform much more than that as well. Therefore, in what follows I will attempt to broaden and elevate the examination of hip-hop and its manifestations: I will engage with and critique hip-hop as a postmodern philosophy using the tools of the philosopher. Textual criticism will, at times, be unavoidable, but it will ever take a role subordinate to the overarching philosophy that informs everything within the rubric of hip-hop.

For present purposes, I treat hip-hop as a musical phenomenon linked with other kinds of music such as jazz, rock, blues, and so on. Treating it as music places it within aesthetic philosophy, which as G. W. F Hegel noted is "the science of sensation or feeling."[16] A philosophy of hip-hop tries to get at its essential objectivity, its being in the world as Heidegger would put it. Slavoj Zizek observed that

> What Rilke said of beauty goes also for music: it is a lure, a screen, the last curtain protecting us from directly confronting the horror of the (vocal) object. When the intricate musical tapestry disintegrates or collapses into a pure unarticulated scream, we approach voice qua object.[17]

Think of Edvard Munch's painting, *The Scream*, in which the artist depicts the unvoiced scream. Its silence brings it to a more visceral reality than an auditory scream. Imagine being in an art museum and hearing a scream: shock, a searching for its cause, but then, a quick resolution. Compare that to staring at Munch's painting for half an hour. So it is with hip-hop, except that hip-hop vocalizes the scream through the curtain of music. What it yields is a close approximation of a concrete space: the cradle of hip-hop, the South Bronx, in its devastation and ghettoization of the 1970s. Hip-hop expressed the reality of urban life under the effects of deindustrialization, decay, racism, and marginalization. Its form and content still reflects these realities.

Hip-Hop's Role in the Public Sphere

Jürgen Habermas postulated a "public sphere," in which "private persons" come together to discuss "the general interest."[18] In this important public arena, even the most marginalized of people, traditionally excluded from the political process, can have a voice on par with that of their neighbor—no matter how privileged that neighbor might be. Hip-hop has enlivened dialogues and debate within the public sphere. It has brought to prominence hitherto unheard voices. As Akilah Folami says, "Hip-hop arose out of the ruins of a postindustrial and ravaged South Bronx, as a form of expression of urban Black and Latino youth, who politicians and the dominant public and political discourse had written off, and, for all intents and purposes, abandoned."[19] Hip-hop not only gave voice to these abandoned voices, but it gave them a platform from which they could address massive, sympathetic audiences as well. It represented one of the first opportunities for African American and Latino voices to rise above the din of the city; it democratized and equalized on a massive scale.

Even in the world of mass production, it's easy to look at today's hip-hop as another empty commoditized product. The meteoric rise of hip-hop into the mainstream has, indeed, been extraordinary: a group with such little societal visibility and resources has managed to carve out a space in a largely corporate-dominated space. They have "managed to provide seeds of resistance that challenge the dominantly held negative view of the gangsta image." While some artists, it is true have positively reveled in the negative image, conscious hip-hop artists have worked tirelessly to re-fashion the image of American Blackness dominated by the (mis)representations of Black youths in the media—and, yes, in rap music as well—as dangerously violent thugs and hustlers. Hip-hop artists have battled misunderstandings fuelled by these images and have put forth their own representations that show Black youth as prophetic, as enlightened, and as community conscious.

The prophetic strain of hip-hop can be found in the works of artists like KRS-One, Gift of Gab, Mos Def, Toni Blackman, Lyrics Born, Brother Ali, Jasiri X, Jean Grae, Talib Kweli, and those other lyricists who succeed in critically analyzing the social systems that surround them, using references to historical and philosophical content, while framing their message in terms that appeal to their audience on the streets. Hip-hop disregards the notion that there is something out there and knowable, as propounded by realist philosophers. Rather it urges us to focus on the present and on our personal everyday experiences. The only knowledge we have comes from within.

To take a single example, Lauryn Hill exemplifies a paradigm in which hip-hop liberation is found in personal self-awareness. When talking of religion, she suggested that "spiritual revolutions occur when existing religious institutions lose their vitality and fail to be relevant to the human condition." Like other rappers, she is a postmodernist and deconstructionist "questioning the epistemological sources of modern societal beliefs and their validity." She rejects traditional European values, turning the dominant American narrative—the capitalist American Dream—on its head.

The economy functions or feeds on creativity. Its value and impact has been framed within economic categories so that creativity has a use-value, but artists have ever resisted this connection of the creative and the useful. Art makes us more conscious of our surroundings, of our communities (local and global), and of that which speaks in a common language across national, ethnic, and social barriers. Must we condemn all human activities to the spectacle of consumerism and alienation as Guy Debord maintains,[20] or can art prove something of an antidote to the malaise of postmodern consumer culture? Hip-hop shows itself to be a powerful avenue of critique on this front. Beneath the broad umbrella of hip-hop, there are countless instances of art that is entirely isolated from the existential anguish that is so apparent to some (turn on the radio to see what I mean). Rampant consumerism and superficiality is more rule than exception when the critical lens is turned on the lion's share of Top 40 radio, but hip-hop, at its best, is a reaction against this; it attacks the blindness at the heart of the culture industry.[21]

Media outlets of all kinds—television, print, radio, online—represent, usually in coherent ways, an imagined sense of community; they speak to and for this community and shape ideas of nation and community in their audience. Chuck D famously said that "Rap is black America's CNN."[22] In his memoir, *Decoded*, Jay-Z agrees with Chuck D, but adds the following clarification: "Hip-hop," he says, "would be boring as the news if all MCs did was report. Rap is also entertainment—and art."[23] It is precisely because it does both of these things that hip-hop is, to quote Chuck D once more, "the worldwide religion of people 25 and under."[24] Just as media outlets like Fox News, the Drudge Report, *The New York Times*, MSNBC, and NPR are powerful sources of political sentiment for baby boomers and gen-exers in this country, hip-hop addressed the generation that followed them—a generation raised in the cradle of MTV that came of age in a point-and-click era—by appealing not only to their sense of outrage, but to their entertainment-driven sensibilities as well. Though consolidated artists like Jay-Z and Birdman are in the position to be power brokers and information filters in the environment that they have helped to create, there is no monopoly in the dissemination of knowledge among millennials; competition from democratic and decentralized sources of information (YouTube, BuzzFeed, Facebook, etc.) is making authority an ever more elusive concept.

Still, even in a largely leaderless forum like the Internet, there are artists who continue to use hip-hop to call their communities to action; artists like Che "Rhymefest" Smith who are focusing the community's gaze upon pressing social issues; artists who are using hip-hop to form sympathetic communities based on an ever-broadening desire for emancipation and enlightenment. Take, for example, the massive success of Macklemore and Ryan Lewis. Beginning with their breakaway smash hit "Thrift Shop," they captured the interest of the broader, less entrenched hip-hop community and, indeed, the music-loving community at large. Once they were firmly entrenched within the media spotlight, they released a second single very different from the first. "Same Love" demands a reexamination on the part of the hip-hop community of their powerful use of language; the language that the song targets is quite specific: the widespread pejorative use of words like "gay" and "faggot." Macklemore doesn't beat around the bush in "Same Love"[25] as he sternly admonishes those rappers and other artists who use antigay slurs on the Internet and akin this type of verbal assault to racist and sexist language that he equally disavows. Macklemore, a 2014 multiple Grammy award winner, equates the ongoing struggle for human rights in the Lesbian, Gay, Bisexual, and Transgender (LGBT) community with the struggle for civil rights that so engaged the Black community for more than half a century. To be sure, hip-hop is awash in homophobic language;[26] the battle rap tradition has leaned on homophobic slurs in such a way that those MCs who are making their way to the top have, too often, engaged in homophobic wordplay so frequently as to entrench it within the lyrical body of hip-hop. Macklemore and Ryan Lewis, by their broad, chiefly non-Black following have brought a massive online following into the fold; they have drafted a response so eloquent and moving—and at the same time, so head-noddingly good—that it increases the number of boots on the ground in the long war against an injustice that has been fought by folk like Tim'm West, Juba Kalamka, Invicible and others with little broad support.

And so the community broadens, but its identity remains visible: the ideal hip-hop artist, I will argue, can be seen as the strange combination of the philosopher king and the dandy—Plato and Oscar Wilde have on few occasions been so close. Much like Machiavelli's Prince, moreover, hip-hop's princes and princesses enchant the masses by the *vertu* of their character. A true hip-hop artist guides and mobilizes his or her community. The artist manages an image, highlighting virtues and (*contra* Machiavelli) highlighting his or her vices as well. The best of an artist builds alliances and speaks on behalf of his or her community, giving voice to their collective will, of which he or she is at times mastermind and at other times representative.

Analysis of past philosophical thought reveals that the concerns and conflicts that animate hip-hop's poetic are not new. In 1932, theologian Reinhold Niebuhr asserted that, while each generation is beset with complexities and issues that feel, to those experiencing them, unique to their century or even generation, the essential struggle between man and his environment, between man and his neighbor, remains ever the same: "Human society," he says, "will never escape the problem of the equitable distribution of the physical and cultural goods which provide for the preservation and fulfillment of human life."[27] Hip-hop is not the first art form to assert itself in this domain, but this does not in any way diminish its importance. Its stance is not one of the simple observer; it does much more than merely point out the issues of oppression, racism, exploitation, and inequality that are everywhere prevalent in America's cities. As a postmodern critique, as a philosophical approach to the malaise of urban life, it offers real-world solutions for the disaffected. Beginning with the call to wake up, to rise up, to stand up, the best of hip-hop demands social change while, at the same time, it empowers agents of that change with knowledge both of the self and what is external to that self. Both can be changed, and hip-hop never tires of ringing the bells of revolution. For those who hear the call, the movement has emancipatory power; it is a movement that cuts to the core of what holds our generation, our century, our species back. It is a movement moving us in the right direction.

Sketches into the Ruminations

In what follows, I will attempt to bring together in new ways the tools of philosophy and the broadly inclusive culture of hip-hop. For the most part, I will engage with hip-hop via its textual element, that of hip-hop poetics. However, no treatment of hip-hop would be complete that did not also touch on the visual representations of hip-hop culture contained in music videos and album covers, the art of graff writers, the acrobatic physical movements of break dancers, and the deft musical stylings of turntablists. I will treat each of these in turn insofar as they are an expression of the underlying philosophy of hip-hop or insofar as the tools of philosophy, when applied to these media, yield interesting results.

I have divided this work into eight "ruminations." Each of these examines in some detail an aspect of hip-hop in relation to a broad selection of key thinkers. In rumination 1, "Of the Beauty and Wisdom of Hip-Hop" I introduce my subject with a narrative tapestry of hip-hop that situates the reader in the eyes of hip-hop, showing what and how it sees. From jazz and the Harlem Renaissance to blues and the urban landscape, this section begins the work that will be continued throughout this work by laying bare the aesthetic and philosophic foundations of hip-hop culture. Knowledge of these foundations is essential to creating and sustaining an argument for investigating hip-hop's various aspects. Of particular interest here is the evolution of hip-hop from a socially conscious and revolutionary poetic into a massively popular commercial entity that, while still revolutionary in tone, quickly began home to increasingly violent rhetoric. This, in turn, shaped (and continues to shape) the way that hip-hop was and is handled in the media.

Rumination 2, "Firebrands and Battle Plans," is at once an engagement with the Blackness at the heart of hip-hop and an examination of the battle rap tradition as it emerged and flourished as an expression of this Blackness. Jean-Paul Sartre's writing on race and commitment are pivotal here as they poignantly express the desire for a distinctly Other form of expression that grounds hip-hop within its context as a material production of inner-city minorities who were struggling to be heard—they felt—for the first time. How they were heard—how they were perceived within and without their communities—is crucial to understanding the course that hip-hop took through the 1980s and 1990s.

Rumination 3, "Conscious Hip-Hop versus the Culture Industry," takes a closer look at the thriving underground scene of conscious hip-hop. Using Adorno and Horkeimer's work on the culture industry, I posit conscious hip-hop as a possible source for the mechanism of reply that the German theorists felt was lacking in the cultural productions of the first half of the twentieth century. Although, for the most part, commercial rap artists conform in every way to their dire warnings about the future of mass culture, there are pockets of concerned and dedicated artists who are working tirelessly to educate—rather than indoctrinate—their audience. They are providing the tools for their listeners to carry on the project of emancipation begun so long ago, and they are, if one is looking for such a cure, the antidote to the insidious influence of materialism and consumerism that has come to dominate so much of the hip-hop industry.

Rumination 4, " Toward a Philosophy of Hip-Hop Education" addresses how hip-hop and the classroom can and should come together. Given just how relevant hip-hop is for today's students, given how ubiquitous it has become in nearly every form of twenty-first-century culture, there is tremendous potential for educators who are willing to explore the many ways in which hip-hop's poetry can be integrated seamlessly into the classroom. Hip-hop, as a legitimate epistemology, can provide the key to unlocking what it means to be human while preserving the individuality of divergent experiences.

Rumination 5, "Lost in the City and Lost in the Self: Sin and Solipsism in Hip-Hop's Dystopia," dissects hip-hop to reveal the dystopian message at its core. Birthed, as it was, from the Black musical tradition of the spirituals and the blues, both of which more often lamented than celebrated the state of the secular world, hip-hop has retained a thoroughly unromantic image of city as a place of sin, excess, and exile. This sensibility keeps the urban space as transient, deracinated, and disconnected to *home*. From the shores of West Africa to the call of the 1865 Emancipation through the Great Migrations that followed, the hope, the quest, the journey north, west, away, ultimately somewhere else is a consistent trope in the Black letters. Religiously, such a hope is couched in Luke 18:16, "Let the little children come to me, and do not hinder them, for the kingdom of God belongs to such as these." How do youth, the most precious elements to both a civil nation and God's Kingdom, become the very ills and fodder for extinction? To this end, hip-hop meets God right where he "gave his one and only son" (John 3:16) and his silence in the garden of Gethsemane.

Rumination 6, "Hip-Hop and International Voices of Revolution," highlights the importance of exploring the role of the hip-hop artists in communicating the broader significance of philosophies of empowerment and emancipation in America and abroad. Hip-hop's power has provided the musical backdrop as well as the poetical platform for various reform-based movements in Ghana, Cuba, the Middle East, and Caribbean. Using postcolonial theory as a lens, this chapter examines revolution as a quest for and acquisition of the power of information. In this century, such revolutions, thanks to broad access to sites like Twitter and Facebook that have become powerful agents of change in developing countries, have started online and spread into the streets as massive collectives supported by sympathetic online communities worldwide. Hip-hop has played a role in these movements, and, with a nod to Homi Bhabha, this chapter asserts hip-hop as an "enunciative space," in which meaning is constituted through the active mode of address through performance.

Rumination 7, "The Artist and the Image," investigates the philosophical implications of concepts that we take for granted in the modern world such as the simulacrum of technologically altered images and the creation of digital-age rap icons. Images, which are the primary foundation of contemporary mass marketing, are no different in their essential characterization then highly transformative aesthetic images. This apparent contradiction forces a reconsideration of the intrinsic inadequacy of the conventional interpretation of "the medium is the message."

Rumination 8, "The Catastrophe of Success," primarily addresses the work of rap artists Kanye West and Tyler the Creator and their complex relationships with fame, its commodification, materialism, and deep-seated feelings of personal inadequacy. Since the new models for artistic authenticity that are discussed in rumination 7 suggest that rigid adherence to the presented reality of the artist is less connected to "keeping it real" than it once had been, Kanye and Tyler the Creator are particularly powerful models of self-representation in the new media. The emotional turbulence that is offered to the listener is at once authentic and manufactured in that it is, at one and the same time, freely expressed and prepared for and with an audience in mind.

So as you enter into *Philosophy and Hip-Hop: Ruminations on Postmodern Cultural Form*, enter with care and patience as you are ingesting the thoughts of a philosopher who appreciates the breadth and breath of this cultural form. This means, therefore, that rather than a form of escapism from pressing matter of daily life, hip-hop is centric to this daily life, it plays a greater role for the individuals involved. It is only by doing so that hip-hop can be seen as a true abode, which houses desires, but which remains in the open: hip-hop is not in hiding, and it does not ask individuals to masquerade anything.

Hip-hop attacks the angst (the neuroses, the darkest fears) that rises over the surface of a postmodern world that insists in the radical premise of atomized individuals. Hip-hop, thus, is a community that accepts the collective fears, but which lives and breathes through the dreams of individuals who seek an alternative to atomization. Hip-hop, originally as an expression of American culture and heritage, is naturally attached to a history but neither does it hide its origins nor does it pretend to be a form of escapism in that sense. As a community hip-hop endures within the history and traipses the world and its peoples where they are. The existence that it proposes is one of reconciliation with the past, with only one aim: the appropriation of a future where the energies that breathe life into man are celebrated and embraced by a community of its peers.

Rumination 1

Of the Beauty and Wisdom of Hip-Hop

Black history is as rich and dynamic as its subject. Blacks in the United States trace their roots to the African peoples who were abducted by slave merchants and marched to the coast, where they were sold and transported, first to America's colonies, then to the Republic itself that was immortalized in the nineteenth century as the "land of the free and the home of the brave." Those words, "land of the free," they were written almost 50 years before Lincoln signed the Emancipation Proclamation. Even if your roots are untouched by the slave trade, the irony of this is palpable, isn't it?

Much of the richness and dynamism of American Black history stems from the fact that Africans, like Europeans or Asians, were not a monolithic people. African slaves were captured from a variety of ethnic groups such as the Biafara, Mende, and Jola. African Americans have ties to one or more of 46 different African ethnic groups (Heywood and Thornton, 2007). Because each of these groups was geographically dispersed, because each had its own discrete traditions, mythologies, languages, arts, and so on, African slaves in America had to develop entirely new ways of communicating with each other; within the rough framework provided by the English language, they developed a heavily coded language and cultural jargon, a language they used to communicate with each other, and to protect each other from reprisals from those they referred to as masters (Alves, 2009, p. 25). The existence of distinctly Black jargons, of languages within languages, is therefore not new. It is part of a long and complicated—and mostly unwritten—history. At least in part, Black history belongs to America, but, thanks to its oral transmission, its coded language, and, of course, thanks to the fact that the Black history of America is still being written, it belongs most of all to us, to those of various Ebony shades.

The creeds and ideals of Harriet Tubman, Frederick Douglass, Booker T. Washington, Zora Neale Hurston, Martin Luther King, and Malcolm X are inextricably linked with our cultural and national heritages, and, therefore, they profoundly impact all of our arts, of which music has always been one of the most prominent. Just as our ancestors were liberated by music from the literal chains that bound them (through soulful sounds of spirituals such as "Sometimes I Feel Like a Motherless Child," "Nearer, My God, to Thee," "Steal Away Jesus," and "Wade in the Water"), we, in the present, continue to liberate ourselves from the injustices of our times through our own music.

Soul music, gospel, and other distinctly Black forms of music continue to lift the spirits of Black listeners, but the most recent and certainly the most commercially prominent form of music that has come to liberate its Black listeners in the last 30 years has been hip-hop. Just as Tubman stealthily led thousands of Blacks to freedom in the North, Black musicians and other artists in hip-hop culture continue the long and glorious tradition of liberation, using rich and sometimes coded language to emancipate both themselves and their listeners from the confines of the present.

Pulitzer Prize-winning writer Isabel Wilkerson posits 1915–1970 as the period of Great Migration for African Americans. While the post–Civil War Reconstruction period after 1869 and World War I, both, created the environment for the exodus of African Americans from the south that Wilkerson calls a fever that "rose without warning or much in the way of understanding by those outside its reach" (*Warmth of Other Suns*, 2013, p. 8), it was a combination of events that led to the relocation of more than 6 million African Americans from the Southern to the Midwestern and Northern regions of the United States during the period that Wilkerson outlines in her book.

Black people were searching for liberty through migration that they didn't find in the Southern states that were burdened with racism. The injuries of racism were bred by the assault of Jim Crow laws and the massive lynching of Black men and women in these regions of the United States. Those who left the South hoped that within the metropolitan spaces of New York and the disparate landscapes of Chicago and Philadelphia they would begin new lives. Though this "fever" of migration that seemed to go unnoticed at its epic was silent, it impacted "every realm of America, into the words of Ralph Ellison and Toni Morrison, the plays of Lorraine Hansberry and August Wilson, the poetry and music of Langston Hughes and B. B. King and the latter-day generation of Arrested Development and Tupac Shakur" (Wilkerson, 2013, pp. 12–13). It also birthed a creative arts movement in Harlem, New York: The Harlem Renaissance.

Even what Black people called themselves evolved from 1915 to 1970. Wilkerson, in *Warmth of Other Suns*, presents the guiding principle applicable to my work in this book: "[T]he word coloured…is a primary identifier for Black people…during the first two-thirds of the twentieth century…into the 1960s, it shifts to the use of the term 'black'…and then to both 'black' and 'African American' in the current era" (p. 13). Also, when I refer to "Blacks" in this context, I denote Americans who were born in the United States—the descendants of African slaves. For my purposes here, I am most interested in the ways in which former American slaves shaped a distinct facet of the American experience in the twentieth century.

To truly understand the roots of hip-hop, especially its Harlem Renaissance roots, it is crucial to acknowledge that Blackness in America is evolutionary. The very act of enslavement assured that Black people forced ashore first in the East Coast colonies— and later, in larger numbers, to the agriculture-based Southern states—were often comprised of men and women from different African ethnic groups. Their experience and the will to survive envelops the study of their ability to create, sustain, and impact cultural forms in America. They are far from what may seem to some a monolithic group, united by the color of their skin and the circumstances of their enslavement and continued persecution in the United States. The varied diasporic story of Black people is evidenced in its cultural art forms. From West Africa to the United States, Black people bear witness to their human suffering and equity-deficit condition through cultural art. The cultural exchange of Black people in the United States is most obvious in dance, music, and literature.

The Need for Art

In 1926 W. E. B. Du Bois posed a controversial question to an audience in his speech "Criteria for Negro Art" for the National Association for the Advancement of Colored People (NAACP). Du Bois was concerned with the formal education of Blacks at the turn of the twentieth century and the 1926 symposium, "The Negro in Art," was published in *The Crisis* as his way of considering the question: "What have we, who are slaves and black, to do with art?" Though Black people in the United States had been emancipated from slavery since 1865, Du Bois used the word "slave" to indicate an ongoing mental state of Blacks in the United States who were uneducated and separate from cultivated beauty. He appealed to an innate sense of longing for beauty through creativity in "Criteria of Negro Art" and called for "artists [to] face [their] own pasts as a people" (p. 511) and allow that past to take on "form, color and reality" (511).

Du Bois writes years before hip-hop, and his "Criteria" was controversial even in 1926.[1] The Harlem Renaissance rests on Du Bois' position of "art as propaganda" to favorably position American Blacks in literature and art. However Du Bois' directive is agitated during his time by writers such as Langston Hughes, Richard Wright, and Zora Neale Hurston in that the literary genre appeal is twofold: it tells the story of a people, in their harsh realities of daily life behind the veil through the art form, but conversely it appeals to Whites as a monolithic view of Blackness in America. This was far from the truth and beauty of Blackness at the turn of the twentieth century and even further at the turn of the twenty-first century. But what remains the same is the quest for identity found in Du Bois' controversial speech about Black art. This quest was visible in the various cultural modes of expression of the Harlem Renaissance and can be seen in hip-hop today.

Bearing Witness

The founders of the Harlem Renaissance envisioned the period as one that would cultivate and showcase Black artistic expression. The development of an oral tradition that began during slavery would now become a transformative means of equipoise for Black art combining the oral and the visual. This semiotic linguist transition began while Blacks were still enslaved. Oral consciousness was awakened by the time Blacks are emancipated and a distinctly Black verbiage—both coded and direct—had been honed.

The Germination of Hip-hop

Contrary to what many people may think, hip-hop did not appear suddenly. The rhythms of hip-hop germinated in many places: in the bombastic sounds, expressive of hope and despair, that rose from the slave quarters at Rose Hall Plantation in Montego Bay; in the expansive rhythms of intelligent and beautiful Nubians from the Ivory Coast; in the long and pronounced rhythms of the South's bayous; and, eventually, in the use of relatively old technologies—microphones and turntables to name a few—to create new sounds in the North's urban centers. Hip-hop has always been a process, a journey. Its beginnings can be found on New York City blocks, but they can be found elsewhere as well. It is a product of the environment, but it is also—perhaps more crucially—a product of the blood's flow and pound within the arteries of the body and into the world at large.

In the first half of the twentieth century, Black Jazz and Rhythm & Blues artists gained national audiences. French-speaking Black writers from African and Caribbean colonies living and writing in cultural centers like Paris lyricized their own experiences and bellowed their chorus from across the sea. In the United States, the Harlem Renaissance, which included such literary notables as Langston Hughes, Zora Neale Hurston, and Claude McKay, gave expression to the Black experience of America, which had, before the 1920s, lacked a literature per se. Jamaican poet, writer, and scholar Claude McKay penned one of the most popular novels of the time, *Home to Harlem* (1928). Not only did McKay's novels, and those of many other talented Black writers emerging in the American Northeast, expose to the reading public the deeply rooted prejudice lurking within American Society, they also spoke to and for Black readers, urging unification for black folks.

In the era of the Civil Rights Movement, Black Americans began to engage in political discourse concerning identity, more forcefully addressing the question "Who am I?" by adopting new ethnic labels (Gallagher and Ashcroft, 2006, p. 59). Negro became Black, Black became Afro-American, Afro-American became African American. After centuries of forced silence, voices, previously timid and fearful of violent reprisals began to whisper, and then speak, and on occasion yell, but ultimately and most powerfully, sing and rhyme. Black Americans, along with West Indian immigrants, and new migrants from Africa, while forming individual communities, also united as one Black America. In venues like the Cotton Club, jazz shimmied and shook its way deep into American consciousness. White and Black artists alike contributed to the development of jazz as a genre, but the first massive celebrities of jazz were almost all Black. The sound of the big bands, Count Basie and Duke Ellington chief among them, made way for the explosion of individual acts in the second half of the century. Improvisation became one of the hallmarks of the jazz sound, and the free range granted to musicians to pursue their own distinct sounds gave artists like Nina Simone, John Coltrane, Miles Davis, Thelonious Monk, and countless others a platform—no less than Carnegie Hall—from which they could expose Black music to an appreciative listening public that quickly spread the sound around the world. Just as the Harlem Renaissance had used the art forms of the novel, the poem, and the drama to address both their own community and a sympathetic reading public, so jazz artists, especially singers (with songs like Billie Holiday's "Strange Fruit," and Nina Simone's "Why? The King of Love Is Dead," so powerfully delivered in a concert three days after Martin Luther King Jr.'s assassination[2]) used powerful lyrics and musical arrangement to strike a chord in the heart of both Black and White America.

Hip-hop, with its elevation of improvisation into a paralleled art form, and its use as a vehicle for powerful social protest, is a clear descendent of jazz. Jazz records, along with funk, soul, reggae, and other distinctly Black forms of music, provided the musical texture for hip-hop's birth. Even the sartorial and physical style of jazz was appropriated by hip-hop artists. The sway of men in the Jazz Age dressed in seersucker suits evolved into the swagger of hip-hop men and women in jeans, polos, and dress shirts. In her book, *The Music of Black Americans*, Eileen Southern states that hip-hop "was the direct heir of R&B, soul, and funk" (1997, p. 598), which would make hip-hop a younger phenomenon with a gestation period lasting only three decades at most. I push the roots of hip-hop back much further than this, back to the 1920s as an expression of an urban, musical poetic that has prevailed since at least the Harlem Renaissance.[3] Somewhat overlooked is the genre of Jamaican Dub, which represents yet another musical parent to the modern movement that ushered in the cultural phenomenon known as hip-hop (Chang, 2005; Forman and Neal, 2011; Ogbar, 2007).

The mid-1970s brought with it the rumblings of something that would come to pervade every corner of the world. Legendary sociocultural educators like the Last Poets moved beyond musings on the country's military engagements to begin the work of motivating a new cadre of freedom soldiers and heroes. Outside of the high-rises of Sedgwick Avenue, and in the streets of 163rd, prophets and MCs directed throngs in rallies. Musical instruments and amplifiers helped to enhance and modulate the voices of the new statesmen in their native "Black and Proud," "Black is Beautiful" tongue. Artists such as DJ Kool Herc introduced a new form of deejaying while performing at parties on Sedgewick Avenue. Serendipitously, he discovered a way of "breaking" the beat on a record to isolate it and then use two turn tables to extend the beat. He helped to give birth to three very important aspects of hip-hop culture by way of deejaying. First of all, the art of deejaying has itself been a constant presence in the hip-hop scene. It continues to expand in new directions, birthing countless genres and subgenres both within and outside of hip-hop. More important to the emergence of hip-hop as an art form with the power to express forcefully and directly the malaise of the ghetto was the blending of the art of the deejay and the spoken word of the crowd-crowd thrilling street poet, the MC. The break, the beat, later the scratch and the loop as well, all gave a new avenue through which the tradition of oral poetry—a tradition that extended back to long before the slave trade began—could express itself in stunningly modern ways. The break beat became the identifying characteristic of hip-hop music. It inspired breakdancing. "Using "breaks" (two break silence for every eight bars) in the music, expanding the music with two turntables and double copies of a record to mix music, and light rhyming, the DJs and dancers who called themselves B-boys and B-girls (with the "B" standing for break) would entertain a street crowd. The syncopated staccato of the break led to the third branch of hip-hop: Breaking, B-boying, or Breakdancing.

Showing their power by whipping through the air on the strength of one arm, dancers would seemingly manipulate gravity, freezing in midair. Whether it was dizzying head spins or windmills and fancy footwork, this form of movement and performance became something that allowed for healthy competition, and skilled dance crews emerged around this new form of dance. Practitioners spent hours rehearsing and devising new dance moves in order to elevate their craft to ever higher levels. Breakdancing as distinctive cultural phenomena became a focus of belonging. It became a part of identity. Through it, dancers and spectators could become agents for positive change, empowered and mobilized for greater action and good deeds. The dancers developed different body tricks like spinning on their heads, contorting their bodies into pretzel-like forms, twirling around on their backs, doing the "uprock" and other athletic moves."[4] Breakdance troupes soon began to emulate gang violence in their dance dramatizations. In these simulated confrontations, or dance battles, "B-boys" and "B-girls" would compete for dominance and popularity. The artistic basis of *West Side Story*—rival gangs dancing through the streets of New York— was suddenly realized in actual life, though with rather different music than Leonard Bernstein's popular score.

Among the new hip-hop generation, graffiti, which had been around since the ancient Egyptians used hieroglyphics as a means to say *I am here*, was adopted as a means of visual expression by youth who often didn't have the luxury of expensive art supplies. Through graffiti, public space became a forum in which the artists announced to the world *I'm here, too*. Ohio-based graffiti artist "Dante" claims,

> I've been a visual artist since before I can remember…I got attracted to the graffiti scene back in middle/high school…Getting older meant more freedoms…at that age I loved the attention my art commanded from my friends…but unless they were in my art classes, people only saw my sketchbooks, rarely the fine art teachers continued to enter into competitions and showcases…and with these new freedoms, my friends weren't chillin' in museums and galleries…we were on the sides of stores, in alleys, at bus stops, etc…I just wanted to be seen by people like me, people doing what I was doing, living MY lifestyle.[5]

Historically, in many urban spaces, and even today, graffiti is misapplied and synonymous with city crime and vandalism. Although the underground nature of this counterculture is still prevalent as rebellious and politically charged, Dante argues that the art has evolved into more respectable circles.

> I remember feeling discriminated against when I'd enter large, bright displays for competition, and would lose to "traditional" looking oil paintings or charcoal drawings…but as time has passed, it's becoming much more the "style of choice"…I'm proud to see graffiti style works in museums and galleries today…it's making a strong case and being accepted by most as a genuine art form these days.[6]

MCs articulated the pains of our past and the agonies of our present, fused them with blues, jazz, and funk, then spun it into their own dialect. Arguably more alluring than its musical parents, and more expansive in its base than any other political agent, and by far the most well-funded, hip-hop can be thought of as the future of urban and nonurban communications speaking to young urbanites through its emphasis on fashion, on language, on location, and on food, all while serving as an entree into the world of cool. Quote a rap song, program a dance show for television; if it is hip-hop, Madison Avenue wants a piece of it. It is already a unifier, and can do much more to unite diverse peoples. Jonathan Scott, author of "Sublimating Hip Hop: Rap Music in White America," says "Globally, hip hop has been loved, appreciated, embraced, fetishized, and widely imitated precisely because of its boldly assertive African Americanness. To the world, hip hop is as brilliantly Black as blues and jazz, and just as important aesthetically."[7] Although its origins are to be found in West Africa, on the coasts of the Americas, and in the rural Southern states, hip-hop became, very much, an urban phenomena and this encouraged its spread at lightning speed within African American and worldwide cultures.

The Advent of Hip-hop

Hip-hop's etymology traces the roots of the word to two slang words: the first, "hip," connotes a sense of what is in vogue; the second, "hop," describes the characteristic physical movements of dancing associated with the musical style—this dance form itself an omnibus art form with roots, which run deeply through a number of ethnic musical genres. Perhaps more important, hip-hop is both an art form and cultural rallying cry that has for the past

40 years encompassed the dreams and struggles of minorities, and Blacks in particular.

As previously stated, hip-hop's cultural roots can be traced back through generations of African American musical and cultural history, through the culture of the Afro-Caribbean nations and through that of Africa itself. Significantly, each of the major American musical trends that can be recognized as playing a part in hip-hop's ancestry is linked to specific political and social movements. As such, these movements—from the Harlem Renaissance to the Beat Era and Black Arts Movement, from the Civil Rights Era to the urban riots of 1967 and 1968 and the current peaceful demonstrations over the murder of Trayvon Martin—show that hip-hop is a nexusin which it meets the arts and struggles of a distinct people.

Just as James Brown's "Black and Proud" was not simply a song, but rather an anthem for Black Empowerment, a moment in time when Black people felt pride in their darkness, hip-hop was rich in similar anthemic sounds and statements of Blackness and pride in that Blackness. The engine of hip-hop is its sound, rooted in transplanted African sounds; the fuel that feeds this sound, the fuel that turns it into an engine of protest and revolution, is the harrowing past of our ancestors who crossed the Atlantic on slaves ships; it is the pangs of an incomplete liberation' it is the mixture of terror and rage brought on by the terrible spectacle of "Black bodies swinging in the Southern breeze";[8] it is the politics of segregations; and, finally, it is the politics of identity that have united Black folks for the last 60 years. Since its inception, hip-hop has been, at once, a raw and a refined mode of communication. Some of the greatest hip-hop music explodes beyond sound and rhythm to involve a people in a musical conversation that began in Africa.

Though there may be some disagreement between critics and scholars as to how far back we are to push its origins, there is some consensus as to the moment of hip-hop's germination. Just as Realism in painting can be traced back to Manet's *Olympia* and Cubism arrived with Picasso's *Les Demoiselles d'Avignon*, hip-hop, appropriately enough, earned its name during a now-famous house party. In 1973, DJ KoolHerc (Clive Campbell) held the first of his legendary block parties,[9] deejaying his sister's birthday party on Sedgwick Avenue in the Bronx. This party became the first of many, and folklore has it that Herc's parties would last

8–12 hours, a true testament to the power of the music to move crowds interminably.

The cultural significance of these events was much broader than KoolHerc's creations.[10] His parties must be seen within their cultural context—that of the South Bronx of New York City in 1973. The South Bronx was at that time a desolate place, crime-ridden and, by many firsthand accounts, it bore more resemblance to a third-world country than it did to urban America. The installation of the Cross-Bronx Expressway radically changed the demographics of the neighborhood. Many of the Bronx's White residents left in hopes of a better, quieter life. As the Bronx's demographics changed, so too did the culture of the area, as it filled with underprivileged inhabitants, mostly Black and Hispanic. Because the majority of the Bronx's inhabitants were poor, crime, drug and alcohol addiction, unemployment, and all the social ills associated with poverty were prevalent. In these rough conditions, poor and despairing residents reacted in one of two ways: some acted out, resorting to unproductive or criminal behavior that only furthered the problems faced by their communities and, in many cases, led to the forfeiture of their very lives; others, though, underwent a "baptism by fire" of sorts; they set out on intense searches for life's meaning, the unequivocal vision quest, working to gather personal strength in order to improve their lots. For many of these seekers, hip-hop was both source and target for their energies; it gave them the impetus to dream big, to find strength, and, finally, to move onward and upward.

The philosophies that arose and continue to arise from these searches for meaning can be considered as the primary and productive motives of life itself. This has been documented in other contexts as well, particularly in Victor Frankl's *Man's Search for Meaning*, in which he vividly describes the psychology of what it took for Jewish people to survive Nazi concentration camps during the Holocaust. In the 1970s in the South Bronx, hip-hop became the medium through which a similar psychological force of survival could occur. It was around this time that DJ/MC/Crowd Pleaser Lovebug Starski started referring to this culture as hip-hop. Given these circumstances, music alone was unlikely to suffice as a response to social ills, but it was the all-encompassing nature of hip-hop as music and as culture that gave the art form the potential to engender positivity where it was most needed—the escape from the overwhelmingly negative forces of crime, poverty, and racism. With the founding of the Universal Zulu Nation by Kevin Donovan, aka Afrika Bambaataa, Black people were given a powerful new collective through which they could express their despair in constructive and musical ways.

In the early stages of the evolution of breakdancing, Afrika Bambaataa, working in concert with local school officials, encouraged a gang called the Black Spades, in which he had a role as "warlord," to negotiate a peace treaty with rival gangs. A trip to Africa had opened his eyes to the need to stop violence in the hood. Upon returning to New York, he organized hip-hop parties. These were intended to create a Universal Zulu Nation where street violence and gang turf wars could be ameliorated by reimagining anger through dance. Although the beginnings of the musical movement preceded his involvement in the New York scene, Bambaataa's movement was the beginning of the political component of hip-hop.

Afrika Bambaataa Aasim was named in honor of an ancient nineteenth-century Zulu chief destined for greatness and a role of influence. The South-African Zulu people were the only "primitive" people to ever vanquish the British colonial army in combat.[11] Bambaataa knew that if the Universal Zulu Nation were to improve the lives of Black Americans one iota, they would need to first be united to fight against both the external and internal forces that were keeping them from their purpose. As Bambaataa himself put it, "if you resisted, sometimes peace came to you violently. We demanded peace; but a lot of gangs like the Ball Busters refused to join. One group, the Casanova Crew, joined...by force. In the end, there was peace, though" (qtd. in Ogbar, 2007, pp. 176–177).

As hip-hop began to spread as a musical and cultural phenomenon in the late 1970s, Afrika Bambaataa, Kool Herc, Grandmaster Caz, and Grandmaster Flash took their street parties to many of the Bronx neighborhoods. For them, it was clear that hip-hop had the potential to be, indeed, already was, much more than a mere musical style popular in inner-city parties. There was, at the heart of the burgeoning movement, a political, a cultural, and yes, a musical significance as well. It also quickly became a commercial enterprise that, almost overnight, provided young Blacks, predominantly men, an avenue by which they could earn ever-increasing amounts of money. Hip-hop proved, in new ways, what jazz had proved in the heavily segregated America of the 1920s: Black culture was not only beautiful, it was commercially viable. The effects of this commercial success on the Black community—indeed, on America—were beyond the wildest imaginings of those who witnessed the birth of the scene in the early 1970s. The commercial success, while it did undoubtedly ease, for some, the burdens of ghetto life, brought with it a host of new issues, mainly of exploitation, but there were problems within communities as well. As Notorious B.I.G. said in 1997: "Mo money, mo problems."[12]

What one did with one's success—newfound or otherwise— became the subject of intense scrutiny in the scene. This scrutiny continues today, as could be seen recently in the widely publicized criticism of Jay-Z regarding his deal with the New York department store, Barneys. Criticism began when racial profiling allegations were brought forth by two Black customers, Trayon Christian and Kayla Phillips. They alleged that Barneys had profiled and detained them, going so far as to get the police involved, after the two made pricey purchases at the upscale store. Since the incidents, the two have filed lawsuits. An online petition and a fury of twitter messages followed from outraged fans urging Jay-Z to cut ties with Barneys. Residents of the Marcy Projects, located in Brooklyn, where Jay-Z grew up, were irate: "If Jay Z continues to do a campaign with this racist store, he's dirt in my book," tweeted Michele Mimi Evans. Another tweeted, "From someone that came from the hood, he should know all that. He knows how hard it is. I don't think he should sell his things there, not at a place where there's racial profiling going on. It's ridiculous." 99 problems? Make that 100.

In response to some of the criticisms of big money's influence on the hip-hop scene—some valid, some hogwash—some hip-hop purists, KRS-One, DMC, and hip-hop writer Kirk Walker among them, have become bona fide gatekeepers of hip-hop as an art form and a cultural expression. Over the course of its history, hip-hop has evolved from an art form little concerned with the trappings of success to one that champions commercialism in unprecedented ways. rappers flaunt their personal possessions in photo and video shoots (often borrowing or renting the more outrageously expensive items), flashing cash, jewelry, cars, expensive liquor, cigars, lavish estates, and private jets to show that they have "made it." Since the Sugar Hill Gang's 1979 smash hit, "Rapper's Delight," made it clear to both artists and record executives just how powerful a commercial entity hip-hop could be, battle lines began to be drawn, separating those artists who were concerned, at times exclusively, with commercial success and those who were carrying on in the spirit of hip-hop's progenitors. Though there is a flourishing hip-hop scene in countless small and large cities around the world, the majority of hip-hop's exposure is granted to those who have strayed from the path that hip-hop legends like KRS-One and Afrika Bambaataa forged when hip-hop was still in its infancy. Instead of creating for love of expression, identity, and pride, commercially motivated artists now largely create in order to become wealthy. Criticism of this practice has become something of a trope within the hip-hop community; there are too many instances of this to mention—nearly every hip-hop record of the last 30 years has in some way or another engaged with the risible figure of the rapper made wealthy by selling their soul to corporate interests in exchange for shiny baubles and trinkets.

For a group of people whose history in this country was predicated on the fact that we were literally commodified by our enslavers, it is perhaps unsurprising that, once the means of attaining power of one's own through material wealth materialized, that opportunity should be so ardently pursued by those who were once held at bay from the fruits of their own labors. Still, this accumulation of wealth on both a group and an individual level comes with a hefty price tag. Kirk Walker expresses the problems of this candidly:

> The elements that defined hip-hop culture are being stripped away in favor of the corrupted and compromised elements of it that wealthy people not of the hip-hop nation (and, unfortunately, an increasing number of indoctrinated wealthy hip-hop nationals) find profitable. The irony of this is that the aspects of the hip-hop culture that are being phased out are the very aspects that allowed it to grow to a point where others such as themselves find it profitable to be involved with. (Femmixx, 2013)

The environment that hip-hop artists—legitimate hip-hop artists—created with their sub- and counterculture is the *sine qua non* of commercial rap. Any attempt on the part of commercially successful artists to divorce themselves and their genre from its hip-hop roots is at best disingenuous. Though commercial success may have distorted the message and skewed the vision of hip-hop, its sound betrays a root system that moves through soil shared by the conscious artists who gave birth to a movement.

Freedom, Authenticity, and the Ontology of Hip-hop

As hip-hop has evolved, the ability of artists to be free to compose and perform as they see fit has involved a type of liberation, not limited to, but centered on liberation from the norms established by the historical oppressors. This is a freedom to form new thoughts and create something new, things linguistically, visually, or physically "'dope' or 'fresh' (to use hip-hop's early vernacular)."

To the uninformed listener, hip-hop beats, especially without verbal accompaniment, might seem like a skipping record; the break is, in essence, a loop of, at most, 16 bars of music from an existing record. However, the musical form itself is something far more than this. It was created by DJs who, in an act of expressing their own freedom, invented something new out of something old through the practice of sampling. Some might see this as nothing more than appropriation of others' work, a lack of originality on the part of the DJ, but turntablism is an art form that takes considerable ingenuity and dedication to do well (let alone master). Though there may be nothing new under the sun, the DJ takes what is old or what has, perhaps, been forgotten and breathes new life into it through his or her art. If one has any doubts as to the veracity of this statement, simply listen to the productions of a DJ Shadow, a Chief Xcel, a DJ Qbert, a Kid Koala, or a Mix Master Mike (Chang, 2005; Foreman and Neal, 2011). Each combines the record and the turntable to create something entirely new. Play their source materials, and you would hardly recognize them as such. They are like the notes on a saxophone or the keys on a piano. Each has been played before, but never quite as they are played this time. They are cut and blended in such a way as to bear the unique fingerprint of their DJ, and, just as the experienced listener can recognize Miles Davis or John Coltrane from the way they play a single note, so the experienced hip-hop fan can recognize a Shadow or an Xcel cut from the way they cut, scratch, and combine their records. Make no mistake; the DJ is an artist.

In discussions of hip-hop, though, the art of turntablism is usually overshadowed by that of the MC. Rap and hip-hop are often misconstrued as the same thing, but the former is actually a subgenre of the latter. Grandmaster Caz, who was the first—the first in a hip-hop context at least—to refer to himself as an MC, moved hip-hop in radically new directions when he realized that the DJ's music needed vocals to drive it. As artist KRS-One powerfully articulated, "Hip Hop is something you live, Rap is something you do."[13] In essence, hip-hop is a culture and rap is a form of music, a verbal form, within that culture.

With its radically new fusion of street poetry and the DJ music, hip-hop became something more than a sound recognizable to its initiates. It became a platform, a voice for the unheard that could address listeners both within and outside of its community. Because it has always been a platform for social change and protest, it can be said that hip-hop is philanthropic, a humanitarian force giving underprivileged and ignored people, particularly youth and minorities, voices and seats at the table of public, intercultural discourse. Hip-hop's explosion out of New York's ghettoes meant that the social and political issues so strongly felt therein were not only being musically addressed, but they were being thus addressed in the broadest of forums as well.

Even White people began to pay attention. For many in the Bronx, immersing themselves in hip-hop culture entailed a resistance to the forces of oppression; hip-hop provided a way to "Fight the Power" (as Public Enemy put it)—the nameless, faceless entities of social control that were, it was felt, continuing the work of disenfranchisement begun centuries earlier. For as long as it was legitimately perceived as a counterculture, a tool with which one could rail against these nameless forces, nearly uniformly it was a unifying and emancipatory force for Black people both within and outside of the ghetto. This was not to last long, though; hip-hop was quickly appropriated, its stars exploited, and its visual and poetic power was diverted into dramatically weakened channels that reinforced rather than challenged mainstream norms. From being the voice of the unheard, it became ubiquitous. There was, it must be said, a mutual influence: the mainstream, especially its consumerism, worked its way insidiously into hip-hop's message, but, at the same time, Black swagger, Black language, Black mannerism, and Black musical styles made their presences felt in the mainstream in a way that they previously had not. As diffuse as hip-hop's emancipatory and revolutionary power[14] became as it entered the mainstream, the widening of hip-hop's national and international audience brought with it newfound attention to the plight of the inner cities of America. On MTV and the radio waves of the nation, the problems Black America faced moved front and center and became part of the country's collective consciousness.

In 1982, Grandmaster Flash came out with "The Message," which highlighted this inner-city struggle. Mainstream America hopped on the hip-hop train for the music, and stayed for the message. Attitudes began to change, as people who had previously been ignorant of the strife of ghetto inhabitants began to understand the existence and persistence of inequality and human suffering. This was—shocking to those who were hearing and seeing it for the first time—happening under the very noses of the sheltered suburbanites who were lapping up records as fast as they could be produced. The unavoidable message of songs like "The Message" was that things were bad in America, and they were getting worse. Many Black Americans lacked the means to live safely and comfortably, a security that many suburbanites had taken for granted.

As hip-hop entered the suburbs of America, White youth, drawn to its rebelliousness and to its captivating new sound, converted in droves to the church of hip-hop. Hip-hop culture quickly became American culture; young White boys could be seen with their hats back to front, gold medallions swinging from their necks. Hip-hop became a way in which rebellious displays, antiauthoritarian attitudes, and explicit language—all elements of the new hip-hop-infused "cool"—could be both marketed to, packaged for, and consumed by an eager—and surprisingly White—public. In itself, this was nothing new: Whites have been appropriating Black swagger, lingo, fashion, and music for almost a century, if not longer. Elvis Presley was seized upon as a White man who could sing—and, perhaps more importantly, shimmy and shake—like a Black one. The fact that it was a White man moving thus—he was, in fact, merely reproducing a style of movement that had popularized by Black performers years earlier[15]—meant that parents could be scandalized by the sexual undercurrent of the moves, but just scandalized enough to raise an eyebrow and *tsk tsk* at the dinner table. The reverse form of racial blending and appropriation is of rare occurrence. Paul Robeson may have sung Bach and Dvorak as expertly as he did "Deep River," but, in spite of this, he was always first and foremost a singer of spirituals who happened to have branched out, not an authentic singer of Western (White) classical music.

White adoption/appropriation of hip-hop culture raises some interesting questions. Foremost of these asks whether the distinctly middle-class White youths who began to speak, dress, and swagger like "gangstas" were, in appropriating this culture of the oppressed, stealing what they had no right to, thus participating in the de-individualization that characterized Black existence before the 1960s in America. Is this the continuation of a historical precedent of appropriation or it a reversal of a historical precedent of a tongue-in-cheek game of dress-up reverting Blacks of objects (things) devoid of subjective and souls from which their art is birthed? The fear of course is in those spaces, rare but still existent, where the extent of Black-White interaction is YouTube or some form of video depicting one certain aspect of Black life. It is the kind of fear the author/activist Billy Wamsatt is speaking of when he is quoted by Bakari Kitwana as saying: "I'm horrified by the aspect of the white hip-hop thing where you can be a white hard-core underground hip-hop kid in, say, Minnesota and not know a single black person."[16]

As hip-hop continued to grow in the 1980s as a commercial entity, American and European urban fashion trends quickly reflected the growing influence of hip-hop—especially among the young. White suburbanites began wearing paint-splattered and graffiti-inspired prints; they began wearing jewelry in an ostentatious way, and parachute pants quickly began to appear in malls and school corridors almost everywhere; pants were slung lower, and high-top basketball sneakers—particularly Air Jordans, the popularity of which was due to yet another Black icon idolized by White America—were *the* must-have footwear.

The way Americans spoke began to change too; hip-hop lingo became part of the common vernacular. Todd Boyd says, "The beauty of hip hop lies in its ability to transform language."[17] Words like "hood" (neighborhood), "chill" (relax), and expressions like, "What's up?" (hello/how are you?) and "Peace out" (goodbye) quickly entered the stream of American mass communication. In *The American Language*, H. L. Menicken illuminates the ways in which the English language is made richer and more reflective of the cultural environment in which it is produced in its permissiveness regarding slang:

> What chiefly lies behind (slang) is simply a kind of linguistic exuberance, an excess of word-making energy. It relates itself to the standard language a great deal as dancing relates itself to music. But there is also something else. The best slang is not only ingenious and amusing; it also embodies a kind of social criticism. (Menicken, p. 557)

Words that were once outside of Standard English have simply become part of our everyday usage. The slang of hip-hop is here to stay, and it, by Menicken's definition, is enriching our spoken language.

More importantly, than sartorial style or linguistic embellishment though, is hip-hop's contributions to the American attitude. Hip-hop opened new lines of communication between the affluent and the destitute, creating affability between rich and poor youth through shared Black icons. In a way it had not been previously, hip-hop made it "cool" for White youth to care about the issues of racism, poverty, and oppression that were an everyday reality for the residents of the ghetto. Kitwana notes, "as people began to talk about white hip hop kids in a public realm, I felt that often it was a form of ridicule, an outdated caricature...and I thought the white hip hop kids were a lot more sophisticated, not just about hip hop, but also about race."[18] Like so many other notable movements in America's musical past (as we mentioned above, jazz and rock and roll are two examples), hip-hop began as something created by and for Black people; what began as "Black music" became, simply, music as it was fused with White culture. Unlike rock and roll and jazz, hip-hop, entering middle age, is still recognized as a distinctly Black form of culture—the Black roots of jazz are still widely recognized as such, though rock and roll's roots are more often ignored than they are explored. While hip-hop has undoubtedly become more acceptable to dominant (White) mainstream culture and its critics, and while Black artists have undoubtedly been exploited by corporate interests (Black and White alike), Black ownership of its sound, its attitude, its lingo, its gestures has never really been challenged. White hip-hop artists continue to pervade the industry, but they are in the minority, and ad hominem attacks of White artists (think Eminem) often begin and end with the fact that they have adopted a form of music that is not in any way their own. To a philosopher this claim is epistemologically untenable. There is a fine line between White appreciation of Black culture and the construction or revival of what could be construed as minstrel culture.[19] As White youth embrace rap music the broadening of the cultural affects provide a common sort of cultural vocabulary for youths from all cultural backgrounds. It thus becomes a cultural imperative for many White youth to embrace rap music in order to fit in with their peer group. Therefore, many felt the message of hip-hop was being watered down. There is an overwhelming sense of Black ownership in the hip-hop scene; this ownership can be shared, but it can never be taken away.

Hip-hop's musical success may have resulted in an increase of dialogue between White and Black cultures and communities, but these new avenues of communication travelled both ways. Even when it was still a relatively new phenomenon, the influence of American hyper-commercialism began to be felt in hip-hop's sound and in the way it was consumed and marketed. As the new decade began, Sugarhill Gang's "Rapper's Delight" announced hip-hop's entrance into the mainstream. In January of 1980, it became the first hip-hop single to crack the Top 40, peaking at 36 on the American Hot 100 and earning top honors in Canada and The Netherlands. Hip-hop's mainstream popularity blossomed almost overnight; soon, Mr. Magic was hosting "RapAttack," the first hip-hop radio show on WHBI. Kurtis Blow was the first rapper to appear on *Soul Train*, a hugely popular national television show. Blow released "The Breaks" on Mercury Records in September of 1980. It sold more than a million copies in the months following its release, almost matching the success of "Rapper's Delight." Hip-hop quickly evolved into big business; major record labels were quick to take notice of its broad appeal, and they quickly began courting and signing rap artists in the hopes of riding the wave of the new music's massive spike in popularity.

The next year, 1981, saw significant developments both above and below ground. Early in the year, Blondie, after meeting Fab 5 Freddy and others, released "Rapture," which included a hip-hop–influenced beat and a rap by Debbie Harry. It was the first hip-hop music video to debut on MTV. Shortly thereafter, the Funky Four + 1 appeared on *Saturday Night Live*, becoming the first hip-hop act to appear on network television. Beneath the surface, hip-hop was adding new skills to its repertoire and exposing them to its audience. Late in the year, Kool Moe Dee took down fellow rapper Busy Bee in a spontaneous, live MC battle. Since that initial contest, battling has become a way for up-and-coming MCs to sharpen their skills and make a name for themselves. Also in 1981, Grandmaster Flash released "The Adventures of Grandmaster Flash on the Wheels of Steel," the first single that captured sound scratching. Like the MC battle between Kool Moe Dee and Busy Bee, the release of Grandmaster Flash's single heralded the advent of a new form of musical showmanship, a new way for hip-hop musicians to showcase their talents, move their crowds, and build their reputations.[20]

Beginning as a project in 1980, though not widely released until 1983, *Wild Style,* a film coproduced by Charlie Ahearn and Fab 5 Freddy, brought hip-hop to the big screen. The film's protagonist was a New York graffiti writer, but it featured other recognizable features of hip-hop culture as well: breaking, turntablism, and MCs make frequent appearances in the film. The film and its soundtrack, which included cuts by the Cold Crush Brothers and a number of others, were extremely well received by hip-hop fans and noninitiates alike; still widely regarded as the first—and by some, the best—hip-hop movie ever made, *Wild Style* birthed a new film genre that resulted in an explosion of hip-hop cinema; *Breakin'* and *Krush Groove,* both of which were clearly modeled on the success of *Wild Style,* quickly followed in its wake.[21]

As the second half of the decade dawned, hip-hop was poised to make more significant breakthroughs into the mainstream. In 1986, hip-hop mogul Russell Simmons introduced his brother Joseph Simmons to the group DMC. Joseph took on the name Run and joined the group, creating the now-household name, Run DMC. In a collaborative effort that helped reinvigorate flagging album sales for Aerosmith while, at the same time, bringing Run DMC into the spotlight, Run DMC remixed Aerosmith's song (already more than ten years old) "Walk this Way" and made one of the smash hits of 1986. Perhaps more than any other moment in the history of hip-hop, this song crossed over between genres that had previously had little to do with each other. Rap music on rock radio stations was a dream come true in terms of album sales and exposure for both groups.

While the mainstream was embracing hip-hop music, a subgenre of hip-hop was emerging that was, for some, a growing cause of alarm. Gangsta rap, characterized by its explicit, crime-promoting, misogynistic lyrics, made landfall in 1986 with the release of Schoolly D's single "P.S.K." The Recording Industry Association of America (RIAA) was, before long, slapping warning labels on rap records for their explicit lyrical content. What was meant to warn the listening public, instead, turned into a veritable feeding frenzy for recording materials that carried the warning label. One of these, N.W.A.'s *Straight Outta Compton*, featuring the anthemic antiauthority diatribe, "Fuck the Police," was a particular target of musical critics and moral watchdogs. Critical responses were by no means unanimous, but it was the lyrical content, especially its glamorization of Black-on-Black violence, that was almost uniformly panned. The band was quick to defend their right to express themselves regarding the very real conditions of the inner city; "Express Yourself" speaks to the need felt by artists such as N.W.A. to speak truth contra societal pressures to conform: "It's crazy to see people be / What society wants them to be, but not me!" gangsta rappers like N.W.A. and countless others were examples of self-expression in a hip-hop context taken to extreme measures, and the subgenre must be credited for its persistent speaking of truth to power, but the tremendous commercial success enjoyed by these artists does raise questions as to the line between what is real and what is marketable. Gangsta rap had turned criminality into an out-and-out commodity; what the market demanded, N.W.A. and other gangsta rappers like them provided in spades; bravado and exaggeration have ever been features of hip-hop, but the lyrical content of gangsta rap took this to dizzying heights. Many, particularly young listeners, felt, however, that this music unflinchingly captured their anger with authority—no matter what shape this authority took. No matter how much it was exaggerated for commercial effect, gangsta rap was too powerful a musical force to ignore. Suburban bedrooms sported N.W.A., Eazy-E, Dr. Dre, and Ice Cube posters. The artists themselves were busy decorating their own walls with platinum records.

The problem that gangsta rap created for hip-hop as a culture is that ill-informed critics equated hip-hop *in toto* with its problem child—an imprecise equation that continues among more conservative critics of youth culture to this day. There are certainly musical similarities, which do little to clear up critics' confusion, but lyrically hip-hop and gangsta rap couldn't be further apart. As the 1990s approached, the relatively lighthearted nature of hip-hop lyrics—even of the beats themselves—gave way to a more aggressive sound and an extremely aggressive poetic. Hip-hop, on the whole, may have been flourishing, but its commercial success commodified Black anger in a way that did little to address this anger in a constructive, community-sensitive way. The profit system that Black musicians became a part of (often as producers themselves) exploited their rage for commercial gains. What began as something undoubtedly expressing a powerful truth about inner-city life became something that smacked of manufacture. As gangsta rap co-opted the hip-hop movement, mainstream audiences fled from the genre in droves. Hip-hop album sales decreased, and hip-hop culture, overshadowed by the headline-grabbing violence of gangsta rap, became an underground movement once again. The change that the late 1980s and early 1990s had brought to the hip-hop scene and its music split the culture in two; both branches would continue to evolve in the coming years, but they were now moving in divergent directions.

Perhaps due to its powerful expressive potential and its often highly intelligent lyrical content, hip-hop has been more able than gangsta rap to at once remain essentially the same and adjust to the shifting sands of commercial music markets. Hip-hop scholars Murray Forman and Mark Anthony Neal have argued that, "Faced with shifting technologies, new aesthetic values and cultural tastes, or revised by industrial standards, Hip Hop's creative workers demonstrate boundless innovation and flexibility, affirming that Hip Hop is not solely beholden to commercial mandates. Hip Hop's most committed advocates reinforce the reality that Hip Hop is anything but static."[22] They, thus, emphasize the obvious growth that has happened within hip-hop culture, and among those who were innovators and pioneers in the genre. They have further stated, "Since its inception, Hip Hop has inflected conditions at multiple scales, and it remains a vital force in the articulation and expression of culture, politics, and identity for literally millions of people around the world. This is to say that hip hop is an essential facet of everyday life and experiential being, a cornerstone of individual and communal existence" (Forman and Neal, 2011, p. 3) hip-hop culture has both flexibility and resilience enough to evolve when it has to without losing its credibility. It has continued to be a mainstay in popular culture, but, because it so often critiques components of this culture, it doggedly retains its outsider status.

The pioneers and moguls of hip-hop have reinvented themselves to meet shifting climates and demands of both themselves and their art alike. Some examples of this resilience within the culture include Will Smith, who started as a rapper, and parlayed himself into an actor in *The Fresh Prince of Bel-Air*, and is now one of Hollywood's most bankable stars. Queen Latifah, who was a rapper, transformed herself into an actor and even a *Cover Girl* spokesmodel. Highly esteemed actor Ice-T, who started as a gangsta rapper, has appeared dozens of times on both big and small screens. Ice Cube, who started as a gangsta rapper with NWA, then broke out on his own as a solo rap artist, also took up a career in acting and now even stars in family-friendly films that appeal to the masses.[23] He also works as a director and producer of films. These performers are not only commercially astute but, using a variety of talents, they have succeeded in reinventing themselves, sometimes several times over as well.

Hip-hop's commercialization cannot be debated, along with all the results that implies. Professor Jeffrey O. G. Ogbar points out the effects that hip-hop has had on the entire structure of music sales and industry strongholds.

> Unlike the hyperexploited black musicians of earlier generations, hip-hop entrepreneurs, for better or worse, have embraced the capitalist principles with zeal, boldness, and business savvy…artist-owned independent ventures have characterized a scale of control over cultural production unseen in any other genre of music. From real estate and film, to restaurants, sports teams, and even oil refineries, these moguls have been ambitious with their investments. From fashion houses like G-Unit, Sean Jean, and Rocawear, young black men have reaped millions in ways that no generation of black fashion designers have. (2007, p. 177)

Ogbar shines a light on the huge influence that hip-hop culture has had on employing and empowering Black youth. He notes: "They have given initial opportunities to dozens of video directors…some

have found success in big movie productions...hip-hop generation professionals have enjoyed unprecedented access to the music
industry's billions, by employing their own" (2007, p. 177).

It is now clear that hip-hop is no longer the counterculture it
was—at least not uniformly so. Hip-hop is no longer just the music
du jour; its ubiquity knows few bounds, and crossovers between
hip-hop artists and rock stars and even country musicians are commonplace enough to suggest that hip-hop is the most protean form
of music in the world. As such, it has come to play a major role in
corporate America, and, since it does, it must toe the line more
often than it did at its birth. Some hip-hop artists persistently
cling to their countercultural roots. They work with the people
they always have, creating a music that resonates in a powerful
way with the disaffected and the oppressed, but, at the same time,
many hip-hop artists are adapting to the times and markets with a
corporatism that rewards the individual artist for exploiting themselves and their message. Indeed, when it is proclaimed that artists
have "sold out" that some say that the movement is completely
controlled by White, corporate America, effectively creating a new
type of plantation. Both of these (opposing) concepts of a contemporary hip-hop culture have elements of truth. DMC (aka Darryl
McDaniels), part of the legendary rap group Run DMC states, "It
was inevitable that hip-hop became commercialized, but along the
way our power got taken away. Now you got the same 12 records
on radio being played over and over again. Lil Wayne, Jay Z ain't
hot, it's just they're programmed so many times people are brain-
washed."[24] Whatever is to become of hip-hop, it has already made
itself a permanent fixture in the modern American zeitgeist.

Rumination 2

Firebrands and Battle Plans: Jean-Paul Sartre, Friedrich Nietzsche, and G. W. F. Hegel

Jean-Paul Sartre in his "Black Orpheus" wrote: "[B]ecause he is oppressed in and as a result of his race, it is first his race of which [the Black man] must be aware. He must compel those who for centuries, vainly tried to reduce him to a beast, because he was black to recognize him as a man."[1] Black poetry, of which rap is a particularly relevant twenty-first-century example, has, since hip-hop's birth, demanded recognition for Black artists—indeed, all Black people—as subjective identities. Just as Sartre recognized the figure of the Black poet who would "tear Blackness out of himself in order to offer it to the world,"[2] so does hip-hop unashamedly offer to the world its own beautiful Blackness, carrying on the proud tradition of Black expression that was begun when the formerly colonized and the formerly enslaved began poeticizing their feelings in the language of their oppressors. Crucially, such expressions of Blackness and selfhood did not demand a place at the table next to enslavers and colonizers; rather, they established a counter discourse through which Black voices could contend not only with racism and colonialism, but also with racist underpinnings of the very language itself. Hip-hop is a continuation of this practice. As James Spady says, hip-hop—Black in its poetics, its politics, its codes, and its rhythms—"mediates the corrosive discourse of the dominating society while at the same time function[ing] as a subterranean subversion."[3] It is a poetic expression of the powerful currents raging beneath the street in the underground. It is a voice for the youth—a voice informed not only by the segregation and oppression of the ghetto, but also by the historical forces of racism that affected our ancestors. Hip-hop is proving itself to be the culmination of Sartre and Césaire's "historic chance that will permit black men to 'shout out the great negro cry so hard that the world's foundations will be shaken.'"[4]

The first step toward developing such a language of return is for Black folks to stop fearing the master. In colonial or slave practice, the "master" is understood quite literally: it is he who physically or psychically controls you, often with violence, threatened or actual. In postslavery America, even in post–Civil Rights Movement America, the "master" is usually understood to be something disembodied, a nameless, faceless force that oppresses in more insidious ways. Controls are economic, social, and political, and, because they are systemic, because the target of resistance is so immane as to seem impervious to our control, it can feel easier—natural even—to allow society to pull us in its currents. As Sartre says in his introduction to Frantz Fanon's *The Wretched of the Earth*, "we only become what we are by the radical and deep-seated refusal of that which others have made of us." Hip-hop has ever been a platform that provides a space in which individuals can use art—be it graffiti, breaking, turntablism, or the poetry of the MC—to carve out a space of their own that either utterly rejects what the nameless, faceless powers of under-representative democracy and soul-crushing consumerism would make of them or turns negatives into positives. In true liberatory fashion, those who use hip-hop in such a way are recognizing who they are, validating their own autonomous existence; they have a voice and, even if *they*—constrained socially and politically—are not completely so, that voice is free.

So, once it has been asserted, what is one to do with this freedom? The language within which we assert ourselves as Black men and women is prejudiced against us. As Sartre says, thanks to that "great Manichaeistic division" that splits the world according to Black and White, "The negro will learn to say 'white like snow' to indicate innocence, to speak of the blackness of a look, of a soul, of a deed. As soon as he opens his mouth, he accuses himself."[5] Hip-hop artists like KRS-One, Erykha Badhu, Arrested Development, X-Clan, and Black Star, to name a few, have continued the work begun by the postcolonial Black poets that Sartre is discussing in "Black Orpheus," all of whom used Blackness to express the divine, the strong, the beautiful, and the sublime. By positivizing Blackness, placing it in new contexts and endowing it with new meanings, they are breaking down "the walls of white culture—its silence, its words, its mores—[that] rise up between [a man's blackness] and him."[6]

Suddenly, communities are formed around powerful words and modes of address that can claim ownership of a language that, while it may branch from the trunk of the oppressors' language, is distinctly a people's own. This language can be overheard and understood—this is a crucial part of its power—but it only addresses the outsider indirectly. It recalls the vivid image of Sartre's introduction to Frantz Fanon's *The Wretched of the Earth*:

> After taking a short walk in the night you will see strangers gathered around a fire, get closer and listen [...] They might see you, but they will go on talking among themselves without even lowering their voices. Their indifference strikes home [...] The fire that warms and enlightens them is not yours, You, standing at a respectful distance, you now feel eclipsed, nocturnal, and numbed. It's your turn now.[7]

The language that is being spoken around this fire—the language that, for the oppressors, can be overheard but never participated in—is today manifested in hip-hop. However, flaming brands have been taken from the fires lit by and for Black folks in the first part of this century; these torches have lit countless fires, around which conversations of a very different kind are carried on, though in the same indiscreet tones. As hip-hop developed as a poetic art form, the speaking individual began to separate himself from his community. Battle lines began to be drawn around the self; the representation shifted from one of collective strength to one of Herculean independence. This was the emergence of battle rap, and few innovations in the field of hip-hop have had as broad an influence as this one.

Battle Rap

As part of the marketing for rapper Big Sean's new album *Hall of Fame*, one of the tracks from the album, "Control," was posted online on August 12, 2013. The track included a guest appearance by Kendrick Lamar, who, in true hardcore fashion, used his verse to both name and challenge his fellow MCs. He claimed that his verses would "raise the bar high" and he asked: "Who tryna jump and get it?" In his verse he placed himself in elite company—Jay-Z, Eminem, Andre 3000—while, at the same time, he called out a sizeable list of his fellow MCs (surprisingly, this list included even the artists, Big Sean and Jay Electronica, who shared billing with Lamar on "Control"). "I got love for you all," he spits, "but I'm tryna murder you niggas." Two elements of hip-hop bravado are at work here: the diss and the brag. The first belittles one's competition, the second self-promotes, even self-aphotheosizes, the MC. Lamar is simultaneously demanding respect from his peers while disrespecting them en masse. This is not a contradiction. This is part and parcel of the MCs search for recognition and respect, which, in certain circles such as hardcore rap, virtually demands that one build their own reputation upon the foundation of the destroyed reputations of others. To understand more fully what is at work with hip-hop circles like hardcore and battle rap, it is necessary to examine both the roots and the philosophical underpinnings of hardcore rap culture.

Street Gangs to Hip-Hop Crews

The diverse amalgam of street cultures known collectively as hip-hop arose in a period of complex economic, demographic, and social change. Unemployment combined with intra-racial tensions resulted in a dramatic increase in the street presence of youth gangs. In his seminal study of hip-hop as a cultural force, Jeff Chang notes that, for a vast number of young people chiefly in the Bronx and Harlem "gangs structured the chaos [. . .] They warded off boredom and gave meaning to the hours."[8] Being a gang member, wearing its colors and emblems, strictly adhering to its codes and rituals, became a lifestyle of choice for many boys and girls in New York City hoods during the first half of the 1970s.

Though the gangs gave both structure and solidarity (even if that solidarity was limited, as it often was, by extremely narrow locational or ethnic constraints), hip-hop, as it entered the milieu of street gang culture, offered the chance for the individual to forcefully assert their individuality while retaining some of the former features of the gang culture. Crews—smaller collectives of like-minded individuals all actively participating in the new art form as MCs, DJs, dancers, or artists—began to take the place of street gangs. Chang notes that these new breeds of "post-gang youths were [...] more interested in projecting individual flash than collective brawn."[9]

Such individual flash can be traced across all of the various manifestations of the new culture. While all members of a hip-hop crew would front a unified image—wearing, for instance, identical colors—the individual within the crew was granted far more power than the gang member was. Graffiti writers, for instance, risked life and limb just to write their own *personal names* in unreachable yet highly visible places so as to become known and recognized among their peers for their bravery as much as for their artistry. MCs, in a brilliant and innovative approach to guerilla marketing, made self-reference a hallmark of the new style, frequently repping both themselves and their crews. In the same way, spurred to do so by perpetual competition, DJs and b-boys and b-girls endeavored at all times to innovate and introduce something unique that could be tied to their name and their name only.

Unsurprisingly, imitators emerged in the wake of nearly every new innovation, but hip-hop's ironclad ethic of individual expression made "biting" another's lyrics, graff-writing style, dance moves, or breaks anathema for its initiates. The quickest way to destroy one's credibility was to transparently model one's style on that of a recognizable artist. Thus, across the wide range of hip-hop's early manifestations, the individual could claim ownership of their actions in a way that the youth gangs' brand of solidarity had positively discouraged.

This by no means eliminated street gangs—they continued, and still continue—to flourish in primarily, but not exclusively urban communities. It did, however, provide a constructive outlet for the desire to rep oneself so strongly felt in the communities in which hip-hop began to make its presence felt. Violence was still very much a reality in these communities, but actual violence, especially in those early pockets of urban America in which hip-hop emerged, often became metaphorical, finding expression in lyrics, in posturing, and in showboating. It was out of this climate, borrowing from culture's past and creating anew, that battle rap began to emerge.

Battle Rap Tradition

There is broad consensus as to the earliest recorded battle rap contest that is recognizable as such. Late in 1981, at the Harlem World's Christmas Rappers Convention, Busy Bee Starski—arguably the best party MC of the time—and Kool Moe Dee each took a turn trying to move the crowd. Busy Bee went first, and, as can be heard in the recordings, the crowd's response was ecstatic. However, when Kool Moe Dee took center stage, he shifted the attention from the crowd to Busy Bee. Rather than exhorting the crowd as Busy Bee had done to "clap your hands" or "scream," or any of the other call-and-response lyrics that had become conventional among MCs, Kool Moe Dee lambasted his fellow MC with lines like, "if you was money, you'd be counterfeit," and, speaking about his opponent's style, "party after party, the same old shit." The in-your-face nature of such insults paired with the Kool Moe Dee's bravado inaugurated a new form of hip-hop that was to revolutionize the way that status was achieved and maintained in the scene. As Kool Moe Dee stated in numerous interviews, he was provoked by Busy Bee's bragging both onstage and off that he was *the best MC* and, virtually, *undefeatable*. Rather than meeting him on his own ground and trying to outdo such braggadocio, Kool Moe Dee used the hip-hop rhyme format combined with his considerable lyrical talent to savagely insult Busy Bee. Busy Bee can be heard on the recording of the battle shouting "shut up, shut up," but this was the sum total of his response to the Battle rhymes. The out-and-out victory won by Kool Moe Dee that evening was so complete that MCs battles became, almost overnight, a staple in the repertoire of the MC.

This milestone in the history of hip-hop brought the art of MCing closer to the other hip-hop artistic expressions such as graffiti and breaking, uniting an entire culture on the basis of a *show* (represent) *and prove* (battle) attitude that is shared by all forms of hip-hop. From that point on, MCing became a symbolical space in which the individual represents himself in order to establish his persona as *ultimate* in relation to all the other inhabitants of that space. This is asserted on a communal level (I'm better than y'all) and on the individual level (you ain't nuthin).

Run-DMC were the first artists to bring this sound to market. In 1983 they released their debut single, "It's Like That," which included as a b-side, "Sucker MCs," that was to become the first battle rap anthem. According to music journalist Peter Shapiro, the artful combination of lyrical mastery, forceful delivery, and distinctly minimalist production on both of the Run-DMC's debut single completely revolutionized the rap music industry, "rendering everything that preceded it distinctly old school with one fell swoop."[10] Rather than using the battle rap format to bring down a single opponent, Run-DMC targeted all MCs who weren't rapping at the same level as Run-DMC, that is, practically everybody. Nearly every major MC of the 1980s was, in some way or another, to follow in the tracks of the new battle rap style and minimalist sound ushered in by Run-DMC. Rakim, LL Cool J, Big Daddy Kane, Slick Rick, Milk Dee of the Audio Two, all of them contributed their own take on this sound, but they didn't stray far from the original blueprint. They all represented themselves as streetwise individuals fighting for recognition on the pure MC level, bragging about their lyrical prowess, flow, style, charisma, energy, and determination, all while claiming that the other MCs lacked the talents they possessed in such abundance.

The one upmanship of battle rap could only be contained within the pure MC level for so long. Battle rap, at its birth, was a purely mental exercise—the content of one's self-representation, like the content of one's disses, was limited to one's flow, one's intelligence, one's ability to move crowds at will, but a new breed of MCs soon emerged that connected the hip-hop world with the very world of the ghetto in a way that had less and less to do with the pure MC level. In the mid-1980s, gangsta rappers like Toddy Tee, Schoolly D, Boogie Down Productions, Ice-T, N.W.A. Geto Boys, and many others began to self-represent in ways very different from their battle rap predecessors. The new breed of rappers delivered raw and vivid depictions of the harsh reality of American inner cities, and, crucially, they placed themselves in the very center of these representations, as active agents in the violence-steeped gang culture of the ghettos. Schoolly D and Ice-T made rap something more tangibly connected to life in the ghetto; they radicalized its poetic and brought to it all the aggressive bravado of the street gangs that had been kept at arm's length from the genre in the early part of the decade. Threats suddenly carried new weight as street cred(ibility) became connected, in unheard of ways, to what an MC *did, could* and *would do in real life circumstances* in order to support his claims of being the ultimate, the best, the baddest, the toughest, and so on.

Recognize: Battle Rap and the Will to Ultimate Power

The quest to be the ultimate that is so often explored in hip-hop lyrics is a product of long-sublimated desires bubbling to the surface, where they erupt with energy-given force by their unduly protracted period of dormancy. One of its early manifestations is the relatively simple demand for name recognition. *Naming is an ontological act* or, more precisely, that *there is no entity without identity*.[11] From the early graff writers to today's hip-hop scene, the name one gives oneself and the recognition of that name by others is a crucial step in the entire enterprise. Innovators who threw up bombs on subway cars or shouted their names out on street corners or in house parties created a distinct *symbolical reality* that allowed them to *be* in it only after he had *established a name* by means of an innovative artistic style supported by "survivalist" values of facing and overcoming *real life dangers* in an artistic/ontological feat.

Once one has a name, the will to power can be made manifest in ways unavailable to the anonymous. In a Nietzschean sense, the will to power that was so utterly opposed during the long period of Black oppression, once given vent, expressed this desire of the determined individual to dominate in the clearest terms: "What is good?" asked Nietzsche. "All that heightens the feeling of power in man, the will to power, power itself. What is bad? All that is born of weakness. What is happiness? The feeling that power is growing, that resistance is overcome."[12] In the realm of the hard-core MC, the battle rapper, the gangsta rapper, life is defined by such rejection of any trace of weakness; it is defined by the constant, forceful, even violent reaction to resistance, and that which is good, that which the MC feels to be *true*, is anything that is free of weakness—for anything that cannot be resisted proves itself beyond reproach. In *The Gay Science*, Nietzsche further explores this feeling of truth as it relates to the exercise of power: "Those who feel 'I possess Truth'—how many possessions would they not abandon in order to save this feeling! What would they not throw overboard to stay 'on top'—which means, above the others who lack 'the Truth'!"[13] The powerless, having once found that power can be manifested simply by its enunciation, will defend their corner with every weapon at their disposal, and, in a world where claims to be anything less than ultimate are viewed as an expression of weakness, that corner will need to be defended almost constantly. This is the world of the Hardcore: everybody is master, yet nobody is.

John P. Pittman, in his thought-provoking essay, "'Y'All Niggaz Better Recognize': Hip Hop's Dialectical Struggle for Recognition," uses Hegel's well-known dialectical *master and slave* relationship that the German philosopher used to illustrate the development of self-consciousness. Pittman argues that any MC who competes for the title of the ultimate cannot achieve complete *autonomy*. Even in the case where an MC is recognized as "master" by all other contestants who are, in turn, his slaves, he remains with each and every one of them locked within the master-slave relationship.[14] In Hegel's philosophy, there can be no master if there are no slaves to recognize his authority, thus proving that the *master is perennially dependent on the slave.* The consciousness of the individual is crucial in subordination to master. According to Hegel's philosophy self-consciousness exists in itself and for itself, only insofar as it exists in relation to another self-consciousness; that is to say, it *is* only by virtue of its acknowledgment or recognition.[15] This means that the superiority of the master depends on its recognition as such by the other (the slave).[16] This dependence reverses the relation between master and slave, making the slave master and the master slave.

Pittman seems to locate an example of an MC who refuses to participate in this dialectic. He cites André 3000's lines from the Outkast's "Liberation": "Can't worry about what anotha nigga think / Now, that's liberation and baby I want it." Pittman concludes that "liberation cannot come from simply refusing the struggle for recognition. Refusing to seek the recognition from those who present themselves as one's peers can easily become a self-defeating attitude that rejects the world altogether" (p. 48). But is that so? André 3000 may have openly refused to even get into the struggle for recognition, but this is hardly representative of a "self-defeating attitude." "Two Dope Boyz (In a Cadillac)" from Outkast's sophomore album of 1996, *ATLiens,* has André describing a situation in which an MC challenges him to a freestyle MC battle. There are many significant motives in this verse.

First of all, André refers to his challenger as an "old sucker MC," who "spit and stumbled over clichés." The MC who is trying to provoke André 3000 into a battle is a representative of an earlier time (and not even a good representative at that). His rhymes are so clichéd that André 3000 has to go back to 1983 to find an insult that fits the bill. Outkast and this "old sucker MC" might as well be from a different planet. The game has changed—indeed, Outkast was one of the groups that forever changed it—and the kind of recognition that comes from making "someone feel low" is something the MC of the new era of hip-hop no longer needs. He is self-realized, self-actualized, disengaged from the mutually binding slave-master relations that, while crucial to hip-hop's development, have become more characteristic of his past than his present. What threat can a sucker MC pose to one who "grew up to himself," that is, one who is truly autonomous.

In a similar vein, Zondo, an MC from the popular Croatian rap band Dječaci (The Boys), dismisses the battle rap tradition and its baggage. In "Kraljevi" (The Kings) Zondo rhymes: "I won't fight a wretch since there is nothing for me to win." He even takes his argument to the ontological level, establishing his ultimate power (that of refusing name recognition) through the strength of his own words: "If I don't mention you, you don't exist." Like André 3000, Zondo has claimed a power above the master-slave dialectic. This is the ultimate power of nonrecognition, of the refusal of the reciprocating power relationships between master and slave. His existence stands apart, no longer in need of recognition and no longer willing to give any. He doesn't just deny his opponent mastery; he denies his very existence. Such is the power of the ultimate.

The MC and Self-Apotheosis

Within the conceptual framework of Hegel's philosophy, which Pittman proposed as an adequate interpretation theory for battle rap, the master-slave relation is a stage in the self-development of the Spirit, but it is not the final one. The ultimate stage in Hegel's philosophy is that of the *Absolute Spirit*—sometimes referred to by Hegel as *God*. Knowing this, we can try to use these concepts of slave-master-God to solve the main problem of the battle rap tradition that Pittman identified.

Close to end of "No Competition," a track from Rakim's 1998 album, *Follow the Leader*, the rapper spits the following: "I'm God, G is the seventh letter made / Raining on rappers, it's no parade / So if you ain't wise, then don't even come / Competition for this and the mixin is none." Firmly rooted in the battle rap tradition, Rakim is claiming himself as the ultimate. His verses are "raining on rappers" coming, as they do, from so high above them. Hip-hop MCs have used this trope so often as to make it a predictable one. Jay-Z, for instance, has built his *representative self* around an alter-alter-ego, Jay-Hova (Jehovah), and Lil B has calling himself Based God since 2008. But both of these, like Rakim's, are thoroughly steeped in conventional representations of the God-MC: in Jay-Z's case, the line, "God MC—me—Jay-Hova,"[17] is imbedded in the middle of lyrics that make light of his competition. He doesn't transcend the need to compare himself with others, he is simply better than the rest—the God of the Old Testament, flexing and demanding tribute. Lil B's image of the God-MC is even more limited. When he raps "I'm the god of rap, nigga, and this here my space,"[18] he is merely expressing a feeling of domination within a narrowly imagined space: that of the street. This is self-praise, but not self-apotheosis in a transcendent sense.

In order to thus transcend the conventional braggadocio of the Battle MC, the MC must represent himself as ultimate without depending upon the Other as referent. Such transcendence would bring a hardcore rap MC into the realm of *pure represent*—a lyrical space within which comparisons are irrelevant. Serbian MC Lou Benny is one of only a handful of MCs who shows a deep understanding of this level of represent. In his track "Dobar rep" (Good Rap), he claims that representing oneself as the best is a thing of the past; The real goal, he says is not to be the best, but to be "absolutely good."[19] He prefers to be a good MC rather than the best one, because "when you are the best, you are not good yet, which means you are not God—and to be God is the main purpose of Hip Hop…The flattest is not flat, the straightest is not straight—that's why I'm not the best, but good, and I'm only looking at myself—I'm not better than you and you aren't better than me."[20] The struggle to be the best keeps, Benny suggests, the MC from realizing the God-potential that exists beyond the outer edges of the consciousness limited by its reference to the Other. The battle rap tradition locks one in an exterior struggle with one's peers, but Godhead comes only from interior struggle, the recognition of and the eventual mastery of the self. Though Benny might say that God "doesn't give a fuck,"[21] this is only in relation to the recognition of others; what Benny *does* "give a fuck" about is the mastery of his art on a pure, absolute level. God "does everything for himself,"[22] Benny says, and it is by himself and for himself that the God-MC transcends the limitations of reference.

Back on hip-hop's native shores, commercial and gangsta rap remain, for the most part, locked in the ongoing battle with the Other. However, in hip-hop's smaller inner circles, conscious hip-hop artists are using their music and their lyrics to explore themes of transcendence. Take, for example, Oakland-based hip-hop duo Blackalicious. The group's debut album, *Nia*, is framed with three tracks marking the beginning, the middle, and the end of the album. The first and the last cuts on the sprawling, 19-track album are poems by the group's lyricist, Gift of Gab. In the first of these, "Searching," he defines man's movement through the world as one of constant change: "Progressing. Changing. Evolving. Growing. From a seed to a tree. From a child to a man. From a man to a spirit to a god fulfilling his plan."[23] The final step in this progression is presented in the middle of the album with a track called "Ego Trip," which features a recording of a 1972 spoken-word poem by Afrocentric poet Nikki Giovanni layered over a deep hip-hop beat. The poem is a pantheistic self-representation of the poet/ MC as a God, that is, the mother of all things: "I am so perfect," she says, "so divine, so ethereal, so surreal, I cannot be compre- hended except by my permission."[24] Taken, as it is, from the body of spoken-word poetry that so influenced the shape that the MCs poetry assumed at its birth, the artists' appropriation of this poem recognizes that the transcendence sought by the conscious MCs is not something new; on the contrary, it precedes hip-hop. This means that the way forward for the MC is at once forward and backward looking. The final track of the album "Searching"[25] rec- ognizes this as they reify ancestral strength as a guidepost toward self-control and strength. The model for transcendence is there for the conscious MC who recognizes that enlightenment is an eter- nal becoming, not something you can just lay claim to without the work that justifies such claims. Standing on "our ancestors shoul- ders" allows one to better see into the future and to plot a course toward that future that begins, first and foremost, with the transcendence of the individual, which, on a massive scale, with the transcendence of the community. Only then will the hip-hop "chant down Babylon one more time." But the race doesn't always go to the swift, and, indeed, "it's gonna take some time."

With this in mind, we can conclude that Kendrick Lamar's attempt to raise the bar high by reaffirming the battle tradition seems to be just a sentimental and weak maneuver of an "old sucker MC." He is as tied to the need to first be recognized and then to dominate is as old as the battle rap tradition itself. If we want to look for transcendent MCs, we may have to look for them outside of the rap game.

Rumination 3

Conscious Hip-Hop versus the Culture Industry

In its broadest sense, hip-hop is understood to mean the culture taken as a whole; the MC, the deejay, the graffiti artist, the breakdancer, and the encompassing knowledge that bring these elements into a cohesive whole. Rap is just one of these elements, something the MC does. It is the verbal element of hip-hop. commercial rap and conscious rap become relevant terms when the young culture began to germinate. As both community and art form began to take shape in the early 1970s, a palpably distinct, shared, and lived experience resonated within the culture. Stylistic differences separated artists, but the antiauthoritarian content of the music, the self-consciousness of the poetry, and the tangible sense of community could be felt throughout the movement. As the 1980s approached, the community began to be pulled in new directions by forces that had once been kept at bay by hip-hop's fierce sense of independence. As Greg Tate points out in his important editorial, "Hiphop Turns 30," the moment that "Rapper's Delight" went platinum, hip-hop as a holistically coherent cultural movement began its decline. An unholy alliance, "the marriage of heaven and hell, of New World African ingenuity and that trick of the devil known as global hyper-capitalism," brought hip-hop culture, hardly kicking and screaming, into the toxic waters of the mainstream.[1] The offspring of this "marriage of heaven and hell" is commercial rap. In lieu of substantive discussions about or legitimate protest against the predicaments of the social, economic, and political consequences of life in the ghetto, the trappings of success (a success defined almost exclusively in financial terms) became the ubiquitous hallmarks of the genre. Sprawling mansions, exotic cars, women, designer labels, expensive liquor, such were not merely the rewards of commercially viable rap, they were the subject of its poetry. The form changed little, but the content was radically altered. Sincere representations of inner-city life rapidly gave way to a self-apotheosis that was little more than an extreme exaggeration of the bravado and posturing that had been an undeniable element of hip-hop culture since its birth.

The magnetism of the mainstream, especially in terms of financial rewards, has profoundly influenced the direction that the stream of hip-hop culture has taken over the last two and a half decades. The mainstream has swelled into a raging current of corporate interests that are in the business of marketing violence, misogyny, and rampant consumerism. And business is booming. However, running alongside the mainstream are much quieter, more dignified flows that take their cues, not from the market and what it devours, but rather, from the early hip-hop pioneers who forcefully expressed profound truths about life on the margins of society. These are the conscious hip-hop artists,[2] who have carried on the proud traditions of musicians like Afrika Bambaataa, thinkers like Angela Davis, and the countless street poets and urban philosophers who birthed and nurtured hip-hop's nascent poetic through the 1970s and 1980s. Hip-hop is a movement so young that its founders can be seen actively participating in its shaping and reshaping from its beginning all the way through to its more recent incarnations. Conscious hip-hop artists focus intently on the fifth pillar of hip-hop culture: knowledge. They have been the inspiration for a movement that is the antithesis of the popular form of commercial rap.

In terms of content, even the most cursory of comparisons between commercial rap and conscious hip-hop reveals a massive gulf between their respective productions. Lil Wayne's "Got Money," the third single from his Grammy-Award-winning album *The Carter III*, contains the following stanza: "I make it snow, I make it flurry / I make it out alright tomorrow don't worry / Yeah, Young Wayne on them hoes / A.K.A. Mr. Make It Rain On Them Hoes."[3] The song is entirely devoted, not to the getting of money (a common theme in all branches of hip-hop), but to the having of it. The anxiety that comes with attempting to eke out a living in marginalized communities is a deeply felt concern residing at the heart of hip-hop. This is the same anxiety so pointedly articulated in early hip-hop cuts like The Furious Five's "The Message." But as the record industry began to recruit talent from the ghetto, and as industry dollars began to make their presence felt in both the verbal and visual content of commercial rap, the message changed from one of "I've carved out a piece of the pie for me and mine" to "I've got more than I know what to do with, so much that I'm literally throwing it away." It's an oft-repeated theme of commercial rap, and it's one of the points through which conscious hip-hop artists have engaged with their community, holding up for ridicule those rappers who imagine that fat bankrolls somehow mean that they have "made it." In their critique of the hip-hop industry, Dead Prez, in their song "Hip-Hop" exhort their colleagues: "Emcee's get a little bit of love and think they hot / Talkin' 'bout how much money they got / Nigga all y'all records sound the same…You would rather have a Lexus, or justice/ A dream, or some substance." The lures of the record industry are just that, shiny materials without substance. They do next to nothing to advance the cause of the community or the emancipation of the individual. This is not to say that conscious hip-hop artists are somehow above the desires for acclaim and financial success that pull so many toward the industry. They do, however, often express a reluctance to acquire the material trappings of commercial success if such rewards come with a cost of compromise.

The works of conscious hip-hop artists make it possible for me as a philosopher to engage with the culture of hip-hop in a meaningful way. Afrika Bambaataa's Zulu Nation and KRS-One's Temple of hip-hop,[4] among other groups, have served as collectives in which articulation of the knowledge-based approach of conscious hip-hop is used to confront ongoing social, economic, and political concerns of local and global communities. Eschewing the superficial in favor of the substantive, the material in favor of the spiritual, the commercial in favor of the communal, conscious hip-hop is emancipating new generations of listeners and fostering communities of self-determined and self-aware individuals who are using hip-hop as a blade to cut through the empty promises of hyper-capitalism revealing the false promises that lurk at its core. Dropping knowledge may not be commercially viable to the same degree as making it rain is, but it is, for those who practice it and for those who appreciate it, of crucial importance. It has brought hip-hop into the academy as a respectable field of knowledge and study. As Daudi Abe notes, hip-hop has burst upon the academy as a field with "unlimited potential for knowledge construction in the classroom."[5] The conscious hip-hop artists who have moved the community forward, while constantly looking nostalgically backward, have kept hip-hop music alive as a historical movement, as a philosophy, and as an articulated experience of the move from bondage to freedom.

This movement necessitates a moment of protest—an outrage toward injustice that is broadly and strongly felt by a portion of the population significant enough in numbers to be politically powerful. But such outrage needs to be powerfully articulated if it is not to become a movement of violence, and hip-hop gives a platform for this articulation. In Tupac's "Changes" the rapper wonders, "is life worth livin'? Should I blast myself? I'm tired of bein' poor, and even worse, I'm black." Tupac is speaking for himself, but, crucially, not only for himself. "Changes," with its references to purse snatching, and crack slinging, is autobiographical, but it is much more than this as well. It is a heartbreaking account of what it is to be a poor Black man in urban America freighted with the historical baggage that makes his life one in which crime is a survival mechanism born of poverty, oppression, but, above all, exasperation. "Sell the crack to the kids," he says, "who the hell cares?" There is a sense of futility and powerlessness in this that reflects the very real social and economic conditions of the ghetto in the same way that his statement, "even worse, I'm black," reflects those self-esteem and racial-esteem issues that have been such a persistent and pernicious problem within Black communities since they were brought to America in chains.

These self-esteem issues in Black communities have deep roots. In the 1940s, Kenneth and Mamie Clark's experiments with light- and dark-skinned dolls showed how Black and White children alike were more likely to equate attractiveness with pale skin.[6] This has by no means been eradicated. At a market in Lagos, Nigeria, one cosmetician told a reporter that 90 percent of her business came from women asking for skin-lightening agents; this trend is worldwide, with flourishing markets for such products in Africa, India, other parts of Asia, dozens of island nations, and, of course, in the United States as well.[7] Dominant forms of media continue to reinforce this prejudice, and its effects are obvious enough considering ever-whitening effects that the spotlight seems to have on many African American celebrities like Michael Jackson and Beyoncé Knowles.

Much of this can be traced to the overwhelming sameness that is present in American cultural productions. Whether it is notions of beauty, of masculinity, of femininity, or of success, the American brand of such products is recognized, accepted, and, in countless cases, adopted in countries around the world. Curtis Mayfield and James Brown used their music to remind their brothers and sisters that black is beautiful, that dark skin ought to be a source of pride and never shame. Hip-hop's roots were steeped in such messages of pride and difference, and it continues to be an art form in which the monotonous sameness of America's cultural output is challenged.

However, hip-hop's once-defiant poetic has been transformed by industry into jingoistic pabulum. Its massively popular bastardized form, commercial rap, has joined the ranks of the endlessly repetitive products of what Theodor Adorno and Max Horkeimer dubbed "the culture industry."[8] As a transparent tool of industry, popular music serves the same purposes as do the glossy advertisements and billboards marketing the latest fragrance or moisturizer that are selling, not just the product itself, but a mode of being defined by conspicuous consumption of consumer goods. The advertizing industry, according to Adorno and Horkeimer, "can pride itself on having energetically accomplished and elevated to a principle the often inept transposition of art to the consumption sphere."[9] While its bastard child has given itself entirely over to the marketing machines of hyper-capitalism, the subgenre of hip-hop music, conscious hip-hop, as an art form with a rich history of critiquing culture and society, has retained its dignity. Corporate dollars, especially in terms of the avenues of promotion and distribution, have turned the mainstream record industry into one of cross-promotion and branding, but conscious hip-hop artists have maintained their independence, refusing to abandon their roles as legitimate and untainted artists who resist and transgresses the flow of the mainstream.

Let me be clear, I am not arguing for an uncritical acceptance of hip-hop as a form of art immune to popular currents. Just as I would not describe all who bring together pigment and canvas as painters in our deepest understanding of the word, I would be loath to call artists all those hip-hop performers who have graced the microphone. The true artist is one who negates, transgresses, affirms, and transforms. As a powerful vehicle of expression and social critique, hip-hop found an audience among an expanding community of the disaffected and the marginalized—those beneath the heel of an ossified structure of power. The emancipatory nature of its narrative made it a thing beautiful even by Socratic standards, for what is beautiful must also be useful, and, by nearly every standard, useful it has been. The MC's microphone as a vehicle of emancipation has been every bit as powerful as the pulpit was in the decades preceding the Civil Rights Movement. As a philosophically inspired movement with revolutionary roots and aspirations, conscious hip-hop is not, in its essence, a product to be sold. It is the counterculture industry.

Adorno and Horkeimer, important members of a select group of influential theorists known collectively as the Frankfurt School, pay particularly close attention to popular music in their massively influential work, *Dialectic of Enlightenment* (1944). The chapter in the book titled "The Culture Industry: Enlightenment as Mass Deception" is a much-discussed and provocative take on popular culture. As much as "The Culture Industry" is a product of its times, certain of its pronouncements remain germane to contemporary conversations about the various forms of popular culture. In particular, their pronouncements about the popular music of the 1940s—jazz is their primary target—can be applied effortlessly to the musical movements of the second half of the twentieth century, including, of course, hip-hop.

More than anything, it was the predictability of the American singers and songwriters of the 1930s and 1940s that drew Adorno and Horkeimer's ire: "[T]he prepared ear can always guess the continuation after the first bars of a hit song and is gratified when it actually occurs."[10] It is impossible to deny that the beats associated with the various forms of hip-hop are as predictable as any of the other conventional forms of popular music. Beats produced by Timbaland, Dr. Dre, or Swizz Beatz—to name a few—may be instantly recognizable as the products of their respective creators thanks to trademark uses of the tools of their craft such as Timbaland's deep-register bass, Dre's idiosyncratic snare hits and palm-muted strings, and Swizz Beatz's clatter and clang of snares and cymbals. In spite of highly individual components in some rap music, there is very little deviation from the handful of overarching songwriting formulas. The sample, the break, the hook, the scratch, all have become so familiar that our pleasure as experienced listeners "moves strictly along the well-worn grooves of association."[11] It is important to remember, however, that the beat serves merely as backdrop for linguistic gymnastics of rap. Deejaying as an art form has its own history—a history that is inextricably fused with that of the MC—but it is the poetry of hip-hop that is my primary concern here. It is not the beat that makes hip-hop music such a rich field of study for the philosopher; rather, it is the transgressive and emancipatory nature of its poetry. Though the beat may be predictable, but the poetry, in many cases, can be anything.

Hip-hop's poetry confronts the monotonous drone of the culture industry head on. It is the "mechanism of reply" that Adorno and Horkeimer could not locate in the 1940s America they were critiquing.[12] Persistent as it is, the culture industry has been challenged by forms of art that, at their very heart, engage the soul-chewing machinery of capitalism. Conscious hip-hop artists like KRS-One, Talib Kweli, Common, Sarah Jones, and Mos Def are oiling the gears and stoking the fires of the mechanism of social change that were part of the protest music of the 1960s and 1970s. They have highlighted the injustices of the system, the economic stagnation that is the ghetto, the inherent racism of policies of economic and social segregation that persist in our supposedly enlightened age. Now, having created a space for their art, they turn to address the individual, the thinking, feeling brother or sister, and they engage them with a philosophy of emancipation that seeks to release from bondage both the individual and the community at large.

Whether one approaches the field as a critic or as an artist, the engagement with conscious hip-hop can be a philosophic exercise. The tragic artist, says Nietzsche, glorified "[c]ourage and freedom of feeling before a powerful enemy, before a sublime calamity, before a problem that arouses dread."[13] Conscious hip-hop may not be exactly what Nietzsche had in mind. It is, after all, a product of a feeling of the individual as he relates to the whole, not as he rises above that whole. It is, though, a head-on confrontation with the dread-inducing malaise of postmodernity, especially as that malaise presents itself among the marginalized and the alienated. It speaks against and across the current of the culture industry. It emancipates the thinking individual and the self-aware community from the grip of the cold machinery of capitalism.

With such revolutionary and emancipatory power, hip-hop has time and again met with resistance from the establishment. As hip-hop was fused into the mass market of American culture, its revolutionary roots and its clearly articulated anger were diluted as it became a vehicle for corporate interests, but undercurrents of hip-hop philosophy that remained true to the revolutionary roots of the movement have always been there for those who are motivated to look for them. What is more, the movement, as it has progressed through time has changed considerably, and this has largely gone unnoticed by the establishment. Hip-hop may have begun as something violently abrasive to the generic Western interests that helped to create the climates of poverty in urban communities, but, since its birth, it has grown into an expression of unity, peace, and collective struggle that, while not always friendly to capitalism and its interests, is not as bent on violent forms of resistance or even illegal means of self-support. Some of hip-hop's less-enlightened critics have crystallized hip-hop, approaching the music and its message as though it can be adequately summarized by those productions that emerged from a relatively short period in the middle of its existence.[14] What hip-hop's most stubborn critics have refused to recognize is that there have always been a diversity of opinions and messages expressed via the MC's microphone. Since the unprecedented commercial success enjoyed by gangsta rap birthed a still-popular subgenre of hip-hop that unabashedly glorifies gangs, Black-on-Black violence, criminality, and positively revels in the trappings—material and sexual—of success, hip-hop's critics have more than evidence enough to merit their exclusion of hip-hop as a relevant art form.

This is, of course, based on only the slimmest sampling of the productions of hip-hop artists. Witness, for instance, the recent right-wing furor when enlightened hip-hop artist Common was invited to recite at a White House poetry event hosted by Michelle Obama. Even though Fox News recognized, in print, that he was a "socially conscious lyricist,"[15] on-air pundits referred to him as "vile," citing a poem from 2007 in which he combined the image of the burning bush of the Old Testament with the image of a burning sitting president of the United States.[16] Sarah Palin foamed at the mouth and, over and over, clips of Common performing next to Obama's former pastor, Jeremiah Wright, were played while the pundits read the few inflammatory expressions their researchers could dig out of Common's catalogue. This was textbook media manipulation of hip-hop to fit a preconceived narrative about what hip-hop and, indeed, all Black urban culture stands for. Never mind that Common has used his celebrity to fund raise for the People for the Ethical Treatment of Animals (PETA) and for AIDS charities, that he has been a staunch advocate for literacy, ghetto mobilization, and for community building in his own both Chicago and New York communities as well as communities around the world.[17] As is too often the case when the media discusses hip-hop, the MC is only cited for his or her most controversial statements—no matter what the context, and no matter what direction their message has taken since the statement was originally made.

The very fact that Common was invited to a poetry event at the White House shows that hip-hop's rebellious poetic has entered the mainstream as legitimate forms of musical, poetical, and philosophical expression. What is more, it demonstrates a willingness on the part of the community to work *with* the upper echelons of elite power structures to overcome the persistent problems of urban poverty in America. However, the response from the right wing of the spectrum was proof positive of the abrasive and antagonistic relationship between the conservative establishment and the hip-hop community. In hip-hop's birth, it was an almost entirely antiestablishment form, and, for those who long for a bygone era of race and class relations, hip-hop will always represent the same threat that it posed to those relations at its birth. All that establishment, conservative interests can remember of hip-hop is the fact that, at one time, it was a popular form of music that glorified criminality. Once speak of killing cops—as Fox News pundits reminded their viewers that Common once did—and that is all these popular branches of the media will remember you for.

In *How Hip-Hop Holds Blacks Back*, John McWhorter condemns the entirety of hip-hop culture based on this kind of long-term memory. In a gesture identical in every way to that enacted by Fox News in the wake of Common's White House invite, McWhorter condemns high schools in Savannah, Georgia, for inviting rapper

Camoflauge to speak to their almost entirely Black students.[18] He chooses one of the rapper's more violent passages as "representative" of his body of work, as though Camoflauge had been invited to incite his young audience to violence, not to reach out to them. In his community, he was as well known for his rap persona as he was for his softer side—he would dress up as "Camo Claus" at Christmas time each year and hand out gifts to inner-city children.[19] McWhorter speaks of revolution and community as "fantasies," of hip-hop's poetry as "doggerel," and he ends his article with a sweeping, anti-intellectual generalization: "Hip-hop creates nothing."[20] Such a statement is typical of the blinkered view of hip-hop that focuses on the softest of targets: the violent content of commercial rap lyrics. As a movement born of frustration and anger with entrenched power structures that either ignored or oppressed urban minorities, violence as part and parcel of hip-hop's nascent poetic is not surprising. What *is* surprising is that hip-hop should be so widely—even intentionally—misunderstood as being adequately represented by now decades-old lyrics by N.W.A, Ice-T, and Tupac Shakur. This is not to suggest that the violent content of rap music has all but disappeared—quite the contrary. But hip-hop artists like Common, KRS-One, Afrika Bambaataa, and many others have long since diverted the flow of the culture into streams of thought, of knowledge, of respect, and of caring; community and revolution are not the "fantasies" that McWhorter suggests they are; they are keystones in the philosophy of hip-hop as a culture of love that is helping it to spread around the world.

In *The Hip-Hop Driven Life: A Genius Liberation Handbook*, Arnett Powell and Adebayo Olorunto, two biracial cousins, write about their experiences as artists, and put forth the concept that "our Love of rap unites nations," meaning that hip-hop is a transracial, unifying global force: "The Hip-hop community," they say, "exists as an international culture of consciousness that provides all races, tribes, religions and styles of people a foundation for the communication of their best ideas and works. Hip-hop "Kulture" is united as one multi-skilled, multi-cultural, multi-faith, multi-racial people committed to the establishment and the development of peace."[21] Under such a rubric, the artist is judged, not according to their bankroll or their rap sheet, but, rather, according to the content of their character. McWhorter brashly suggests that hip-hop "lyrics turn money into the ultimate validation."[22] In a lecture about philosophy and the origins of hip-hop, KRS-One warns: "Those running after money are running away from their real power...If you don't understand your divine rights, the world will do whatever it wants with you."[23] KRS-One's notion of power and rights demands that one be self-questioning, self-reliant, and self-empowered, thoughtful, feeling, and behavior-conscious. Under such conditions, hip-hop has the power to be a fertile soil from which philosophers can emerge and empower both themselves and their communities. This is hip-hop as a force of natural awareness that permits men and women the freedom to be democratic and philosophical in a way that corporate America does not. Financial security is a need like any other; one must be able to provide for oneself, but financial well-being ought not to be the be all and end all of any career. Viewing financial success as the ultimate goal of a foray into hip-hop is the chasing of the corporate America's dream, which entails a compromise that the true artist as philosopher should not be willing to make. The desire to be financially independent too often entails a compromise of principles—a compromise that is born of fear more often than it is born of desire. Claiming one's freedom as an artist is fraught with difficulties, but it is the path of integrity, not security, that is the path of the true philosopher. Skewing one's priorities for the sake of financial gains is the dreaming of someone else's dream, the enacting of another's vision, and the creation of another's art.

The spirit of hip-hop is the antithesis to this kind of corporate slavery. British hip-hop commentator Anthony Thomas identifies five tenets of hip-hop, all of which in some way embody this movement from bondage to freedom:

(1) Keep it real
(2) Speak truth to power
(3) Change the game
(4) Represent your hood
(5) Express your self[24]

The key holder to the Temple of hip-hop is uncompromising. His truth, even if it is his alone, is the relief—the sacred graffiti if you will—on the Temple walls; it subverts the order of that which is external to the artist and his community (broadly or narrowly imagined), while, at the same time, it affirms that which is interior to both. The necessities of life demand that artists play some form of role within capitalist power structures, but, as Thomas's tenets make clear, the hip-hop artist must find a way to navigate the power structures in their market while, at the same time, maintaining the fierce brand of independence and inflexibility that endows their art with power and keep the truth at the heart of their art entirely their own.

Thus, it is crucial to adjust our pedagogical and philosophical lens when examining hip-hop. Students who identify themselves as hip-hop fans may have already been exposed to the work of idea-shaping and community-building artists—the holders of the keys of the Temple. At the same time, hip-hop as a term has been applied so broadly to a sonic texture rather than the message of the artist, that it is just as likely that the student is being exposed to nearly transparent advertisements for liquor and clothes, to glorifications of consequence-free violence and promiscuity. It is only in the analysis of the lyrics, in the examination of the authentic thoughts, feeling, and expressions contained therein that one can know whether through those headphones speaks a free human being espousing hip-hop's core elements, or a mere automaton of corporate interests. If the former, then the work of education has already, in many ways, begun for us; if the latter, it is for us to begin.

Rumination 4

Toward a Philosophy of Hip-Hop Education

Hip-hop and the classroom can seem uneasy, not to say unnatural, bedfellows. Firmly embedded notions of canonicity and classroom-appropriate language left un-critiqued leave little room for hip-hop in either its popular form or its more intellectually savvy underground manifestations. Educators with boots on the ground in the inner city however, are confronted with an anything-but-ideal reality: America's education system, especially in the inner city, is, no matter how you judge it, failing to produce high percentages of passably competent students.[1] Results-based education, an unfortunate byproduct of the No Child Left Behind policy that rewards high-performing schools while punishing poor performing ones.[2] The edifice of new educational systems—when it is constructed at all—must be constructed upon the ruins of the last one. Such an interpretation often serves as justification for the total and systematic dismantling of public education (which I am not a proponent of) but it does buttress the fact that resources, or the lack thereof, render these failing[3] schools as vulnerable. Students have been guided to the place we meet them now by educators equipped with few tools to engage urban youth in a language that resonates with them, and the failures of such a long-standing disconnect are present in the classroom. But rather than trying to be educational archeologists and reverting back along the path that got us to the place where we are now—this path travelled backward, of course, leads us back to still more problems of canonicity and inclusion—the classroom, which is willing to actively engage students on their own ground will find results that can lift both students and educators off of the plaster dust and broken columns of our failed schools.[4] Classrooms ought to be and can be a space in which students and educators alike can investigate and articulate what was and what is using the most powerful tools at our disposal to do so.

While it may be relatively uncontroversial to blame educators for America's troubling test scores, I want to examine the possibility that, in the inner-city classroom, a change of learning materials may work to close the ever-widening gap between educators and their students. Hip-hop offers us, as educators, a chance to engage with students on their own ground with material that is intellectually rigorous without being divorced from the lived reality of the inner city. It is here that both Dr. Chris Emdin and Ladson-Billings converge. Where Emdin cites, "his process is enacted with the embracing of the finiteness of the teacher's knowledge and a validation of questions from students around these topics as points for further research" (2011, p. 291) and Dr. Ladson-Billings asserts that highly effective classrooms are those where teachers and students "maintain fluid student-teacher relationships and demonstrate connectedness with all the students" (1995, p. 480).

Ask American students about the issues facing the education system in this country, and you are confronted with an overwhelming sense that students are aware, sometimes awkwardly so, that they are being treated with kid gloves; They yearn for—and need—a more poignant and pragmatic pedagogy. John Dewey, a progressive American educational reformer of the early twentieth century, was an early recognizer of the disconnect between educational practices and the real-world experiences of students: "How many," he asked in his 1938 educational treatise, *Experience and Education*, "came to associate the learning process with ennui and boredom? How many found what they did learn so foreign to the situations of life outside as to give them no power of control over the latter?"[5] In the 75 years since John Dewey recognized the problem, we have little addressed it; indeed, the issue has only been exacerbated by a system ill equipped to handle diversity in the inner-city classroom.

Look, for instance, to the classroom in which the student is introduced to literature. It takes a gifted educator indeed to blend draw distinct parallels that students feel the truth of between canonical literature and inner-city life. Is it any surprise that such students frequently fail to draw parallels between their own experiences in the world and that of the protagonists to whom they are being introduced and asked to critically analyze? Whether it is Harper Lee's *To Kill a Mockingbird* or Shakespeare, blackness is something alien in those pages. If anything, it contributes to what Dubois so poignantly referred to as the "double consciousness" of Black Americans: "this sense," he says, "of always looking at one's self through the eyes of others, of measuring one's soul by the tape of a world that looks on in amused contempt and pity."[6] No matter how sympathetic the portrayal of minorities may be in canonical literature, such portrayals inevitably speak *of* minorities, not *to* them.

What is more, such texts inevitably speak in—and thus demand to be responded to in—a language that only further divides the environment of education from that of experience. According to Earnest Morrell, if we are to engage in a profound way those students who are located well outside of "dominant" or "mainstream" cultures, then we "need to examine non-school literary practices to find connections between local literacies and dominant, academic literacies."[7] To excel on par with our high hopes and expectations for all students, these same students need to feel they are collective "participants in and creators of" the material they are presented with; only then will they recognize "a logical connection between [their] lived experiences and the school culture."[8] This connection must be formed through more than just subject matter. It must occur, as well, at the level of the language in which the students are both addressed and in which they are expected to respond.

Rather than "literacy," Morrell speaks of "literacies" in the plural, and the attitude-shift this represents towards our students and the way they use language(s) to communicate in separate spheres is important to recognize.[9] Vershawn Ashanti Young, an expert on how African American's use and experience language, represents the new school of thinking, which does away with previously permissive attitudes when it came to code switching (the process whereby minority students are encouraged to speak separate languages in domains that are kept separate by the process—home and school). Code switching, he says, has become "out of sync"[10] as understanding and promotion of plural literacies increases in the classroom. One of the hallmarks of this progression is the inclusion of hip-hop in the classroom. Since, as Young argues, many

English speakers "may not have as big of a choice as we believe they have in choosing the ways they speak and write," educators have a responsibility to their students to not privilege one manifestation of language over another. Young encourages educators to allow, even to encourage, their students to "code mesh" rather than code switch, to "color their writing with what they bring from home," enlarging thereby the vocabulary of the classroom; this fostering of literacies will, he continues, "multiply the range of available rhetorical styles...and make us in the end multidialectical as opposed to monodialectical."[11] Hip-hop's language may not be academic, but this could also be said of the vast majority of written and spoken language in the United States. Hip-hop is a different lexical set—one of many among subcultures and minorities in this country. Its rhythms depend on elision, enjambment, on meaning more often than not understood rather than clearly enunciated. It draws on, and, if included in the classroom, can develop skills quite different from, while also incorporating those frequently taught in literature classes.[12]

Hip-hop can thus be used to enlarge the classroom vocabulary as students are encouraged to respond in class in a language they are comfortable expressing themselves. What is more, the introduction of the rhythms of street language and its unique vocabulary can effect a similar gesture, but in reverse. Rapper Dead Prez says: "I got my diploma from a school called records."[13] Student coloring the classroom becomes classroom coloring the student. Hip-hop can be used as a tool to transform exclusive classroom practices into inclusionary ones for Black students but, certainly, it can do more than this as well. If it is literacies that are being promoted, and if these literacies are going to be truly inclusionary, hip-hop's language ought to be promoted in classrooms in the same way that Elizabethan English is introduced to classes as they study Shakespeare (Bailey, 2011; Hill and Petchuaer, 2013; Love, 2013; Morrell and Duncan, 2002). Just as Shakespeare would not be Shakespeare were his plays to be re-written to conform to a trochee foot rather than an iambic one, just as Shakespeare is not Shakespeare without his Elizabethan vocabulary, just so is hip-hop not hip-hop if it is somehow translated into a language and a rhythm alien to its origin. Hip-hop's powerful message is lost if it is rearticulated or diverted into "standard" English, which, as Allen N. Smith assured us more than 35 years ago, "is mythical."[14]

If hip-hop is to be a continually relevant and powerful classroom tool, it must be presented as a device through which students can actively engage in "code meshing," not translation (Richardson, 2006). Stanford scholar Samy Alim refers to this language acquisition as Hip Hop Language Nation (HHNL). In an interview with author and pedagogy scholar, Bettina Love, she points out that "HHLN, most notably found in rap, is a subgenre and discourse system of African American Vernacular English (AAVE)" (Alim, 2009). According to Richardson (2006), AAVE is an outgrowth of "slavery, colonization, neo-imperialism, migration, wars, global technological processes, and diasporic crossing, [and through this language] Continental Africans and their descendants participate in the (dis)invention and global flow of Black discourse" (p. 2). Thus, Black discourses act as "ways of being in the world; they are forms of life" (Gee, 1996, p. viii). As a contemporary subgenre of AAVE, HHLN is rooted in "Black oral tradition of tonal semantics, narrativizing, signification/signifyin, the dozens/playin the dozens, Africanized syntax, and other communicative practices" (Smitherman, p. 4). Thus, HHLN recreates and reshapes language rooted in the past- and present-day experiences of African American life and as a result, HHLN is a frequently changing dialect that influences how African Americans behave, interact, think, speak, read, and write (Alim, 2009).[15]

Still, there are a few objections to hip-hop's use in the classroom that need to be overcome if hip-hop is to be a broadly used pedagogical tool. Allan Bloom's criticism of rock music in the 1980s continues to echo through conservative critiques of hip-hop as an art form that articulates anything more than rage, misogyny, and greed. In rock music and videos, Bloom saw "a nonstop, commercially pre-packaged masturbational fantasy,"[16] and rap has replaced rock as the outrage *du jour* among conservative commentators on culture. Violent music videos, video games, song lyrics, and so on are all turning adolescent consumers—so the argument goes—into mindlessly violent, sex-crazed simpletons. Putting aside violent video games, it is most often the products of Black culture that are examined as though they pose some kind of threat to America's gaping masses. The connection of hip-hop with the expression of Black rage in the 1970s and 1980s is examined only in terms of the rage itself—never the oppression, inequality, and voicelessness that produced it. Could it be possible that hip-hop is not the cause of violence, promiscuity, and criminality, but, rather, an expression stemming from preexisting conditions of violence, poverty, and inequality in urban America? Some 15 years after Bloom published *The Closing of the American Mind*, Noam Chomsky, lamenting that any respect whatsoever had ever been given to Bloom's critique, dismissed the latter's work as "mind-bogglingly-stupid."[17] Still, those who imagine that there are clearly defined antagonists and protagonists in the ongoing culture wars seem to never tire of laying the blames for America's declining test scores and escalating violence rates[18] are laid at the door of popular culture in general and hip-hop music and artists in particular. Not only is hip-hop broadly characterized for being violent, misogynistic, and shallow, but it is also declared to be immature, even unintelligent. Hip-hop educators can expect significant resistance if they fail to recognize that the language of hip-hop and the classroom setting are not always compatible so long as hip-hop is represented as a culture of youth rather than one of experience. "Pedagogy," say Henry Giroux and Roger Simon, "authorizes the voices of the adult world, the world of teachers, and school administrators."[19] If only examined in its commercially successful incarnations, hip-hop might seem to fly in the face of the mature world of pedagogy. While the teacher often trains students to speak in the language of this adult world, the language of hip-hop is powerfully felt as a language into which this adult world and adult language can little penetrate. This is especially the case when popular culture, youth culture, and subculture expression are merged, as in the world of hip-hop. Giroux and Simon quote a passage from Dick Hebdige's 1979 study of subcultures, the findings of which are as relevant now to the world of hip-hop as they were then to the world of punk. According to one of Hebdige's subjects, there is a powerful desire to mystify and confuse the adult world: "You really hate an adult to understand you," says the subject, "That's the only thing you've got over them, the fact that you can mystify and worry them."[20] When teachers, identified as representatives of the outside, adult world, attempt to put their students' tastes in music, dance, or art under the pedagogical microscope, there will always be a significant amount of resistance to any attempt to penetrate the interior life of students as it is thus culturally expressed. However, as hip-hop has matured, as its messages of self-betterment and education have been heard both within and outside its community, educators are beginning to emerge who are as steeped in the language of the street as they are in the language of the classroom. Rather than what Iain Chambers refers to as the "patronizing academic mind that seeks to explain an experience that is rarely his or hers,"[21] educators hip—as it were—to hip-hop's sensibilities present educational institutions with a unique opportunity to form a bridge between educators and students, to offer the latter a forum in which to explore exegesis and hermeneutics with material that they feel to be an expression of their lived experience rather than the expression of thinkers whose lives are utterly disconnected with their own.

What must be kept in mind when considering the inclusion of hip-hop into the classroom is the reactionary nature of bureaucrats, parents, fellow educators, and even students themselves when it comes to the perceptions and misperceptions that surround hip-hop culture. Not everything that fits within the hip-hop's rubric is appropriate in a classroom setting. "Keeping it real" is, of course, crucial, but not at the expense of one's credibility as an educator. If we are asking students to develop their tools of critical analysis and comprehension, of reading between the lines of a popular form of culture, it is important to recognize when there is, indeed, much of value between the lines of a particular artist or piece of work. A graffiti artist does not count everything scrawled on a subway car as "graff"; a b-boy or b-girl will not be willing to say that anyone spinning on their back is breakin'; an MC is more than just a man with a microphone and a platform. A hip-hop artist of any sort might be superficially identifiable by a certain artistic style, a sound, a posture, or a pose, but, like any craft, hip-hop mastery requires a nearly absolute dedication to one's craft. Commercial success is no guarantee of such mastery, so the educator must be careful when selecting his or her materials. Exclusionary practices of canonicity are, in some small way, replicated in deciding what merits discussion in the classroom and what does not.[22] It is important to engage with materials that promote autonomy and on critical analysis of both the self and one's environment. This runs counter to the hand-holding of many contemporary educational practices, many of which turn a blind eye to the consequences of a blinkered world view; hip-hop as a pedagogical tool, though, demands in the clearest terms that the individual take accountability for themselves and for their education—an education that must navigate either through or around a system that is undoubt-edly failing America's Black youth. When I spoke with friend and colleague Bettina Love of the University of Georgia, she noted:

> The crux of Hip Hop scholarship in education rests within the pedagogical frameworks of critical pedagogy, culturally relevant pedagogy,[23] cultural modeling,[24] reality pedagogy,[25] and culturally sustaining pedagogy.[26] Each of the aforementioned educational ini-tiatives concludes that students learn best when their everyday lives, cultures, languages, customs, and ways of learning are affirmed and sustained in school curricula and teachers' pedagogical prac-tices.[27] This assertion has produced a rich body of Hip Hop-Based Education (HHBE) and scholarship that illuminates student-cen-tered educational outcomes when Hip Hop is linked to formal school curriculum and practice.[28]

Hip-hop offers a strategy through which students can be engaged in the classroom, and, rather than sloughing off responsibilities and consequences, it has the potential to enlighten students as to their responsibilities both to themselves and their communi-ties at large.[29] A hip-hop–inspired pedagogy seeks nonconformist approaches to curricula and policies; it undermines the institu-tional ethos that so little serves urban youth, giving them a voice within the system rather than one that is merely railing against the system. It serves students, but it can serve open-minded educators as well.

Primarily, hip-hop can serve educators as a bridge: as I have already suggested, it can be a bridge between educators and their students and vice versa. It can connect students to the classroom environment, and, through the responses elicited both in assign-ments and in classroom discussion, it can educate the teacher as well, giving them a glimpse through the lens through which the student views the world. When Earnest Morrell introduced hip-hop into his classroom, he not only asked his students to critically evaluate lyrical content of hip-hop songs and compare songs to canonical poetry, but also asked them to participate in a way more germane to hip-hop as a culture: they were encouraged to be hip-hoppas, to write their own lyrics and perform these lyrics in front of their peers, to judge and be judged by their classmates for both the content of their poetry and the means of its delivery.[30] Nothing was so revealing to him as this simple exercise of performance and critique.[31] It gave him a better handle on his students' experience of the world than any previous attempt to reach them had. Hip-hop was the bridge between he and his students' experiences, and it helped them to become better students and him to become a better educator.

But this is not the only type of bridge that hip-hop can form in the classroom. In more concrete terms, hip-hop can be a bridge to difficult—and more canonical—material that educators are finding it more and more difficult to introduce to students who are not convinced that such material speaks in any way to them as a living, experiencing human being. The poetry of hip-hop resonates deeply due to the fact that it addresses the student more directly than does, say, British or White American literatures. There is a familiarity with this material that can be a powerful tool for educators who wish to coax their students onto the path of textual exegesis. Hip-hop educator and one of the foremost authorities on pedagogy Emery Petchauer says, "For hip hop collegians, developing critical sensibilities alongside hip hop was entirely more sophisticated than simply adopting wholesale specific lines in songs…Experiencing hip hop as critical text was connected to personal experiences of loss, inequity, or oppression" (2012, p. 103). Once profoundly engaged in the hermeneutics of deep reading—or listening, whatever the case may be—students are much more likely to be prepared to expand the scope of their newfound skills.

This can, in turn, be broadened to include the overarching theme of knowledge that lies at the heart of inspired hip-hop culture. Hip-hop master visionaries like KRS-One and Afrika Bambaataa have been stressing the need for students of hip-hop—adult or adolescent—to use hip-hop as a tool of awakening (Parmar, 2009). By examining the philosophies that empower the conscious hip-hoppa in the classroom, bridges can be built to a radically new world of philosophical engagement and awakening.[32] Understanding a text or a lyric is not enough. It is the implications of this understanding that need to be fully comprehended, but still, understanding is the first step in the process. Students may think they have a grasp on familiar material; they may feel they have already mastered its message, but, in the classroom, new critical tools can be developed in order to both broaden this meaning and place it in context within a broader range of literature and philosophy.

As a graduate student, I found myself making similar connections between the world of hip-hop and that of philosophy. In Cornel West's class at Harvard, I read Samuel Beckett's *Waiting for Godot* for the first time. At the play's heart is an existentialist cry of despair and the tedium that its characters face as they realize that their objectives are meaningless. Until the crack of doom, all they can expect is to be distracted from the endless ennui and tedium of existence. Jay-Z expresses a similar weariness in the chorus of "Encore." He asks: "What the hell are we fighting for?"[33] His query speaks of the tedium that humans face in light of the realization that their struggles are, in essence, meaningless. We simply wait, and wait, and become distracted by the mundane and the daily grind before death. French existentialist Albert Camus describes this as the life of *absurdity* where Monday becomes Tuesday, Tuesday becomes Wednesday, and so on, *ad infinitum ad nauseam.*

With this connection and others like it in hand, I have entered the classroom and bridged the world of hip-hop with that of philosophy. The answers to my questions posed in exams reveal students considering hip-hop in a similar way: when engaged with hip-hop, students are pushing themselves to the edge without losing their heads. This is particularly true for students who are intellectually gun shy, which is to say students who may have either not held their feet to the fire of intellectual rigor, or, those who, when challenged, have withdrawn from the task. As an oblique paradigm to the educational, literary, and philosophical canon, hip-hop helps students to wrestle with the single master pedagogy that encompasses master themes and processes.

My students often respond with statements like, "This is cool and deep too, doc!" While there may be some truth in that statement, I rarely take it as such and see the "depth" as being attributed to the student-as-tourist within the space of the material taught in academic form. Whether it is that I have offered them an oblique pedagogy that works against some master form of teaching, or that I am simply acknowledging the ubiquitous nature and activity of hip-hop by bringing its poetry into a classroom setting, I am encouraged by these words. I ask students and teachers alike to take heed to the words of Jay-Z and Eminem in their Blueprint Classic, "Renegade": "Never," they say, "be afraid to say what's on your mind, any given time of day."

Malcolm X was fond of saying: "I pray that you will grow intel-lectually, so that you can understand the problems of the world and where you fit into that world picture. And I pray that all fear that is evident in your heart will be taken out" (X, 1965).[34] A hip-hop pedagogical tactic offers students the chance to do all that Malcolm X wanted for his brothers and sisters: it offers them the chance to understand the world as it is, to see through the appearances of the superficial and to engage with language in a profoundly personal way. Such engagement can be, at first, a ver-tiginous experience for both educators and students, but, moving past that fear, doors open onto a world of expression and expansion that moves well beyond the walls of the school. The Black body, formerly rendered anonymous when confined to predominantly black spaces, has been, through art, catapulted onto the plane of human existence. From the aggressive chest-popping of krumping (Curry, 2009), to the aerial assaults that taggers and graff artists display high upon bridges or deep within the urban tunnels; from the verbal gymnastics of the MC to the physical of the b-boy, hip-hop announces its presence to a world that once rendered the bodies that perform it invisible.

There is something deeply existential within the soulful cry of a Mystikal screech of "YIKES," the visceral grunt of Rick Ross or Master P. Sonic-studies scholar, Regina Bradley suggests: "Framing black men's narratives through a combination of instrumentals, vocals, and other relevant sounds like grunts, laughter, and wails, 'Hip Hop Sonic Cool Pose' negotiates signifiers of black male life through a sonic framework. It is the improvisation of black masculinity through sound, making space for the performance of otherwise silenced, supposedly non-normative feelings and expres-sions"[35] (2013, p. 61). Puts it another way, an artists' use of their creative tools and their meaning is both in question and unasked for to question presupposes a separation from the very culture that birthed it. Such powerful articulation, and an investigation into it, can be—and has been—used to engage students with their own experience of their bodies, of their lived experiences, and of their place within their communities. As educators in the new America, what could be more important than fostering such expression in our classrooms?

Rumination 5

Lost in the City and Lost in the Self: Sin and Solipsism in Hip-Hop's Dystopia; St. Augustine, Toni Morrison, and Paul Tillich

Hip-hop originated in the urban streets of New York in the 1960s.[1] Through the decades, hip-hop did not just became a music or art genre; it also became a global social movement, whose influence has permeated almost all aspects of life outside music, such as dance, literature, arts, advertising, the general way of life, and the discourse of many societal issues, such as race, gender, and identity.[2] Hip-hop was not just street poetry turned music; it was the voice, the very pulse that the so-called ghetto environment breeds.[3] As the genre has evolved, many have interpreted hip-hop and these interpretations rarely failed to depict a society that is full of violence, chaos, and discrimination. Why this depiction of violence and pessimism in hip-hop?

Rumination 1 identified hip-hop as a form of dialogue, birthed from the Black musical tradition of the spirituals and the blues, adopting a pragmatic migration to a northern city. This analysis will take two approaches: literary and theological. It focuses on "Sin City", a track off of *Cruel Summer*, the 2012 album featuring a host of different artists from Kanye West's GOOD Music Collective. This song becomes the fulcrum that balances the production of this rumination. The song clearly deals with the problem of excess and pleasure and locates sin as the place where the characters in the song reside and feel affirmed but yet acknowledge the need for a salvific intervention. Although Kanye West himself does not make an appearance on this particular track, Kanye's musical corpus continues to traffic in the body, pleasure, erotic urges, vanity, and consumption, typically calling for some type of celestial interruption or encounter. Originally crafted as a lecture outline from my research assistant, Dalitso Ruwe, this rumination pedagogically uses theology and literature. The city in this song is interesting in that it paints a picture of the world of debauchery yet seems always to seek a way out. In that vein, this Rumination argues that the track includes a call for redemption is beholden to the tropes of Christianity that demand redemption for the sin-filled body.

"City" as used in the song, describes a literary "place" that situates the song's themes and metaphorically anchors them. "Sin City" as described in the song could be likened to St. Augustine's City of God, the Greek's Atlantis, or Batman's Gotham City. All three talk of a place, a location, whether it is an imagined location or an actual location. All three also depicts a kind of Sin City—in relation to the time these places were created. Batman can't be taken out of Gotham City the same way Gotham City can't be taken out of Batman. The interdependence between Batman and Gotham City is essential because Batman's story cannot be explained without the depiction of Gotham, its dark-lit and crime-ridden streets.[4] The streets of Gotham, where Bruce Wayne witnessed the murder of his parents, became the reason why he is obsessed with battling crime.[5] Gotham City is a fictional place—superfluous, exaggerated, and over the top. As much as it is a fictional place, Gotham City bears a resemblance to real-life places—the dark alleys where invisible evil lurks, the drug- and crime-infested ghettos and cities, and poverty-stricken slums. Moreover, Gotham City depicts social realities, such as poverty, inequality, the unequal distribution of wealth, poor living conditions, and corruption.[6]

In Gotham City, Bruce Wayne lives a dual life—a playboy philanthropist by day, a law enforcement hero at night. Bruce Wayne, who has lived a solitary life, haunted by the death of his parents, tries to correct the "wrongs" of his city by day by sharing his wealth through his Wayne Foundation. This act, though, does not seem adequate to help his city, so at night he dons cape and mask and fights off villains. Bruce Wayne/Batman has a bipolar relationship with his city, Gotham City. It is the city that bears him so much pain—a lonely childhood without his parents and a superfluous adult life where trust is something difficult to gain, echoed in "Sin City" as "Fake friends, forgive 'em for they sins." Gotham City is a city of sins, a city of drugs and earthly pleasures, but like the characters in Kanye's song, Bruce Wayne/Batman cannot take the city out of him, as much as cannot take himself out of the city. No matter how painful and difficult it is for him, the city already defines him and the person he is, and justifies his obsessions.

"Here is where her heart belongs, Her heart belongs to me," Teyana Taylor sings in the second stanza of "Sin City." A shout, not of resignation, but of a sense of belonging; despite the acknowledgment of the presence of sins in her city (in the first stanza), she belongs in the city because her heart is in the city and the city's heart is in hers. Similarly, with Bruce Wayne/Batman, the frustrations he experiences over his repeated failures in improving his city or in redeeming his city from evil cannot extinguish the fact that he continues to reside in the city, or if he did escape for a time, he came back to live, to belong, in the city that holds his heart. Such is the message that comes out from the song, "Sin City." This is also an expression of the abiding message that the hip-hop genre aims to convey to anyone who listens—that this is my music, the expression of my heart. Let us also not forget the uncanny parallelism of the literary symbolism that is Gotham City. The place was used as early as the fifteenth century to refer to places with foolish inhabitants.[7] In American literature, the place was picked up by Washington Irving in his 1807 New York satire titled *Salmagundi*. Gotham City is clearly a fictional place, but in modern literature and through depictions in countless Batman comic books and movies, the city seemed to point as reference the Big Apple, where the hip-hop movement started. *I'm here and I won't go*, Teyana Taylor cries.

Hip-Hop's Resistance to Dystopia in Search for Atlantis

Just as "Sin City" has hints of Gotham City's stylized literary place of alienation and belonging, it also evokes the perhaps-mythic city of Atlantis. The dynamics between the individual and the collective in relation to the definition of an ideal society is a topic broadly explored through many perspectives, and the philosopher Plato wrote on Atlantis, a mysterious, if not mythical island, that vanished due to the society's eventual decline in ideals. World literature is full of similar stories of societies that vanished and one example is the city of 'Ad,[8] in the Quran, which was removed by a sandstorm with powerful winds. While the city of 'Ad was eventually discovered, Atlantis was never found despite the striking details that made Plato's description far more believable than any picture offered by Homer in the *Odyssey* and *Iliad*. Given the fact that the nineteenth- and early twentieth-century archaeologists used Homer's descriptions to locate a variety of cities, such as Troy, Mycenae, and Pylos, it seemed only natural to use Plato's account for the search for Atlantis. He was a philosopher after all, not a poet, and surely did not lie about the past; Plato's description of the architecture, topography, and social structure on the island held the promise of a real place for archaeologists to track down. Despite Plato's reputation and his detail, the island has not been found. In fact, the majority of Classical archaeologists doubt it is even a place to be located.

Professor Darlene Brooks-Hedstrom, an Ancient Egyptian expert, surmises that "Plato's words have sparked numerous identifications of sites as Atlantis including locations in the Aegean; on the coasts of Crete, Cyprus Sardinia and Sicily; and most recently off the coast of Spain. What they all share is evidence of cites and islands with partial destruction due to fierce environmental forces. The island of Santorini, home to the city of Akrotiri, was destroyed in 1628 BCE[9] by a volcano.[10] Its central city was covered in dense ash and hidden entirely until excavations in the late 19th century and work continues to this day."[11] When asked about any contemporary research being done on debunking or proving aiding in the understanding of the Atlantis phenomenon, Dr. Brooks highlighted that "most recently, archaeologists working in Spain have used satellite technology and underwater archaeology to aid in the discovery of site they think could be the basis for the Atlantis myth.[12] It remains to be seen if this is Atlantis."[13] Those of us, vaguely interested in the mythology can lament at this discovery and conclude that "Atlantis" itself, or other geographical localities were lost to nature's evolution.[14] Search for the actual island still takes place and whether or not any certainty as to its historical reality may never exist but historians and archaeologists like Dr. Brooks-Hedstrom have benefitted from the substantive research.[15] Nevertheless, given that the majority of Classical archeologists doubt that Atlantis can be located because they believe the city is only used as a medium for Plato to illustrate his philosophical ideals. Atlantis, many Classical archeologists[16] believe, is what Plato described as an ideal society.[17]

The ideal society, utopia, depicted by Plato[18] segregated its citizens according to vocational classes, such as farmers, warriors, and rulers shunned luxury and worked toward the common good. Plato believed that human beings, specifically Olympians, are rational beings who can decide for themselves what is right and what is wrong. Contrary to popular fiction at his time, Plato believed in peace and order, even among the gods and goddesses that ruled the citizens. Plato believed in the good more than the bad, and in justice more than in inequality. He depicted Atlantis as the ideal society that is orderly and just. In Plato's philosophy, a just man overcomes his anger and does not let negative emotions command his action. On the other hand, an unjust man is easily swallowed by negative emotions. Plato suggested that the statesman must be a philosopher because a philosopher knows what is just.

Atlantis vanished as a result of a natural occurrence, swallowed by the sea, which are typical occurrences in Greece, where numerous earthquakes, seismic sea waves, and volcanic eruptions have been recorded since ancient times.[19] The ideal society that Plato described will vanish when there is disorder and when there is injustice. A state deteriorates when the statesmen and the citizens are no longer working for what is the common good. The deterioration begins when individuals no longer have the capacity to act for themselves, as individual actions result to collective repercussions.

A sociological approach would see disempowerment as a loss of individual agency, also known as the capacity to act and influence one's own life. The song "Sin City" serves, however, as a commentary on the overemphasis on individualistic desires in a system that has managed to maintain itself by offering too much individual agency. In the song "Sin City," Malik Yusef blamed himself for the deterioration ("I did some wrongs") but he did not correct his wrongs, whether it's because he is no longer capacitated to do the correct things or he is apathetic ("I wouldn't dare right"). The Atlantis, the imaginary utopia, the ideal society, will vanish when the individual has prioritized individual desires over the greater good.

God Bless the City

Theologically, "Sin City" presents itself as a schizophrenic cry for redemption: as Teyana Taylor and John Legend soulfully plead for mercy, while Travis Scott and CyHi da Prince seem to bask in their sinful bravado. Certainly, the myriad voices present themselves in moral contention. For example, following Taylor and Legend's tragic moral appeal ("I beg for mercy today…Wash these demons away"), CyHi enters the track with a boastful laundry list of illicit behavior ranging from drug slinging to womanizing. These contradictions in lyrical content—from the penitent hook ("Wash the demons away / Wash the demons away") to Scott's declaration that sin is inconsequential—highlight the track's greatest conflict: to live in Sin City is to live in a paradox, a paradox that entails conflict. The artists who speak on "Sin City" present characters and figures who are embroiled in personal, ethical, and moral turmoil. The very pleasures that divide them also, paradoxically, empower them.[20] They are torn between the amoral dismissal of sin and Judeo-Christian moral codes, between solipsistic gratification and communal redemption.

St. Augustine wrote *City of God* as his reflection on the sacking of Rome by the Visigoths in 410 AD. In the book, he defended Christianity from those who blamed the religion for Rome's hardship at the hands of the Vandals to the defection of the Roman gods to Christianity. He then described two cities: the City of Earth and the City of God. Augustine acknowledges from the beginning that the two cities are "inextricably intermingled one with the other."[21] However, Augustine's writing is dualistic in nature describing one city as sinful, filled with those who deny God and whose eschatological reality includes complete separation from God; and one city as heavenly, filled with saints and those who desire to reside with God for all eternity.

While Augustine knows that the present world contains both sinners and saints, and thus acts as the stage upon which both cities are enacted, his complete distinction between the two is in stark contrast to Kanye's vision where everyone is simultaneously sinner and saint. The song "Sin City" portrays a single world where the City of Heaven and the City of Earth are coterminous; the distinction between sinner and saint is vaporous and conditional. The dualism displayed in Augustine's analysis is missing. On the one hand, Kanye presents certain voices reveling in the debauchery and sinfulness of their lives. On the other hand, during the chorus, voices cry out for redemption and healing. While it is tempting to view this contrast between the sinner and those crying for mercy with an Augustinian dualistic view of humanity, it is also possible to interpret these voices presenting two sides of the same person/people. Within the history of Christianity (or even humanity) there has always been a sense that people commit certain acts by night, which is a metaphor for the "Sin City," and feel sorrow and desire redemption by light of day. Paul himself described this phenomenon.[22]

Augustine argues that our end, our goal, should be to dwell eternally in the City of God.[23] Acknowledging, as Paul did, that we are driven by our desires, which may not be in line with or lead to the end we desire, we are to abandon the types of activities that many of the schizophrenic souls in Kanye's songs glory in committing. Augustine firmly believes that only by God's grace are we able to conquer the demons that we submit to in the dark, where no one can see. Of our own power, we are slaves to sin; depending on God, we are already living in the City of God, even while inhabiting this world.

Sin and Solipsism: Morality in the Unfair City

Living in a city develops as a thought experiment, where we must churn morally adjusted behavior while on a carrousel of changing circumstances. In the city we are islands, yet we must adhere to an interminable list of explicit and implicit rules and contextual cues—from red lights to bike lanes and pedestrian walkways. In the city we are free from the judgmental looks of parents, neighbors, and the small-town priests, but are, in turn, bound to the strictest of disciplinarian codes of conducts, fruit of capitalist work relationships.

Explanations of this outcome that we, as urban dwellers, must face are not difficult to find. We have, for instance, the structuralist (and later Foucauldian) approach, where the problem is characterized by the metaphorical figure of the panopticon: we live within a regime of control, which gives us relative freedom in exchange for our life energy (bio-politics), and for our souls; in such a system of top-down control, freedom is little more than market choice. There is also the psychoanalytic approach, with its traditional focus on the ego: repressive institutions, starting with our authoritarian fathers and father figures (teachers and bosses), control our bodies and suppress the libido. The result is that we are all prey of our own personal neuroses, which, in the end, are but coping mechanisms we use to defend ourselves from the morality of urban life.

And there is too the positivistic take, which reminds us that we were made, through turns of evolution, to be hunter-gatherers. Our morality is limited to familial faces, and strangers will for the most part be met by our lizard brain: we flee or we fight. The city is an artificial unit, which differs too much from the tribal groups that our ancestors were a part of for thousands of years. I can hear the retort that says that these are too easily fabricated straw men, which hide the complexities and details that these perspectives entail. Even as this may be the case, the heart of the matter is that a more complete picture is not what is lacking. It is not lacking, because the purpose here is to highlight a centric element that crosses through any such approach. This central aspect is the conviction that Modernity has occurred, and that it is a concluded project. In other words, the fact that we are Modern subjects living in societies designed for modern life is what makes of discontinuities a paradox: we are convinced that we have finally separated science and politics successfully, and, hence, that questions of morality are essentially irresolvable, due to their subjective character, while faith in science will eventually resolve the economic and environmental issue that would underlie moral claims. But, what if, like Bruno Latour, we take a step back and say: "we are not modern; we never were and never will be." What if modern life is not a life that has been perfectly molded to make us speak objectively? If the devil's greatest trick is convincing the world that he doesn't exist, modernity's trick convinces us all that it does. This is an attempt to explore this possibility, and will do so by putting forth a series of motifs or figures that characterize the way in which traditional moral stances face this incomplete modernity, whose exemplar topology is the city. Philosophically, hip-hop takes this moral conundrum to the limit; it gathers these different motifs, ever bearing the traces of their influence, but its path wends its way through, over, and around those approaches that have come before it. By this token, the reading will help to make Latour's point of showing that modernity cannot indeed be taken as a complete project; without that implying that action must be taken in that direction. What we must conclude from such a discontinuity is that the need to understand the gaps in our knowledge is an irrational one, and further we begin to recognize the essential incompletion of modernity as a project and as a foundational premise for thought. Morality, in turn, will not be prescribed, but explored: moral action might appear in these motifs as difficult as requiring reflection at times, while simultaneously encouraging playful intuition at others.

Causal Mechanistic Motif: "Machines Have No Souls"

Returning to the "Sin City" track, it opens with an exposition of blatant wrongdoing as Travis Scott somewhat casually details his business in Sin City. It is not so much an admission of guilt or an acknowledgment of sin as it is an explication of amoral cause-and-effect: "the cops behind us" because we "ran that red light;" his girlfriend "stepped into hell, because winter got cold." Run a red light and the police will pursue. Step into hell because the winter is cold. For Scott, these issues are bound in amoral practicality; they are causal relationships devoid of morality. Events seem to develop separately from their protagonists. Moral action is unlikely, and further, unnecessary, for the logic of events would be prior to its agents.

Toward the end of his verse, Scott radicalizes his amoral pragmatism, actively refuting and ignoring moral evidence. Scott spends most of his verse detailing his drug-fueled exploits-pleasure-seeking consumerism that moves from blatant drug production ("She see the glasses, so obvious") to egocentric gratification ("All of those drunken nights then fuckin' every night"). And while Scott views his actions through a solipsistic frame of cause-and-effect, his amoral stance slips at the end of the verse, revealing what may be in the back of his mind: a latent fear that his actions are taking place in a moral universe. Following what seems to be a persistent reiteration of amoral causality, Scott warns: "Don't look in her eyes, you might see straight to her soul." Despite his insistence throughout the verse that the world follows a simple cause-and-effect pattern, Scott seems to backtrack as he acknowledges the potentiality of a moral "soul." In order to maintain his amoral framework, Scott warns against looking anywhere that may suggest a moral presence. His warning is not cynical, but more of a strategic choice, perhaps even the only sane choice, of surviving this leviathan: this machine we call the city.

The city can make us cynics, but surely not in the Greek sense. Solipsism can be seen as cynical and as selfish: the individual would crawl upon himself—Wittgenstein's last line in the *Tractatus* is illustrative of ethical reflection: it amounts to climbing the ladder and kicking it behind you. The city amoral solipsism is a true innovation for our species. We shrug off our moral duties, yet we do so, not through claims of epistemological skepticism,[24] but through a newfound cynicism that finds an aid in modern social science. As true believers of modernity's riffs between society and individuals we attribute causalities to social processes: institutions have created uniformity and, thus, transgression can only be but an expected symptom, and one that may actually have a positive connotation even, because in them our calls for freedom (be it moral or amoral) ring out. Or we say: "We are all clogs of the capitalist machine," where the only true commandment would be "thou shall consume until the day of your death" and, hence, moral action is but a thing of the past, a thing that only appeals to our nostalgic sense of community.

It is true, however, that the logic of profit and the self-disciplined masses are fundamental for the city's life; there is, unfortunately, no hidden reality to unveil—Marx has done that already. The city functions without us. The city does not need us and will not miss us. The city is truly a machine. Is it not understandable then that we become cynical and reclusive? How can we be part of a machine and still reserve the label of moral beings for ourselves?

Theological Judeo-Christian Motif: "Forgive Me, For I Have Sinned"

From a theological perspective, "Sin City" presents itself as a schizophrenic cry for redemption: as Teyana Taylor and John Legend soulfully plead for mercy, Travis Scott and CyHi da Prince seem to bask in their sinful bravado. Certainly, the myriad voices present themselves in moral contention. For example, following Taylor and Legend's tragic moral appeal ("I beg for mercy today…Wash these demons away"), CyHi enters the track with a boastful laundry list of illicit behavior ranging from drug slinging to womanizing.

These apparent contradictions in lyrical content—from the penitent hook ("Wash the demons away / Wash the demons away") to Scott's declaration that sin is inconsequential—highlight the track's greatest conflict: to live in Sin City is to live in a paradox, a paradox that emits conflict. As previously mentioned, themes found in Black aesthetic productions, and the human experience proper, present characters/figures who are embroiled in personal, ethical, and moral turmoil. The very pleasures that divide them also, paradoxically, empower them. They are torn between the amoral dismissal of sin and Judeo-Christian moral codes, between solipsistic gratification and communal redemption. Sinfulness itself is the result of our incarnational nature. As the great twentieth-century theologian Karl Rahner states, "Our human existence is caught between the sinfulness of all creation . . . on the one hand, and the redemption of Christ on the other."[25]

From a religious perspective, where individual behavior always takes place against a moral backdrop, redemption is called upon while temptation seems to lurk in every corner. We become, in pure diachronic fashion, postmodern Jobs, located in the middle of a battleground that seems not to be our own. Judeo-Christian morality is markedly different from the self-disciplined subject churned by modern institutions. While the city asks us to restrain from affecting others with our actions, our Christian roots would remind us that morality and pragmatism do not go along well—you can only serve one master. Postmodernity is filled with philosophies by those who repudiate religion as the basis for moral decisions. These philosophies represent the moral vacuity of the city as the ultimate result of the divorce of morality from faith.[26] The city is indeed the cradle of pragmatism; we cannot suspend with our actions the functional dynamics of city life. In the city, protesters must raise their demands in a designated place, homeless souls must wait politely for the rich man's scraps to fall off the table, and bankers, who epitomize bourgeois morality, are in charge of keeping the industries of transgression alive.[27] It is in this discontinuous reality that calls for salvation and redemption seem to be in place.

With this motif of "Sin City"—namely being "lost" in the postmodern, ambiguous moral-indifference—there is a sense of desperation in longing for some sort of redemption to free oneself from the chains that bind one to such a city. Notice the intentional use of direction in reference to where one is in the City: *lost*. What shall we say then? What is this "City of Sin," and whence has it come? As Kanye West espouses an amorally ambiguous philosophy concerning existence and ontology, there is an underlying theme that is rooted in the nature of every human being. This too can be read between the lines of his songs. In the 2004 single, "Jesus Walks," Kanye expressed a deep understanding and knowledge of sin, within postmodern culture, and how it separates us from God; he states: "You can rap about anything except for Jesus. That means guns, sex, lies, video tapes, but if I talk about God my record won't get played? Well let this take away from my spins, which will probably take away from my ends. Then I hope it take away from my sins."[28] Whether Kanye was trying to work toward getting some of his sins taken away, in point of fact, it was a crucial issue to Kanye in wanting "some of his sins taken away" to begin with.

In the New Testament, sin is translated from the Greek *harmatia*, which literally means "missing the mark." Strong's Concordance described it to wit: "*Harmatia* is the most comprehensive term for moral deviations. It is used of 'sin' as a principle or source of action, or an inward element producing acts."[29] Albeit *harmatano*[30] arguably expresses itself actively in humans, whereby an action is produced, through the moral defect, and makes it more difficult to do the right thing. It represents an entire macro-cosmological framework as well. For as "the Israelites [wandered] around the land in confusion, hemmed in by the desert" (Exodus 14:3), so do Kanye West and his companions wander around the "Sin City" where "are all unwelcome." All may be unwelcome, but still, the "population increases."

"What a wretched man I am!" cried the Apostle Paul. "Who will rescue me from this body that is subject to death? (Rom 7:24). Stricken with grief over the apparent conflict between his flesh and spirit, Paul makes a clear distinction between true righteousness found in God alone, and the sinfulness of the flesh. And again, "We know that the law is spiritual; but I am unspiritual, sold as a slave to sin. I do not understand what I do. For what I want to do I do not do, but what I hate I do" (Rom 7:14, 15). Hence, we must understand the importance of the bondage of the will; namely, that because of sin, all men are born into a fallen state, constantly "missing the mark," and are utterly and completely sold over as slaves to sin. Harmatia resides within all people. This is, in fact, the precise argument the Apostle Paul makes throughout his New Testament letters. Harmatia serves as a thread weaving through his correspondence. "Therefore, just as sin entered the world through one man, and death through sin, and in this way death came to all people, because all sinned" (Rom 5:12, c.f. 1; Cor 15:21).

It must be understood that sin, as a consequence of its very nature, brings death (Rom 6:23). Furthermore, the law should not be understood as sinful in and of itself; however, its sole purpose is to show man's sinfulness more clearly by contrasting the righteousness of God, with man's ability to only "miss the mark." Paul confirms this when he states, "I would not have known what sin was had it not been for the law. For sin, seizing the opportunity afforded by the commandment, deceived me, and through the commandment put me to death. So then, the law is holy, and the commandment is holy, righteous and good" (Rom 7:7b, 11–12). Whither are the tenants of Kanye West's "Sin City" traveling to? *Nowhere*—they are slaves to sin, thereby consequentially reaping for themselves nothing but death. For they themselves have admitted, "we broke all the commandments."

Whereas Augustine of Hippo, 1,500 years ago, bewailed over his sins in order that he could more appropriately give glory to God, "Sin City" appears to be a twenty-first century appendix to his *Confessions*. Although he entitled his massive theological treatise *City of God*, Augustine realized that, for others, everywhere around him was still the City of Sin.[31] "[My will] did not show the presence of another mind, but the punishment was my own. Thus it was no more I who did it, but the sin that dwelt in me–the punishment of a sin freely committed by Adam, and I was a son of Adam."[32] Understanding that as a son of Adam, all are held in bondage to sin, Augustine didn't recognize the problem of evil, sin, and suffering as the absence of God, but rather, he recognized these issues as giving credence to God's omnipotence. Adam brought death into the world through sin; Jesus Christ, however, remedied the effects of sin by defeating the works of Satan, thereby offering an entrance back to the City of God for some (Col 1:13, 1; Jn 3:8), and a cage in the City of Sin for others (Prov 16:4; Rom 9:22). Augustine expounds on these precepts in the *City of God:*

> Though good and bad men suffer alike, we must not suppose that there is no difference between the men themselves, because there is no difference in what they both suffer. For even in the likeness of the sufferings, there remains an unlikeness in the sufferers; and though exposed to the same anguish, virtue and vice are not the same thing. For as the same fire causes gold to glow brightly, and chaff to smoke; and under the same flail the straw is beaten small, while the grain is cleansed; and as the lees are not mixed with the oil, though squeezed out of the vat by the same pressure, so the same violence of affliction proves, purges, clarifies the good, but destroys, ruins, exterminates the wicked.[33]

And again, Jesus confirms the truth of a City of God and "Sin City," coexisting yet separate by and by, in the parable of the weeds.

> He said to them, An enemy has done this. The servants said to him, Will you then that we go and gather them up? But he said, No; lest while you gather up the tares, you root up also the wheat with them. Let both grow together until the harvest: and in the time of harvest I will say to the reapers, Gather you together first the tares, and bind them in bundles to burn them: but gather the wheat into my barn. (Matt 13:28–30)

Hence, we can see that although the entire creation and cosmological order of the universe is groaning for salvific redemption from their bondage (Rom 8:18–23), there is a remnant that obtains the righteousness of Christ, notwithstanding the entire fallen world and race of Adam. For those stuck in "Sin City," are bound to the entire law they have broken inasmuch as sin works through the law (Rom 3:20).[34] However, for those born outside "Sin City"—and not underneath (for those "caged in by age ten")—they have been crucified with Christ, whereupon they receive righteousness *apart* from the law (Rom 3:21).

Although postmodern American culture proclaims, "all are tares!" it's evident the mingling of the wheat with the tares is intentionally done to create an amoral set of values where "tares" really don't exist anyway. Again, notwithstanding the attempt to herald the philosophical worldview that "cocaine killed Abel." It must be clear that even though there is the overt presence of "Sin City," there is the subtle presence of the City of God as well. As the LORD commanded the Israelites long ago: "Distinguish between the holy and the profane; between the unclean and the clean" (Lev 10:10). Regardless of the desire to do well, righteousness will not, and cannot be obtained through the law. It must also be remembered that the City of God which can be equated with the biblical notion of "kingdom of God," or "reign of God," is not a place or state but an action. In Jesus' preaching the kingdom of God is the cumulative deeds that make God present in our world. Therefore, the City of God exists on the same plane as the Sin City but has the additional character of a future, eschatological fulfillment.[35]

Thus, it follows that all who are born through the city of sin will die through the city of sin. In essence, "Sin City" produces what it punishes, and punishes what it produces. As the effects from the

city are not only felt on an individual basis, they are wholly influential on the transpersonal level as well. Physically, and metaphysically, "Sin City" affects all transpersonally—regardless of gender,
race, or sexual identity—just as those in the Body of Christ, in the
"City of God," are affected transpersonally as well: this, too, is not
a matter of status, gender, or race (Gal 3:28). The point, however,
is that those stuck in "Sin City" need not more "will-to-power,"
but need a deliverance from the very power that holds all those
chained to the city in the first place. Regardless of the postmodern will to "transvaluate morality," there lies a deep-rooted sense
of condemnation, guilt, and shame for all those residents in that
deceptive city. A spirit of fear and culpability, wherein they cry, "I
beg for mercy today…Don't let us die in vain."

For the residents of sin city however, many have the life that so
heavily takes a "toll on ya," accepting that someone has to "pay
the price." Nevertheless, the very vices that are so cherished in
spite of all their sufferings were actually paid for through Christ
by His sufferings. His sufferings on the cross, outside of the city,
on-top of Golgotha, opened a door, clearly visible from "Sin City,"
a door that opens onto the city of God. Although the presence
of evil, suffering, and injustice are often used as a presupposition
against the existence of God, Christian existential philosopher,
Paul Tillich, eloquently argues the contrary.

> How can an all-powerful God who is, at the same time the God
> of love, allow such misery? If God has produced a world in which
> physical and moral evil were impossible, the creatures would not
> have had the independence of God, which is presupposed in the
> experience of reunited love. Actualization of one's potentialities
> includes, unavoidably, estrangement; estrangement from one's
> essential being, so that we may find it again in maturity. Only a
> God who is like a foolish mother, who is afraid about the well-
> being of her child that she keeps him in a state of enforced inno-
> cence and enforced participation in her own life, could have kept
> the creatures in the prison of dreaming paradise. And, as in the
> case of the mother, this would have been hidden hostility and not
> love. And would not have been power either. The power of God is
> that He overcomes estrangement, not that He prevents it; that He
> takes it, symbolically speaking upon himself.[36]

Although "Sin City" is both title of the song and a lived reality,
the City of God is equally an ontological reality. The sufferings,

pain, and misery felt in the fallen world of humanity could only be possible by an all-powerful God, who prepared people to strive for paradise and freedom, and thereupon receive it through the power of Christ, who bore such misery, pain, and judgment on Himself. "In the city that is as unfair as life," tenants, no matter how removed they may feel from God's grace, can boldly ask for His forgiveness and blessings.

The Realistic Reappraisal: "Ultimately We Are All Part of Something Greater Than Ourselves"

CyHi's verse stands in stark opposition to an amoral and mechanistic perspective. While on the surface, his lyrical content seems to parrot Scott's opening verse, glorifying a debauched lifestyle of drug dealing and pleasure chasing, CyHi subtly acknowledges the collective problem of Sin City. CyHi's verse moves beyond Scott's solipsistic amoralism and indicts an entire culture. Although he still brashly glorifies the benefits of drug dealing and immorality, CyHi acknowledges the presence of a Judeo-Christian ethical code when he asserts, "We broke all the commandments." It would be a stretch to say that CyHi's lyrical persona attempts to follow the ethical code, but he goes beyond Scott's initial amoral conveyance and acknowledges the reality of a Judeo-Christian moral order.

It is important to note the subject of CyHi's sinning: it is not the solipsistic "I" voice or the guilt deflecting "you" that pervades Scott's verse. CyHi incriminates the communal "we." For CyHi, sinning is a transpersonal problem. For example, he accuses the community for breaking all of the commandments (assumedly, the Judeo-Christian Ten Commandments: "we broke all the Commandments"), later noting that "sex, drugs, and playin' dices are our favorite vices." If the presence of a moral value system was not evident throughout his verse, CyHi ends with a final declarative plea: "God bless the city, amen." With typical swagger, CyHi's "prayer" comes off simultaneously as a heartfelt appeal to a moral God and a brash command. Despite the conflicting (and predictable) blend of social consciousness and arrogance, it is important to note that CyHi is asking (or demanding, depending on your own degree of cynicism) for a heavenly blessing on the community. He has lumped the communal "us" in with his sinning, has acknowledged sin as a transpersonal issue, and attempts to rectify the quandary by asking for a redemptive presence in his community. If before I have said that causality and epistemological separation lead to indifference, it is still true that cynicism emerges only after certain despair has been left behind. If the city would ask us to tolerate vice are we not to get fed up with it all at some point? "It is not natural to live in such way!"

Informed by a vein of Aristotelian (or Thomistic) realism, morality and ontology become correlated terms, mediated by a third one: Nature.[37] The role of human nature in Western thought goes indeed back at least to Socrates.[38] Every being has a natural state and life is but a constant tending toward it. For humans it is the tempting power of sin, what acts as a contrary force that keeps us, or deviate us, from fulfilling our natural calling. The city is an almost perfect expression of this temptation; the city with its love of money, its unlimited offer of sensual pleasures, has truly led us astray from our nature as social beings, as ethical beings, as rational animals. Unless we bring light into darkness it will be impossible for the higher things in life to become our reality. Moral realism absorbs reality as a whole only to filter the wheat from the chaff. If morality under this light is an ally of reactionary forces it is because of their mutual love for order, for uniformity of kind, and for a teleological view on the "we," the "us," to be fulfilled.[39] Moral realism, therefore, would demand for a benevolent dictator in the best of cases, and a vindictive oppressor in the worst. Only through force, it seems to be the lesson of this motif, can morality be attained.

The Nihilistic Sublimation: "My Game, My Rules"

CyHi's shift away from an explication of personal sin to transpersonal sin pits the content of his verse against Scott's lyrical vantage; additionally, the progression of CyHi's verse reflects a similar evolution. Paying homage to his personal transgressions, CyHi details his lavish lifestyle. What opens as an archetypal hip-hop boast (bitches, drugs, and money), turns toward a communal reckoning. Like Scott, CyHi opens his verse with a solipsistic "I" voice, emphasizing his rags-to-riches success ("I used to run with the have-nots / Kept the ave (nue) hot just so we could have knots"), before turning to the communal "we," the voice of transpersonal awareness.

The story told by CyHi in "Sin City" is a story of personal success is amoral at its core: it is amoral in the relativistic sense by which the individual becomes the measure of what's real and what's not, and it is amoral in that the lesson it provides for others is that success depends, almost axiomatically, on the will of the individual—not on family, not on friends, not on the church, and not on weak, but on the strong. Despite how close this perspective comes to Nietzsche's "will-to–power," it is in the end a story about the city as a community. What I mean with this is that the story of self-made success is the mythical story of American capitalism. It is surely not unique to CyHi, but it is certainly not a phenomenon, which we can make sense of from any other perspective besides the individual's perspective. Indeed, Nihilism as a sublimation of the self, as a true calling, is today, as Nietzsche indeed foretold, a powerful moral force. The Nihilistic motif seems to suggest then that morality matters inasmuch as my morals/interests matter.

The Nostalgic Reactionary: "Innocence Belongs to a Long Lost Past"

By the midpoint of his verse, CyHi transitions from personal to plural pronouns. Even when his voice slips from the communal "we" back toward the personal "I" perspective, it is still with an eye toward communal awareness. For example, after CyHi notes that the community broke all of the commandments, he moves back to a seemingly egocentric perspective, promoting his own individuality: "Authentic, I'm hand-stitched." CyHi continues to riff on this solipsistic point of view: "Come spend a day in my Hamlet / My city lost; some say it's Atlantis." Topically, CyHi seems to be spinning his wheels in stereotypical hip-hop egocentrism (by employing a voice that seems brash and possessive), but the illusory depth of his lyricism alludes to something greater: CyHi is acknowledging the shared weight of a community, the transpersonal nature of sin.

CyHi lays claim to the community: it is his hamlet;[40] it is his city. But rather than a boastful flow of entitlement, CyHi takes responsibility. It is his city, his community, and his shared problem. The use of the Atlantian myth suggests a multiplicity of readings. As he linguistically drops the "is" from his flow ("My city [is] lost; some say it's Atlantis"), CyHi puns on the geographic incomparability of Atlantis: sunk beneath the ocean tides, it cannot be found. Additionally, if CyHi's wordplay is to be taken at face value (the "is" is not a stylistic omission, but a grammatical intention), then the line may be interpreted as loss, failure, and defeat (a theme that also fits with the myth of Atlantis). In an abstract moral/ethical reading, the line may be heard as a woeful acknowledgment; it is CyHi's admission that his city is axiologically bereft, slipped into a pattern of moral decay.

The city is lost. There is so much emotional weight, so much discontent in this assertion. There is a true air of nostalgia, which the presence of "moral decay" brings along with it. Weren't we different before? Wasn't the city once a better place? Moral coherence on a massive scale appears such a far-fetched thing that it would seem that only by travelling back in time could we actually get to experience it. If the great narratives have disappeared, if God is dead, if symbolic exchange has been replaced by utilitarianism, and if the revolution of the people will never come, what is left to say but "my city is lost." A postmodern stance is not entirely freed from moral constraints, but its iconoclasm does make it prey to for nostalgia and, ultimately, to despair. It is not solipsistic, however. On the contrary, it simply has made of collective morality an impossible achievement for the society. By almost confessing that it sees no point in individual virtue that despair becomes an actual form of morals. "Live and let live," seems to sum it up.

We go back to the origins of the hip-hop movement. It was birthed, not just from the Black musical tradition, but from Black tradition. The song is morally conflicted, with some singers glorifying their wrongdoings and the other begging for mercy and redemption. One of the most powerful authors on the topic of redemption is Toni Morrison, who in her book, *Home,* delved on the subject that could easily be found in "Sin City." *Home* follows the journey of a war veteran, who avoids going home, to Lotus, Georgia, with whom he bears childhood hurts, but was forced to come back to attend to an ailing sister. One who has traveled far in search for "luck," the journey Frank Money, the main character in the book, took back to Lotus gave him a deeper understanding of humanity, in the process of understanding himself, and gave him his own definition of "home."

Frank Money's travel back home was dotted with encounters that questioned his morality and affected his mentality. Throughout the book, and more so during his travel to Lotus, Frank Money showed signs of having posttraumatic stress disorder, which could be signifying the mental stress that the Black race is undergoing after the decades of discrimination, abuse, and violence. *Home* touched on the moral and the amoral—a conflict that is present, not just in literary creations, but also in real situations. "Sin City" also tackled the conflict on morality and amorality. The song opens with an exposition of blatant wrongdoing without the admission of guilt or the acknowledgment of sin to imply that what was happening was the result of an action that occurred before hand. In short, to Scott, what happened was devoid of morality, just an event that is bound to happen as a result of their actions. Scott's play of words also plays with his views on his actions and the lack of moral evidence, but he warns not to seek evidence of morality ("Don't look in her eyes, you might see straight to her soul"), which illustrates a conflict between his amoral actions and his acknowledgment that if moral evidence is sought, there might be a different repercussion to his actions. Scott justified his sinful actions by taking out moral evidence. He seemed resigned to committing sinful actions because "we lost in the city where sin is no biggy."

In a Sin City—illustrated through Gotham City, the mythical Atlantis, and St. Augustine's City of Earth—one is bound to be burdened with too much pain—emotional and spiritual—that one needs to take a journey to take them back "home," a place where one is safe and secure, a place to rest. Morrison illustrated this journey in her books with the character owing up to his wrongdoings, understanding one's self, and gaining knowledge along the way. CyHi, in the song, owned the city, claiming it as his hamlet.[41] But rather than a boastful flow of entitlement, CyHi takes responsibility. It is his city, his community, and his shared problem. His use of the Atlantian myth suggests a multiplicity of readings, one of which could be read as a woeful acknowledgment—that his city is morally lost. The once thriving and decadent city has slipped into a pattern of moral decay. Despite the admission of moral decay of CyHi's city, he owned the city and owned his sins. Atlantis already lost, sunk deep into the ocean, CyHi's owning up of his responsibilities to the city he calls his own is parallel to the journey that Frank Money took in *Home*, a journey he thought would be an individual's journey to some place he dislikes, yet in the recesses of his mind, to some place that could offer him redemption because this is his own place, his city, his home.

Rumination 6

Hip-Hop and International Voices of Revolution: Brazil, Cuba, Ghana, and Egypt

Throughout time, historians have noted and charted rare, and surprisingly synchronized, shifts in culture, leadership, ideology, and politics and labeled them in one of two ways. They have been either seen as a renaissance or as a revolution. Both comprise a dramatic societal facelift and both can foster an international tsunami. Typically when reviewing eras of renaissance and revolution, we see familiar elements and telling transitions. We turn to the professionals—philosophers, sociologists, historians, and cultural critics—to help us understand what it is we are witnessing. Precedents are cited and models from the past used to assist in interpreting these momentous events. Certain sets of conditions seem to lead to renaissance and others to revolution. When we consider the late eighteenth-century emergence of Romanticism, we can see it as the seditious counter to the First Industrial Revolution and the precursor to the Victorian era with its unique values. How do we understand the relationship between the intellectual discourses and the politics of a given era? We look to the professionals to guide us in our understanding. However in the case of hip-hop we cannot use the model of preconditions applied by historians to other renaissances or revolutions. The rise of hip-hop is an anomaly in history.

Hip-hop, one of the most far-reaching of postmodern insurgencies, is mistakenly tagged solely as an art form. In essence, it appears in every sense of the word to be a revolution and a renaissance.

And if it is determined to be so, it is likely to be recorded as one of the most pervasive and successful cultural transformations in the twentieth century. The question is whether hip-hop is a renaissance or a revolution. Could there be a flaw in the process of weighing this "art form" as even a candidate for the label of renaissance or revolution? Ascertaining its worthiness to be labeled in this way depends on its makeup and whether it mirrors past moments of awakening or revolutionary fervor. Perhaps too little weight has been given to its effects. Has hip-hop transformed the world, its politics, its wealth, and people's minds and ways of thinking, globally? Has hip-hop been appropriately regarded? Are hip-hop artists true agents of power and should hip-hop be regarded as a legitimate revolution? Can they be seen as revolutionaries rising up in arms against the internal colonization of Black America? Or has the corporatism of the Hip-hop industry de-radicalized any movement to the point of it no longer being revolutionary? R. James Ferguson, a professor of Economics and International Relations, wrote: "How power is defined, used and assessed is one fundamental theme in the analysis of states, nations, diplomacy and war. Likewise, the guiding role of ideas is also crucial in analyzing historical trends and their meaning."[1]

Just before a revolution, or in the wake of a renaissance, people look at their lives and their conditions and speak of them, agonize over their condition, and cry out for change. Then it happens! The bold, the courageous, and often the crude and less politically savvy who have nothing to lose charge ahead to make something happen. The power they possess does not lie in their courage. Instead, their newly garnered power is in the collective voice they now represent. It is a common experience that unites them together for the cause, a lived experience that they have all endured and survived together. For Black Hip-hop artists, this experience could be characterized as internal colonialism.

Yes, our rhymes can contain violence and hatred. Yes, our songs can detail the drug business and our choruses can bounce with lustful intent. However, those things did not spring from interior imaginations or deficient morals; these things came from our lives.

They came from America.

Shawn Corey Carter, Jay-Z[2]

Blacks' lived experience of crime, violence, and drugs as it is described by Jay-Z above defines life in the ghetto, which has been characterized as one space of internal colonialism within the United States. "The culture, the State, and particularly the ghetto constitute the racial system…The ghetto depends on small and large capitalist enterprises, which are controlled by whites, for jobs and for purchasing most goods and services" (Bohmer, 1999, p. 1). African American proponents of internal colonialism theory (ICT)—the majority of whom were writing in the late 1960s and 1970s, in the final days of the Civil Rights Movement—suggested that the system is reliant on ghetto residents' cheap labor, and thus exploits the black community, prolonging its oppression for the benefit of the white majority. "Its inhabitants must sell their labor power and buy necessary commodities at inflated prices from these enterprises" (Bohmer, 1999, p. 1). While the notion of Black America as an internal colony is a powerful metaphor, the Black-White dichotomy that was perpetuated by scholars like Blauner (1969, 1972) and Carmichael and Hamilton (1967) is problematic in its simplification of the dynamics of the ghetto and racial relations in the United States. Moreover, ICT fails to account for the changes that *have* occurred related to racial inequality in America since the end of the Civil Rights Movement. Proponents of this theory, Bohmer (1999) explains, tend to represent "the structure of racial inequality [as] fixed and unchanging," and their view of contemporary "government laws, policies and practices as either repressive or co-optive effectively denies that the Civil Rights, Black Power and other movements won anything significant" (p. 1). There is no denying that racial domination persists in very real and troubling ways today, but to completely discount the gains that have come about in the post-1960s United States fails to reflect the more complex reality of racial relations in America today.

Certain scholars like Jared Ball (2009) have built on ICT by exploring the role of mass media and popular culture as mechanisms complicit in the oppressive capitalist system. Ball (2009) and Palast (2002), among others, argue that record companies and music conglomerates threaten the free expression of hip-hop and rap artists, functioning as cultural regulators of a capitalist, neo-colonial system. As in many other industries, the monopoly sustained by the three major record companies in the American music industry clearly limits the options of musical artists in *any* genre—not just hip-hop, and not just those artists of African American descent or that belong to an ethnic/racial minority. The challenges of becoming successful in the music industry are similar to the challenges of finding success in any other competitive, capitalist industry within the US economy. To be sure, there exists economic oppression and structural inequalities remain in place that seriously handicap the economic progress of minority communities like the African Americans, yet labeling record companies as neocolonial regulators grants them too much power, and fails to recognize the true achievements of countless racial minority musical artists in the hip-hop community and beyond.

This integration of experience in Jay-Z's rap as a definition of what constitutes life, which is then connected to its source or origin (*They came from America*) and is embodied with strong racial overtones—America in this verse could easily read Black America—is a powerful one. Jay-Z uses it to contextualize and justify his "rhymes," his artistic output, and his production. The central role of language, as the site of this articulation of the self, and image is also clearly stated. The idea of the hip-hop artist, of self, and of life in relation to the nation is a complex one, and in framing his work in this way Jay-Z opens up a dialogue that speaks to a much broader modern/postmodern philosophical and cultural theoretical questioning. In so doing, these lyrics speak for a cadre of disciples that now represent a constituency and a power base. Despite his mainstream success, Jay-Z still finds ways to incorporate messages of social and political protest within his record-selling albums.

A voice, which people can relate to, which addresses their pain, their desires, and their dreams attracts a following. An organization that promotes such a voice on a world stage amasses a world audience. And when that voice directs action, a revolution can be the result. History has demonstrated that those who control the minds and the will of people have power. This is the very power Ferguson refers to in the quote above. This applies regardless of whether control is attained by choice or by force. The only relevant issue in this argument is the control. History has proven that control is achieved through the management of information. It is words and images that communicate fear and that create feelings of nationalism and superiority, which express understanding, engender unity, cement solidarity, and ultimately set the stage for a revolution or invite a reawakening. To this end, journalist and editor Jared Ball advocates for a discussion not of lofty ideals of democracy or freedom, but rather of "the political nature of communication, the political nature of media in the context in which hip-hop developed" (San Roman, 2011, Part 1). That is the goal of this section, an examination of the potentially revolutionary nature of hip-hop as a form of communication and a voice with the potential to unite a collective and spark a moment of transformation.

When it comes to the conflict between local and global interests, the use of technologies has also presented another set of important social phenomena to postmodern thinkers. The ideology of communicational transparency (testified by the label World Wide Web) clashes, however, with the interests of states, which appear as obstacles in such processes (Lyotard, 1984, p. 5). The authority of the state as political regulator is, in turn, challenged constantly by heterogeneous communities such as hip-hop, although the cultural regulation of mass media and corporatism within the music industry attempt to limit hip-hop's radical forces. Understanding how this conflict of local and global interests develops is a matter of great importance.

Postmodern art and literature are often defined in terms that suggest it as playful, parodist and pluralistic, combining styles and opinions, which make them less classifiable[3] and certainly not politically legitimate. Consequently, the work of hip-hop artists and producers, who often change genre from track to track, can clearly be seen and appreciated for combining influences such as r'n'b, folk, alternative, synthesized pop and classical music. Some artists like Jay-Z, Kanye West, and others use sampling from very nontraditional sources such as Daft Punk, Shirley Bassey, Aretha Franklin, and so on. This way of combining genres, old and new, and taking bits and pieces from several artists with different backgrounds may be viewed as postmodern playfulness. However, this idea of playfulness, in the hip-hop artist, tends to diminish the actual magnitude of it as a politicized act. Hip-hop artists often string together the work of the artistic statesmen of our musical past and present. Our clandestine activism roots come alive in this art form. Bhabha asserts, "the enunciative attempts repeatedly to 'reinscribe' and relocate that claim to cultural and anthropological priority (High/Low; Ours/Theirs) in the act of revising and hybridizing the settled, sententious hierarchies, the locale and the locutions of the cultural" (Bhabha, 1992, p. 57).

Bhabha's analysis throws new light on the significance of the mode of address and language as it is articulated in the enunciative act. His emphasis on *enunciative agency* is particularly revealing in exploring the role of the hip-hop artist, where meaning is constituted through the active mode of address through performance. Here the *enunciative* site is an ambiguous and dynamic space. In his theoretical restaging of Saussure's arbitrary signifier, Bhabha locates a "cultural space for opening up new forms of agency and identification that confuse historical temporalities, confound sententious, continuist meanings, traumatize tradition" (p. 59). Bhabha speaks of a "time-lag" between the symbol and sign, that in each attempt to define a symbol of cultural identity, there is a repetition of the sign "that represents the place of psychic ambivalence and social contingency." It is in this ambivalence that the postmodern and postcolonial subject is open as a location of different meanings through language and as a strategy of empowerment. In his performance, the hip-hop artist can be seen as shifting authoritative forces and, from their enunciating positions, calling on their audiences to hear and be moved by their words, relocating and dispersing authority in all directions. Again, this validates the magnitude of the voice and the influence.

Not recognizing the impact of change that hip-hop constitutes is not unprecedented. Typically, whether a movement is a revolution or renaissance is not known until generations have passed. It is only through the passage of time that the changes are truly understood. When we are close to or in the midst of change it is difficult if not impossible to identify its true nature.

Revolution and the Arab Spring

In his 1976 book *Keywords* Raymond Williams explains how the term "revolution" underwent significant semantic shifts during the last five centuries, beginning with its scientific sense and eventually taking on the specific political connotations associated with revolution today (Williams, 1976, pp. 270–274). The modern notion of revolution, especially since the 2011 Arab Spring uprisings, has been largely tied to ideas of political change and the overthrow and replacement of an old order for a new one. "Revolution" also has the related sense of physical reversal whereby what was once on top now moves to the bottom and vice versa.

In addition to our changing notion of revolution we understand the term through television advertisements that bombard viewers with "revolutionary" products suggesting groundbreaking or innovative qualities within a particular field or market. With these more recent meanings of revolution it is easy to overlook the historical sense of the word as a revolving movement in space or time, a returning to a point of origin, where revolution relates to the continuation of a cycle rather than an interruption or overthrow. Scholars and music fans alike will notice that these different definitions are all applicable to discussions of hip-hop culture and rap music and specifically to analyzing politics, power relations, and/ or artistic innovation within these musical genres.

It is, in fact, nothing new to speak of hip-hop in terms of its revolutionary character. Historian Robin D. G. Kelley insightfully asserted that "the most radical ideas often come out of a concrete intellectual engagement with the problems of aggrieved populations confronting systems of oppression" (2003, p. 8). Kelley is right, and his own message is just as universal and revolutionary as that of artists like Tupac who espoused ideas consistent with libertarian theology.[4] Academic studies on hip-hop culture in the United States and abroad have also cited the resistant voice of hip-hop, frequently alluding to its "revolutionary" nature (Alim, 2009; Baker, 2005; James, 2005; Kahf, 2007; Perry, 2004; Terkourafi, 2010). The term is tossed around loosely enough in scholarly literature, but one might ask what is actually "revolutionary" about hip-hop? More importantly, what has made, and continues to make, hip-hop an ideal outlet for participating in, reflecting on, and making sense of revolutionary movements? Why has hip-hop been employed on an international scale to protest, invent, and question the cultural and political norms of a given society? A look at hip-hop's global resonances might help to answer some of these questions.

Over the past three years, issues such as those with which Blacks have had to contend in the past and which have found productive expression in rap, were confronted in the seismic political and social change throughout the Middle East, particularly during the Arab Spring. The revolutions in the Middle East are not unlike the hip-hop revolution. African Americans used hip-hop as a means of revolution through political and emotional expression and political activism leading from social unrest to political action. Early hip-hop groups such as Dead Prez or Public Enemy provided listeners with a bridge from passive musical consumption to active political involvement. "M1 of Dead Prez mobilizes their chosen audience: 'We want to create an urgency about freedom…We're here for all the people, not just the political militants, but the people who need to be awakened to become political militants'" (James, 2005, p. 72). By emotionally compelling people toward political action, hip-hop and rap songs functioned as advertisements and campaign tools, if you will, with the campaign being the overall improvement of the social/political state of affairs. The events and revolutionary nature of the Arab Spring are merely contemporary examples of the revolutionary nature. Rap was adopted in the region as an expression of revolutionary fervor. The culture was imported from America where hip-hop had roots in the revolutionary movements of Black Power and the Black Panthers of the 1960s and 1970s.

Since the inception of the Arab Spring, activists have used rap music as a means of dual expression, both as a genre to connect with fellow pro-liberty activists and to send out a plea for aid and solidarity among liberals throughout the world, and most strategically, from those in the United States.[5] Arabs used rap and hip-hop to reinvigorate Arab nationalism or pan-nationalism, both of which began in the early twentieth century.[6] Arabs used rap and hip-hop to intelligently link the disenfranchised and oppressed people of Tunisia, Libya, Egypt, as well as those from other countries. It is important to note that the use of a certain type of rap music— gangsta rap in particular—within the revolutionary context acts more as a social ill than a productive political tool. Nevertheless, despite the great amount of violence occurring in the Arab world, rap music has often been used to *condemn* violence, rather than to praise it. This distinction is critically important since in the post-9/11 period, Arabs have often been viewed by others in a stereotypical manner, based upon a racist notion that all Arabs and Muslims are violent. Being acutely aware of this misperception, many Arab artists have taken great care to create a dialogue through their music to evaluate not only their emotions about the oppressive regimes under which they live, but also the politics that are foundational to how Arabs and Muslims are viewed by the

West, and how they can strategically campaign to obtain assistance from Western nations to liberate themselves.

Within the last decade hip-hop communities have sprung up throughout North Africa and the Middle East in Morocco, Tunisia, Egypt, Lebanon, and Palestine, each boasting its own rappers, deejays, graffiti artists, and breakdancers (Abbas, 2005). Arabic-language rap in particular has received much global attention for its politically vocal artists, among them Tunisian rapper El Général, whose 2011 song "Rayes Lebled" (known also as "Mr. President") earned him a brief stint in jail. El Général's song was soon being referred to as the "anthem" of the Tunisian uprising that ousted President Ben Ali in 2011 and sparked subsequent revolts in Egypt (Gana, 2011). As the revolutionary spirit swept through the Middle East, hip-hop found itself used more and more by Arab youth looking to voice their opinions about police brutality, increased food prices, government corruption, and other issues.

In recent years, the resistant voice of Arabic hip-hop has been portrayed in several films, among them Joshua Asen's *I Love Hip-Hop in Morocco* (2007), Jackie Salloum's popular *Slingshot Hip-Hop* about Palestinian rap groups (2008), Ahmad Abdalla's *Microphone* (2010), and Nicholas Mangialardi's documentary *Egyptian Underground* (2012), the last two dealing with rappers in the Egyptian cities of Cairo and Alexandria. These films depict Arab youth responding to adversity through artistic means that not only challenge existing political, social, and cultural conventions but also borrow traditional elements from the local culture, reemploying them in ways that prioritize the artists' goals. When the Cairo-based deejay known as Fat Sam samples old clips from Abdel Halim Hafez and Fairuz (two popular singers of classical Arabic music) to produce a new beat, he is not simply creating a hybrid product of old and new, Egyptian and Western. He is also expanding his audience so that even those who do not listen to hip-hop can enjoy his tracks and relate to the melodies.[7] In this way, he is returning to his predecessors for inspiration rather than trying to abandon the musical tradition altogether. Fat Sam is not unique in this regard. Rappers from Morocco to Iraq are finding innovative ways to mix old and new sounds, ways of using language that resists simple categorization into colloquial versus standard Arabic. The Egyptian revolution of 2011 coincided with a significant increase in the number of rappers, live concerts, music videos, and fan pages in the small, but growing, hip-hop communities of Egypt (centered primarily in the capital city Cairo and Alexandria in the north).[8] Although Egyptian rap traces its roots back to the early 2000s, the development of revolutionary activity in 2011 served as a catalyst for many artists to contribute their verbal skills to the uprising. This is by no means to suggest that hip-hop guided the Egyptian revolution to success or that rap played a direct role in the ousting of Hosni Mubarak.

Such claims are denied by Egyptian rappers themselves. However, many see rap as having spread positive messages during the popular uprising, thereby encouraging some Egyptians, particularly youth, to take part in the protests. While rap songs may have served as inspiration for the listeners, the number of people who follow hip-hop in Egypt is still quite limited compared to the popular and widespread *habibi* music found emanating from most cafes, car radios, and cell phone speakers).[9] Rap music may not have been the key element in toppling a 30-year dictatorship in Egypt, but many artists felt the spirit of hip-hop manifested in revolutionary activity during the 18 days of protest that began in January 2011. Some rappers reported attending demonstrations and composing rhymed chants for crowd members to shout. Other groups, like the Arabian Knightz, protested in Tahrir Square but also recorded and released songs about the revolution during the uprising. Their song "Rebel" was posted online with the hope of encouraging people to band together, be educated, and take a stand against oppression and injustice.[10] But why do these young Egyptians choose hip-hop? Why not rock or jazz or heavymetal?[11] This would suggest that part of hip-hop's attractiveness for those engaged in protest lies in the issue of physical space.

The Egyptian revolution of 2011 was an uprising of enormous proportion with much activity planned and carried out through various oft-cited technologies like Facebook, Twitter, and text messaging. However, the ultimate demonstration of the people's strength took place in the streets of Cairo, Alexandria, and other urban centers. The street corners, sidewalks, squares, bridges, medians, alleyways, roundabouts, and other public spaces were major arteries for the flow of revolutionary activity, also serving quite literally as stages for protest and performance. That Egyptian youth find hip-hop an ideal tool for protest is not surprising. Hip-hop is, in many ways, a musical reflection of the streets and the city more broadly. Hip-hop is freestyling and beatboxing while you wait at the bus stop. It is the graffiti under the bridge by your house. It is the piece of cardboard beneath your shoes as you perfect a top rock. Just as the streets offer a critical space for protest, so too do they represent a locus of hip-hop culture where music and other art forms do not need to be cleaned up, censored, or beautified.

Perhaps the most revolutionary aspect of Arab rap and hip-hop during the Arab Spring and its current reawakening is that it has given a voice not only to men but also to women in the region. When one takes a minute to stop and think about this fact, it should become very apparent how radical and revolutionary it is for women to be involved in rap and hip-hop in the Middle East, and specifically within countries in which Islam has become more fundamental. Faced with rape, mutilation via acid attacks and the like, the stakes for women in the Middle East have been and continue to be particularly high since the beginning of the Arab Spring, suggesting that women's involvement in crafting art through this cultural form is bold and unfortunately, in some cases, life threatening. If this is not a testament to rap and hip-hop's revolutionary flavor and liberating power, what exactly is?

There is then a natural link between protest and hip-hop, namely the street as a common space of performance. However the more one considers the relationship between the two, the harder it may be to separate them from one another. Perhaps the question we should be asking is not how does hip-hop interact with protest on an international level but rather, how can hip-hop and protest be viewed as representing much the same thing—the act of taking a stand, making your voice heard, and tracing your roots to the street.

Hip-Hop Culture as Transformative: Ghana and Sub-Saharan Africa

The continent of Africa embodies the roots of all those individuals across the globe who belong to or identify with the African diaspora. As a region that has suffered from exploitation, conquest, and colonization for centuries, different forms of oppression still seem to plague the majority of African nations to this day. Economic oppression persists, particularly in those independent nations that are former European colonies. The residue of colonialism remains in the financial control and monopoly that corporations associated with the former "mother" country wield over African nations like Ghana or Nigeria today. This notion of modern-day economic colonialism is often referred to as neocolonialism, a concept coined by Ghanaian politician and scholar Kwame Nkrumah (1965). Ghana is one of few African nations to have maintained a peaceful existence and democratic politics since its independence from Britain in 1957. However, like many other neighboring countries, despite the decades that have passed, Ghana continues to suffer from economic and cultural domination by Britain and other former colonial powers. Just as popular culture and traditional music and performance played an important role in bringing about the revolution against Britain in the 1950s, hip-hop culture and rap music play an important role in raising awareness and fomenting resistance against neocolonialism in modern-day Ghana.

Ghana became the first sub-Saharan colony to gain its independence in 1957, which led to the creation of the new Ghanaian Republic and the election of Kwame Nkrumah as the free nation's first president. Nkrumah encouraged the growth and strengthening of Ghanaian nationalism through the promotion of different cultural traditions and activities, including music, dance, and football (Darby, 2002). Thus, the culture surrounding traditional Ghanaian music and other forms of performance and orality played an important role in the country's successful independence from Britain. Musical culture is consequently already rooted in revolutionary ideals, and vice versa, within Ghana, and many other African nations. It comes as no surprise that modern-day Ghanaian hip-hop embodies many of these revolutionary ideals advocating for change and progress.

A popular movement in the Ghanaian music scene in recent years is "hiplife," a hip-hop spin off of the early twentieth-century West African genre of "highlife." Highlife was associated with an "up-tempo, synth-driven sound" (Asante, 2008, p. 110). Asante explains, "As hip-hop spread across the globe, it infused itself into much of the continental African music, including highlife" (p. 110). Thus was born hiplife, a contemporary musical genre that spins rhymes in local Ghanaian languages over imported hip-hop rhymes and beats. The music of Lil' Kwesi, a local MC in Accra,

Ghana's capital, is representative of the hiplife movement and its revolutionary undertones. One of his songs, performed in the local Twi dialect, addresses the economic oppression under which, according to Kwesi, Ghana is still living. Kwesi explained, "We are still not independent. That's what my song is about. The British still control our country in many ways…They come here, take our goods, pay us nothing, then sell our stuff in Britain, the so-called mother country, so we don't even benefit, as a country, from the fruits of our own labor."[12]Kwesi's music, exemplary of the popular hiplife movement in Ghana, evidences the awareness and nonconformity of the younger generation with the status quo.

A more well-known Ghanaian hip-hop artist, D-Black, born Desmond Kwesi Blackmore, has successfully made the crossover from African to United States audiences and now raps primarily in English. His breakthrough into the US commercial hip-hop industry poses its own challenges, including the pressure to conform to the gangsta rap/depoliticized mainstream hip-hop style in order to be signed by one of the three main record companies. Ball (2009) suggests that this pressure to "sell out" in order to succeed in the industry is reflective of the US "monopolized capitalist and/ or colonial economy that necessitates control of cultural expression by that society's elite" (p. 620). Nevertheless, as asserted earlier, this view of the all-powerful music industry is problematic, and fails to allow for the agency of musical artists that challenge the control of said record companies. In the case of D-Black, the international attention he has gained through his musical crossover has proven to have many positive consequences for the rapper and his home country so far. D-Black is the first Ghanaian rapper to be nominated at the Black Entertainment Television (BET) Awards, and he is recognized as the United Nations' celebrity ambassador in Ghana.

The Ghanaian hip-hop artist's commitment to bringing awareness about African and Ghanaian culture to the international community, as well as to inform the world about the threat of deadly diseases faced by millions of Africans today, is reflective of a different form of cultural and social movement through hip-hop. For example, D-Black was joined by Nigerian performer 2face Idibia (Nigeria), and fellow Ghanaian rappers Kwaku-t and J-town on the collaboration song "STOP IT" that promotes the United Nations Millennium Developmental Goals including poverty and domestic violence awareness, women empowerment, and HIV/ AIDS awareness. The song's chorus repeats, "You are truly on your own now / You are responsible for whatever you do / Better watch it, and stop it / You cannot trade life for bling, yeah / You've got to do the right thing, yeah." The singers call for a stop to irresponsible, risky lifestyles that can lead to life-and-death situations such as contracting HIV or becoming involved in domestic violence. D-Black and company are associated with "Gh rap," a hip-hop movement in Ghana where artists mainly rap in English or in pidgin English.[13] This type of collaborative, socially transformative music is perhaps not revolutionary in a strict sense, but does reflect a more international collective movement for progress and change within African society.

Scholar Marc Perry (2008) explains that the rise of thriving local hip-hop movements in sub-Saharan African countries like Ghana, Senegal, Kenya, and Benin "suggest that African youth today are increasingly engaging in the black signified cultural space of hip-hop as a medium of critical self-expression" (p. 652). Perry continues, "The very real, structurally conditioned hardships that much of sub-Saharan Africa continues to live through have no doubt shaped the social commitments and political urgencies found in much of the hip-hop produced on the continent" (p. 653). Perry and others, including Perullo (2005), recognize that rap has become an important avenue for urban African youth to critically question current social issues including unemployment, state corruption, and AIDS/HIV.

For African nations that have endured brutal internal warfare, hip-hop assumes an even more critical role, striving to simultaneously make the world aware of the horrific slaughter of their people, while also serving as a voice of hope and a vehicle of remembrance for their nation. Consequently, the role played by hip-hop in countries like Somalia, as Mitchell and Pennycook (2009) have asserted, is one of cultural revival. This contrasts with the conviction of other scholars (e.g., Ntarangwi, 2009; Pritchard, 2009), who argue that the presence of hip-hop and rap in African nations is a manifestation of cultural imperialism, or some form of globalization or Americanization. The case of Somali-Canadian MC K'naan is particularly relevant due to the important role he plays as an advocate for his people in the international arena. As he explains regarding the title of his 2005 album, *Dusty Foot Philosopher* is a phrase that "means the one that's poor, lives in poverty but lives in a dignified manner and philosophizes about the universe," and these individuals' worth and value stretch far beyond the clinched photograph of their dark-skinned, dust-covered feet captured by a foreign reporter (Mitchell and Pennycook, 2009). K'Naan's repositioning of himself and his fellow Somalis from "undignified" poor people to dignified philosophers is a political statement, challenging the dominant West's understanding of the world by asserting their dignity through their ability to articulate and comprehend more than an outsider could ever appreciate.

K'Naan's self-assigned role for Somalia is aligned with that of hip-hop artists in Senegal like the crew Daara J. Rather than be influenced by the gangsta rap glorification of the ghetto and poverty present in some mainstream commercialized rap in the United States—a phenomenon some blame on the "Musical OPEC" of the monopolizing corporations in the music industry (Ball, 2009; Palast, 2002)—MCs like K'naan and Faada Freddy (member of Daara J) deliberately work against it. According to Faada Freddy, Senegalese hip-hop has moved beyond imitating US rappers, focusing instead on the issues of their people. "We live in a country where we have poverty, power, race...you know, ethnic wars...So we couldn't afford to go like Americans, talking about 'Bling Bling'...rap music was about the reality and therefore we went back to our background," he explained, recognizing that "rap music is a music that [can] help people...solve their problems" (Mitchell and Pennycook, 2009). As Joy James affirms, "The revolutionary impulse in hardcore and underground rap and political theory exhibits...an ability to contextualize struggle within a political and historical framework of radical resistance" (2005, p. 74). This framework operates today within a global hip-hop community that has taken up the musical genre as a tool of resistance.

Like the group Daara J, K'naan strives to speak directly to the Somali people, aiming for his lyrics to serve as oral forms of remembrance and education for today's generations and those that come afterwards. In his song "In the Beginning," K'naan rhymes about the Somalian public's sacrifice of its youth for unwarranted, selfish acts, "We don't see em / See them for their worth at all. / That's why we lead em / Lead em to these wars and what is it we feed em / Feed em our impurities and who it is we treat em / Treat em like the enemy humanity will need em / Need em like the blood we spill," alluding to the brutal Somali civil war that began in the 1990s (K'Naan, 2005). It was the war that forced him and his family, along with hundreds of thousands of their compatriots, to flee the country. The "impure" politics of Somalia is evident in the reigning chaos and political instability that persists in K'Naan's homeland today. Similar to their Ghanaian and Nigerian neighbors, Somali and Senegalese artists like K'Naan and Daara J, respectively, "are 21st century digital artists who draw on and change traditional, cultural forms; they are part of the global Hip-hop movement, identifying with and also rejecting different aspects of its global formation…remain[ing] highly critical of Western ways of viewing the world and of the bias in particular forms of historical reasoning" (Mitchell and Pennycook, 2009). Thus, rather than evidencing a continuity or resignation to cultural imperialism or neocolonialism, these African artists simultaneously embody, and communicate a need for, change and rupture within and outside of the geopolitical borders of their homelands.

Cuban Hip-Hop: It's a Political Thing

Similar to socially conscious hiplife and Gh rap artists in Ghana, the work of contemporary Cuban rappers reflects a strong criticism of forms of political and economic oppression. Sujatha Fernandes (2003) notes that "transnational rap networks constitute a vehicle through which Afro-Cuban youth negotiate with the state and build strategies for survival in the difficult circumstances of the contemporary 'special period' of crisis" (p. 576). Referring to the period following the collapse of the Soviet Union that spun Cuba into an economic crisis from which it is still digging its way out today, Fernandes explains that Cuban rappers have been influenced by African American rappers who spit a form of "conscious" rap projecting socially critical messages to their audiences. "Cuban rappers offer strong criticisms of neoliberal globalization…rappers also highlight causes of racial justice within Cuba and make demands for the inclusion of marginalized sectors in the processes of economic and political change" (Fernandes, 2003, p. 576). Like African American rappers in the United States, race is a prominent theme in their raps as racial tensions and violence are a constant reality in Cuba.

Interestingly, rap did not gain momentum as a cohesive movement in Cuba until the state began to sponsor the genre during the 1990s (Fernandes, 2003). Prior to the 1990s, rap in Cuba was a grassroots occurrence, but beginning in 1991, institutional resources were provided to promote Cuban rap through concerts at local cultural centers on the island. Many of the cultural events surrounding the rap movement were sponsored by the Associación Hermanos Saiz (Brothers Saiz Organization, AHS), which was the youth cultural wing of the state-funded youth organization representing the ruling party. Geoffrey Baker (2005) asked the question that many scholars have pondered upon learning that this "revolutionary" form of music had been appropriated by the Cuban state as representational of national culture, wondering, "How a musical form recently imported from Cuba's ideological arch enemy [the US], and frequently voicing a high degree of social protest, has not only been assimilated into Cuban national culture but has come to be positively promoted by the state within little over a decade of its emergence" (pp. 368–369). While this is a polemic in itself, the seemingly contradictory nature of the merging of state and "revolutionary" interests—albeit in a country that itself purports to be revolutionary and progressive, but acts as a totalitarian state in everything but name—through rap is fascinating. This phenomenon reflects the adaptive nature of rap and its ability to work with or against political and social transformation, depending on the context in which it is presented.

The Cuban rap scene has expanded and diversified greatly since the early 1990s, and the state is now only one of the entities subsidizing the movement, although the government still maintains a certain level of control over all cultural elements within the country. Ariel Fernandez (2002) identifies two distinct groups within the larger Cuban rap scene—the "commercial" and the "underground" artists (p. 43). Somewhat comparable to the divide seen between underground and mainstream/commercial rappers in the United States or Europe, the main issue that differentiates these two scenes is a desire to stay true to the roots of the local music and culture, and the socially and politically conscious messages they choose to contain or not. "Commercial" Cuban rappers attempt to become accepted by the mainstream Cuban public through the incorporation of "popular Cuban rhythms," while "underground" artists "focus much more on an integration of politically committed lyrics with the social context" (Fernandez, 2002, p. 43). Earlier "underground" Cuban rap groups like Los Paisanos and Amenaza addressed local issues including political corruption. In their song "Hip-hop," the rap duo Los Paisanos addresses issues including racism and revolution, flashing a Che Guevara tattoo inked on someone's arm in their corresponding video. "One fist raised, and the other holding the mike," they rap (in Spanish), proclaiming their revolutionary political and musical stance within Cuba.

Los Paisanos belong to a group of 18 Cuban hip-hop artists called The Cartel that is committed to rap that addresses genuine issues. In a song by another Cartel group "American Dream," the duo called Anonimo Consejo rap, "the plight of the poor is the fault of the rich," alluding to economic oppression and inequality, particularly the large economic gap between the upper and lower classes in Cuba. Arlene Tickner (2008) labels this type of rap "progressive rap," explaining that it provides a "critical political and social commentary...but also condemn[s] the dominant social order" (p. 130). In Cuba in particular, the progressive or conscious rap discourse dialogues easily with Cubans' contemporary lived experience of impoverishment, scarcity and oppression, and is "considered more appropriate for nurturing more 'authentic'" rap forms (Tickner, 2008, p. 130).

However, Cuban artists spitting conscious or underground rap tread a fine line. In a communist state, rappers must choose their lyrics carefully, or they will be faced with censorship. At Cuba's 2002 national hip-hop festival, several rappers openly condemned the government and, as a result, were banned from performing on the island for six months.[14] Many of these conscious Cuban rappers say they support the Cuban state, calling their criticism constructive. So Andres del Rio, a member of the group Hermanos de Causa, explained, "We're not focusing on the problem with a point of view that's looking to overthrow the President...We're simply saying that such a thing is bad, such a thing could be better, we're Cuban too, and we have rights."[15] The precarious relationship between state, hip-hop, and revolution is undoubtedly complex in Cuba, which just so happens to be the only (fully) communist country in the Western hemisphere, but also provides for a thriving and diverse musical movement.

Brazil, home to some of the poorest and most violent slums (*favelas*) in the world is also home to a thriving musical and artistic culture that transmits the harsh reality of the Brazilian people to an international audience. Hip-hop has long influenced this nation—yet another former colony with its history rooted in slavery and racial tension—and the culture surrounding it has served as a crucial outlet, particularly for Brazilian youth. While Brazilian hip-hop musical artists like Xis, Thaide, and Rappin' Hood, among others, are well-established performers, many visual art and dance movements have also been influenced by hip-hop culture. Street and graffiti art, in particular, are inextricably tied to the hip-hop movement that made its way to Brazil in the late 1980s, when urban themes like graffiti tagging and youth dancing were popular images associated with the burgeoning rap and hip-hop music scene (Alonzo, 2012).

It is out of this scene that the twin brother artists, Otavio and Gustavo Pandolfo, known as OsGemeos, emerged. Bringing Brazilian street art to the international stage, the work of OsGemeos is colorful and fantastical, largely influenced by different movements rooted in social and political discontent, including hip-hop, break dance, as well as local traditions like Brazilian folk art and pixação (a style of hypergraphic graffiti writing unique to Sao Paolo and linked to the lower class). Consequently, "their works simultaneously evoke the world of their dreams and the favelas (ghetto) in which they were raised. In this sense, both pixação and OsGêmeos draw upon the same political and social discontent felt by much of the population in São Paolo" (Khu, 2010). Also committed to portraying the vibrant Brazilian culture, their work embodies themes including "familial love, national pride, and the desire to precipitate change, [which] are represented with equal importance as political unrest and extreme poverty" (Khu, 2010). Evidencing the political roots of much of their work is a mural that portrays two graffiti artists tagging political protest messages on a wall, one reading, "Corruption…a country for all." As with music or dance, the street art of Los Gemeos veils its political messages rooted in the social discontent of the Brazilian lower classes with the aesthetics of their craft—including the signature bright yellow coloring of their youthful figures and dreamlike elements incorporated into their pieces. Yet even in the midst of their international success, hip-hop inspired street artists to continue to maintain that rebellious, socially transformative element that is synonymous with conscious rap and other mediums of resistance within hip-hop culture.

In sum, Whether on the streets of an impoverished Cuba, amid the revolutionary fervor of Tahrir Square, or immersed in the trauma of war-torn Somalia, hip-hop and rap have time and again served as the vehicles for social, economic, and political protest and change, embodying a spirit of revolution that is fundamental to human kind. What is true for the existential being on the streets of Lagos, Accra, or Dakar is the same for the African American youth in 1970s New York, and the underprivileged residents in urban spaces throughout the Americas. Rising up in opposition to external and internal forms of oppression and facing the constant pressure of conforming to the mainstream, de-radicalized hip-hop culture, hip-hop artists from diverse backgrounds, experiences, and historical moments have persevered in their mission to deliver transformative, radical messages in a way that uplifts and unites oppressed, marginalized, or underrepresented peoples into politically informed and invested communities. This spirit of revolution is at once a global, yet deeply personal/contextual/situational, response of a people, a community, and a nation in search of recognition, justice, or inclusion.

Rumination 7

The Artist and the Image: Ervin Goffman, Marshall McLuhan, and Roland Barthes

In the last couple of centuries, art has primarily been seen as a manifestation of lived experience by a particularly gifted individual, upon whom a special status is often conferred. For instance, the Romantic "genius" was seen as having a unique and innate essence that endowed him with a special quality of vision which allowed him to penetrate the world and express truths about its essence. In the contemporary world, most audiences of popular culture such as hip-hop music still experience and consume texts as the products of a single "personality." Artists and their music are fused into a single body. This is one major pillar of celebrity culture, at least as regards artists: audiences are curious about their personal lives as sources of insight into the art they produce.

Since the late nineteenth century, philosophers and theorists have by and large rejected this conventional perspective, replacing it with a variety of viewpoints that view with varying degrees of skepticism the expressive power of symbolic communication, and, moreover, the very existence of the "true self" that is so often taken for granted. An early manifestation of this skepticism was the work of George Herbert Mead, a sociologist, who observed that symbols were becoming increasingly crucial to social life. He argued that identity, rather than being something innate and inalterable in the form of a *soul* or spirit, emerged from interactions between individuals through the use of symbols—something that is prevalent in present day hip-hop music through both lyrical and visual images.

Mead made his observations after the Industrial Revolution, which had lifted rising numbers of the poor out of subsistence living into the lower-middle classes, giving them greater access to and control over symbolic representation. As the mediatization of everyday life accelerated, observations heavily influenced by or building upon Mead's were being made in various spheres of life. For instance, in Walter Lippman's analysis of public decision making, he concluded that the average person, dealing with a growing tide of information, had no choice but to construct a world of simplified stereotypes, quick sketches rather than deep portraits of people and situations around him. In an even dourer mode a few decades later, Guy Debord satirized the *society of the spectacle*, in which rational thought was being displaced by mere affective engagement with images.[1]

This skepticism came to have an ever more profound impact on social theory, which increasingly abandoned any sense that individuals have a concrete substance that is distinct from their media environment. Starting in the 1950s, Jacques Lacan talked of the "symbolic chain" of modern life as constitutive of individuals in a way directly analogous to Sigmund Freud's "unconscious" of a half century earlier. In other words, the totality of cultural symbols had supplanted the "family drama" as the key component in shaping human individuals into acting subjects.[2] On the one hand skepticism of the power of symbols to genuinely communicate truth became "baked in" to the basic model of communication in media studies—a model in which the sender, message, and receiver represent not intimately linked moments in a connected chain, but a series of disjunctures ripe for failure in the perpetually troubled quest to reach some kind of true understanding.[3]

On the other hand, there were more optimistic takes on the situation; for example, Marshall McLuhan's basic position was that not only mass media (as commonly understood) but a variety of technologies that compressed space and time, were simply "extensions" of human powers rather than primarily complications of those powers. And, working against the psychoanalytic tradition of which Lacan would become the major proponent, Gilles Deleuze and Felix Guattari asserted the primacy of human beings not as mere products of social processes, but as beings invested with particular creative desires and powers that resisted the disciplining forces of society and media.[4]

When translated into the realm of art, this skeptical position, vis-à-vis the media in general, has led to an increasingly prominent view of art as a kind of automatic process, with the artist taking on the merely contingent role of filtering and combining ideas and aesthetics that are part of the zeitgeist—the artist as curator, rather than as unique producer of genius. These perspectives have become increasingly easy to identify in reality, both in the rise of identity-driven consumerism in the twentieth century and more particularly in the increasingly ephemeral nature of culture consumption. Particularly relevant to the current work has been the rise in the hip-hop industry of competition between artists increasingly driven by volume of output rather than craftsmanship. The ultimate example of this is Lil' B, a rapper who grew to popularity by releasing a myriad of mixtapes through social media.

Celebrity culture continues to draw the affective interest of many, but the media environment has, in reality, made celebrities the ultimate manifestation of Mead's ideas about the importance of symbols to identity. For instance, while it is beyond the scope of this discussion to establish whether there ever was "real" access to celebrities at the dawn of the media age, the intensely managed nature of the interaction between celebrities and the media has quite clearly ended that. What we experience as an audience is an entirely poststructural "subject" produced in the interaction of cultural institutions and manifested through media—no longer a person, but what Jeffrey Alexander has called a *celebrity icon*.

This poses a substantial challenge for artists working in cultural forms that rely on the privileging of personal experience or on unique individual talent, but who achieve prominence within a celebrity system that constantly fragments their image and distances them from audiences. This conflict was made manifest in the troubled lives of figures like Janis Joplin, Jim Morrison, and Kurt Cobain, Whitney Houston, and Michael Jackson, all of whom struggled to come to terms with a self that existed at the same time as a radical, gifted individual commodified as an incomplete image. The discourse surrounding cultural forms sets the terms for such experiences—many other examples could be added to those above from the realm of rock music, a genre that has frequently claimed legitimacy either through ideas of "genius" or on the basis of an artist's unique experience.

As hip-hop has come to supplant rock music as the most influential form of popular music, it has to some extent achieved détente with the phantasmal nature of modern celebrity and communication. For instance, in contrast to rock's historical ambivalence to wealth and its tendency to regard the musician as a unique genius, hip-hop music by and large endorses materialism and often posits the artist as a hardworking journeyman. At the same time, hip-hop has at moments placed great emphasis on skill, particularly on lyricists' skill with intricate or engaging wordplay and even enlightened political and social criticism.

More importantly, hip-hop relies on a discourse of authenticity for legitimation, and this is very much a classical understanding of personhood. In forms of discourse including lyrics, interviews, and reporting, claims to authenticity are a constant feature of hip-hop artists—invocations of one's roots, lyrics relying on details of personal experience, or simply the demand to "keep it real," all work to craft an image of credibility based on consistency and authenticity. This emphasis on authenticity in hip-hop is rooted in the experience of economic and social oppression in the African American and Latino Bronx community that gave birth to hip-hop. Hip-hop gatekeepers often express anxiety—justified by a long history of appropriation of exploitation of Black commodities—that this music of struggle would be co-opted by other groups as it became commercially viable.[5]

Expression, Symbolization, and Hip-Hop Poetics

Language is central to the art of hip-hop music. Rhythmically spoken lyrics are without doubt the element that has most thoroughly marked hip-hop as truly innovative in the sphere of Western popular music, and, for many audiences and communities, a rapper's lyrics are the main factor in evaluating their skill and worthiness.[6] These words, while powerful artistic expressions, are also the foundation of a rapper's public persona, the way they stake a claim for their public identity or their role as part of an artistic community.[7]

As is the case for much of popular music, the world of hip-hop requires that MCs maintain these lyrically constructed public performances outside of the music as well—in interviews, in concert performances, and even in public interpersonal interactions.

This blurring of the line between the person and the performer has been perceived as more extreme in hip-hop than in, say, rock music, mostly because of the greater social distance between rappers and the bulk of their public. In its first flush of commercial success wholly unexpected by the mainstream powers that be, there were persistent problems with critics mishearing hip-hop's social critique as the glorification of an antisocial lifestyle.[8] The mingling or confusion of self and artistic persona was particularly acute due to hip-hop music's status as a threatened subculture, which, especially after its commercial explosion, was faced with a variety of outsider-led attempts to exploit its sound for commercial gain. Like an organism threatened by infection, hip-hop developed antibodies to combat pretenders and exploiters.[9] Among them was the preservation of the authenticity of discourse or "keeping it real." This was an important defense of street culture from commercialization.[10] As hip-hop became increasingly commercially successful, artists had to carefully manage an anticommercial public image even as they sold millions of records. Those who successfully kept it real in hip-hop's golden age came in several varieties. The Afrocentric hippiefied Native Tongues were in many circles as respected in this regard as the grittily "realistic" N.W.A.

Of course, NWA pointed to some of the contradictions in discourses of authenticity, since principal lyricist Ice Cube chronicled a nightmarish, bullet-riddled, destitute South Central Los Angeles after growing up in a stable two-parent household. Like many artists and musicians before and since, Ice Cube adopted a voice and character as a way to express a greater truth, in his case, the true presence of a broader Black underclass and of persistent racism. Between the violent deaths Notorious B.I.G. and Tupac Shakur[11] and the public humiliation when details of Vanilla Ice's hard-knock life were found to be manufactured,[12] hard-core criminal/gangster image and "real-world" credentials became the dominant mode of artistic self-construction through most of the 1990s. It was frequently forgotten that the exaggerated, frightening picture of Black masculinity peddled by gangsta rappers began as a satirically skewed reflection of racist stereotyping and forced impoverishment.

After nearly four decades of hip-hop's growth and eventual dominance of American popular culture, though, the complete correspondence between rap persona and artist seems to have become less of a necessity for audiences. For example, the "out-ing" of Rick Ross as a former corrections officer[13] seems to have done no harm to a career that is built upon his self-depiction as a violent, outlandish drug kingpin. Generally, the diversification of hip-hop has led to an expansion of available identities, including of particular note those of the hyper-rich mogul and the emotion-ally wrought pop poet. Still, rappers negotiate a complicated set of priorities when managing their artistic identities, and think-ers attempting to understand the stakes of hip-hop can't take any aspect of the relationship between art and artist for granted.

Text and Self, Identity, and Expression

There are two obvious and opposing ways to interpret art's rep-resentational relationship with the artist. We can take an artistic expression as a direct manifestation of lived experience or a crafted artistic vision of the world. On the one hand, this can be reduc-tively described as a "Romantic" view of art, one that valorizes the personality, creativity, and craftsmanship of the artist and places on the reader/listener a responsibility to divine the author's profound intent. On the other hand, it may be that we can never truly know the intent behind the representative images an artist produces. If we take this view, which can again be reductively termed "postmodern," there is no responsibility for a viewer to penetrate to the particular-ity of an artist's vision. Artistic production may be purposeful, but the emergence of meaning in the encounter between object and viewer is fundamentally disconnected from artistic control.

Romanticism was a nineteenth-century reaction against the rationalism and valorization of science that formed the core of the Enlightenment. Against rationalistic Enlightenment, Romanticism emphasized the poetic sensibility and the irrational or purely instinctual encounter with nature and the overflowing power of suffering or romantic love. This gives prominence to the idea of the "genius" in the artist who produces original viewpoints on the world from nothing, based only on his (at that time, usually his) experience and spiritual insight.[14] The positioning of the romantic author was very specific, often inviting "the reader to identify the protagonists with the poets themselves."[15]

This Romantic conception of art as an outpouring of the indi-vidual soul remains an important part of Western frameworks for understanding art, especially in popular discourse, and underpins the idea of authenticity or "keeping it real" in hip-hop. Despite a growing appreciation of rappers as being capable of role-play and of distancing themselves from their crafted personae, they are still broadly presumed by audiences to be "representing," in a very direct way, their experiences, emotional states, and background. For instance, the case of Rick Ross[16] exposes persistent prejudice as much as new openness; it would hardly be considered news if someone suddenly found definitive proof that Marlon Brando was not an actual mob boss, but the "exposure" of a rapper projecting a false public persona, due to hip-hop's fiercely maintained codes regarding authenticity, remains somewhat scandalous.[17]

For much of the twentieth century, theorists of art and representation have been arguing that such outrage is utterly alien to the reality of the processes of artistic production and reception, which has been increasingly reconceived as providing no direct access to the intent or experience of the author. This notion became clear with the concept of "the death of the author," a phrase coined by Roland Barthes in 1967. More than the unique expression of a single person, Barthes saw texts as drawn from "innumerable centers of culture,"[18] with the author more of a weaver of many threads than the singular creator of a new whole. Soon after, Michel Foucault would further push against Romantic identification between artist and art with the idea that the "author function" was a metatextual construct that he saw emerging in discussions of art. For Foucault the author function may be necessary to consumption of a text, but in the end it can only refer to a reader or critic's idea of the author, rather than the reality of a person.[19]

These assertions about art are rooted in broader changes in thought about the nature of language and representation. Anthropologists including Franz Boas and Edward Sapir challenged the idea of language as merely descriptive or expressive, highlighting instead the duality of its role as a mediator that actually changed what it represented, particularly when attempting to communicate between cultures.[20] Ferdinand De Saussure further de-naturalized language and its functions, arguing that language and other symbols had an arbitrary relationship to meaning. Again, this was particularly true in intercultural scenarios—the fact that the Spanish "arbol" could encompass much the same ideas as the English "tree" highlighted that symbolizations coalesced only through collective social processes.[21] The "linguistic turn" that followed from Saussure through Foucault and many others[22] also had impacts in sociology that are important to the analysis of artistic performance. Irving Goffman used theatrical language to describe his new schema of personal identity, one that, much like Saussure's, repudiated the old metaphysical philosophy of pure expression for one that was specifically social and intersubjective, in which the individual consciously shaped others' perception of him or herself.[23]

But the most significant developments for the discussion of an art as self-conscious are the more specific investigations of the functions of signs and signification *per se*. Theorists of communication and culture[24] merged semiotic and social frameworks, focusing on how symbols functioned as both channels and barriers, the relative power and autonomy of messages and audiences, and how other dimensions of human interaction inflected semiotic functions. Against a long-standing "hypodermic" model of cultural transmission that owed much to the same transcendent conceptions of communication that the linguistic turn had reacted against, the media theorist Stuart Hall advanced what may be the most general and comprehensive theory on the contingent nature of symbolic communication in culture. Known as the "encoding/ decoding" schema, Hall's model starkly separates the stages of making cultural meaning into production, circulation, use, and reproduction, which he pointed out are relatively separate from one another, while still embedded in relations of power at each stage.

For Hall, audiences are not predictably positioned in identical ways relative to the meaning of a piece of culture. They arrive at any cultural object from different structural positions (class, race, and gender, but also more unique personal backgrounds) and carry with them different semiotic codebooks than those that were used to "encode," or create, the message. As Hall puts it, "degrees of identity/non-identity between the codes [may] perfectly or imperfectly transmit, interrupt or systematically distort what is being transmitted."[25] Hall provided a classification scheme for audience decoding frames, including particularly "dominant" and "resistive" frames, according to which the members of an audience might either accept or reject the interpretation intended not just by artists, but by institutions or industries of cultural production. So, just as the relationship between a simple symbol and its meaning were arbitrary for Saussure, Hall argued that there was "no necessary correspondence" between a more complex cultural expression and how it would be perceived, interpreted, or used by an audience.[26]

This model is productive, and for many quite challenging, when thinking about the contrast in reactions between those who brought sympathetic and dominant frames to the reception of art. Because it is so attendant to the role of social power, it is very difficult to think in Hall's framework of any mode of interpretation as being the "correct" one. Each encounter with a cultural text, rather than some attempt to divine an author's intent, is instead embedded in a much wider struggle for social power. This struggle is of course acutely significant in hip-hop, where convention demands that the self be held in tension between a dominant, oppressive culture and a locally grounded (but also global) community of the oppressed.

This "intercultural" aspect of hip-hop, its position at the boundary between different code systems, is vital to understanding the relationship between artist and art. On the one hand, hip-hop artists must constantly reinforce the "code of the street"—a phrase with double meaning, both moral and linguistic. On the other hand, the imperative of pop appeal has become stronger and stronger, especially as hip-hop's status as a music of resistance has eroded. These competing codes may leave the artist very little space to strategically represent, much less romantically express, a distinct and textured version of him or herself within a sphere of commercial viability.

There are, however, spheres in which the imperative of popular appeal is felt less powerfully. Conscious hip-hop artists like Lyrics Born, Gift of Gab, Lateef the Truthspeaker, Aceyalone, Jean Grae, Abstract Rude, and Eligh—to name a few—are more divorced from market forces than are those artists for whom record sales and radio play are the be-all-end-all. In artists such as these, the erosion of hip-hop's status as a music of resistance is held, at least partially, at bay. Messages of authenticity are more often than not couched in terms of philosophical integrity, of lyrical mastery, of adherence to vision rather than the material trappings of success displayed so openly by those who have travelled the path of least resistance by working with record and marketing executives to craft and market a sellable product. Conscious artists avoid these pitfalls, just as they sidestep the (often patently false) claims of authenticity put forth by gangsta rappers; the violence and criminality of the street may occasionally enter into their lyrics, but they represent themselves as active resisters of this violence and criminality—never agents in it. Through tireless self-promotion and consistently high-grade content, many of these artists have built small but loyal followings that are as sensitive as any other group in the industry to even the most subtle of changes in an artist's image or sound. Authentic self-representation without deviation is rewarded with loyalty; anything deemed inconsistent or disingenuous can leave an artist grasping at straws in the communities of the hip-hop faithful.

The key component in a poststructuralist hip-hop philosophy of representation moves beyond the acknowledgment of the arbitrary nature of the symbol and of the loose interpretability of cultural objects to systematically reanalyze our relationships with symbolization after the debunking of the metaphysics of expression by the linguistic turn. A pioneer of this analysis was Jacques Lacan, who combined Saussure's semiotics with Sigmund Freud's analysis of the subconscious. For Lacan, the subconscious was "structured like a language," in fact somewhat violently colonized by the symbolic system of the society into which a child happened to be born.[27] So, while all symbols remained arbitrary, Lacan saw that they had a kind of fetishistic hold over their users. For him, the power of the word was attended to more closely than the power of the phallus in Freud's more simplistic, sexual schema of socialization.

The word does not replace the phallus. In Lacan's argument the desiring relationship to words and representation has everything to do with our complex and intersubjective desiring relationship to other human beings. In a much broader version of Goffman's ideas of performativity, Lacan argues, in essence, that we all long for the kind of acceptance and belonging that we imagine we felt at our mother's breast, and attempt to relocate or reconstruct that feeling in our own social world by adopting a symbolic self that will appeal to others around us. But these images that we adopt to appeal to others are never in any natural or given way connected to either our own selves, or even the desire we are trying to appeal to. In fact, Lacan argues, we are likely to orient our self-creation toward the most opaque expressions of desire by others,[28] and what we pursue is equally spectral. Love is the gift of what the Other does not have.

This is particularly true because those others whom we angle so ferociously to appeal to are themselves embedded or entangled in linguistic and symbolic systems that have long predated us, and therefore can have no relation to our own radical presymbolic uniqueness. Lacan even calls the semiotic system the "signifying chain," with full overtones of repression and entrapment. Lacan uses this language of alienation to describe the experience of adopting the self-as-image, a sacrifice we make in the hope of appealing to those around us, but which tragically "symbolizes the I's mental permanence, at the same time as it prefigures its alienating destination."[29] In essence, then, we are driven by desire into subjective positions that precede us, comfortable identities that we occupy as bolsters for our sense of self. What emerges in Lacan is a view of the relationship between representation and reality that evades the simple dichotomy between romantic expressionism and postmodernist "absence." Instead, close attention to the functional elements of language and symbolization describes a more dialectical process in which the striving for expression finds limited success in the face of a symbolic order that restricts the speaker/artist's freedom: "By coming into the letter's possession—an admirably ambiguous bit of language—its meaning possesses them."[30]

This certainly seems to illuminate the dynamics both by which artists relate to themselves and audiences relate to artists. In his description of the desiring human relationship to the image, Lacan describes the human forces that both encourage our mistaking of the artist for his or her own representation and encourage the artist to enable that mistaking. The artist, particularly in a popular, commercial form like hip-hop, is necessarily driven to pursue the acceptance of an audience, but that acceptance requires to a great degree that the artist's image coincides with images and archetypes that preceded him or her. One subtext of "keeping it real" is often that a rapper can't get too aesthetically or thematically unconventional before being somehow unacceptable or illegitimate to a core audience. This dynamic is in turn driven by the fact that the audience premises its *own* identity on the symbols being produced by rappers. Whether in the form of bodily performance, dress, language, or by way of the affiliation of fandom, rap fans use the symbols produced by rappers to articulate some element of their experience of selfhood.

The seductions of hip-hop signification are not categorically different from those of other art forms, though the over-determined social meanings of blackness and masculinity have arguably narrowed the range of affective associations available to rappers. This is how hip-hop audiences can easily fall victim to the trap of the image, drawn in to "feeling" the music and, at the same time, the self-representation of the artist on an emotional level, even if in different moments they might rationally comprehend that an artist is not the same as his art. Take, for instance, the recent incident of a female fan attempting to publicly fellate rapper Danny Brown,[31] whose raunchy on-record persona apparently has little to do with who he is in real life.[32] This sort of moment clearly arises partly out of a listener's desire to identify themselves with the image being presented. Rather than a monological relationship from artist to listener, the listeners often take on the image, become the image, sharing the microphone and stage (and other things) with an image creating a dialogical nature of the Black aesthetic.

Wearily, self-consciousness about the imagistic status of the form, and perhaps some skepticism about the risks of fetishization, are built into the legacy of hip-hop and the way audiences consume it. Richard Shusterman has said that "if rap has an underlying metaphysics, it is that reality is a field of change and flow rather than static permanence."[33] This postmodernist detachment has a specifically linguistic element. Innumerable critics have linked hip-hop to the African American legacy of linguistic encoding under conditions of oppression that demanded misdirection and concealment,[34] and the related tradition of "signifying" in which linguistic creativity is used to gain leverage at the wrong end of a power imbalance.[35] From this perspective, late-period hip-hop's overblown narratives of excess and violence may be read less as empty, hedonistic boasts consumed by aspiring dupes, and more as a canny performance for the enjoyment of an often savvy audience, who see it for the escapism it is. That would certainly explain why the "exposure" of Rick Ross was met, in the end, with a yawn, confirming his status as the "Teflon Don"—impenetrably, hilariously, gloriously false.

But those who have opposed hip-hop have never decoded it with attention to the strategic exaggeration at its core, or with much respect for its audience's ability to distinguish entertainment and reality. Though it is unlikely that more than a few audience members have ever actively considered the question, in practice, it was hip-hop's harshest critics who were most likely to fully conflate the "I" of hip-hop narrative with the person holding the microphone. In a very real sense, this puts the C. Dolores Tuckers of the world on the same page as a group who have, in the later stages of hip-hop's history, attempted to construct two dichotomous kinds of rap—one "conscious" and positive, and the another "mere" entertainment or, worse, a vector of actual spiritual degeneration and propagator of violence. The mistaking of hip-hop's engagement with the culture of violence for the violence itself was dramatically demonstrated by mass hysteria over rap concerts in the 1980s,[36] but equally by certain of the so-called backpacker movement of the 1990s. "Backpakers," including some affiliated with the Native Tongues Posse, positioned themselves as bearing "conscious," positive messages, in contrast to the violence and excess of "mainstream" rappers—at once an invocation of longstanding discourses of authenticity that opposed commercial success to artistic legitimacy, and a conflation of the surface of a text with its contextual meaning. The underlying assumption of both positions is that there is no distance between artist and expression that might allow their narratives to be seen as reflexive, satirical, ironic, double, or coded. This is a strange assumption indeed in the context of the history of Black rhetoric.

Positions vis-à-vis the "realness" of hip-hop expression around the complete identification of artist with art, or their distance from it are taken by particular stakeholding populations within the hip-hop community. As hip-hop has become a global phenomenon, it has been common for international artists and audiences to regard American hip-hop as more "real" or "authentic" than local versions.[37] Even some critics, subscribing to a very limited romanticist view of hip-hop as metaphysically expressive of a limited set of "real" experiences, have aggressively shut down the idea that hip-hop arising from different experiences can "keep it real."[38] But other commentators have more openly explored the nature of the dialectic of borrowing between African American artists and the globe,[39] while global artists have similarly begun to articulate local versions of "realness." A stirring example of this is "What's Hardcore," by Somali-Canadian rapper K'naan, who uses the ultraviolent situation of his homeland to challenge a strain of hip-hop rhetoric linking violence to artistic legitimacy. A similar challenge would seem to confront female emcees, who must construct their own "realness" within a realm that particularly valorizes stereotypically masculine attributes such as assertiveness. A large subset of female artists do this by simply adding female details to hypermasculine discourse, as when Amil declares "Late nights, candlelight, then I tear the cock up...my coochie remain in Gucci name" (Jay-Z, "Can I Get A..."). It seems particularly clear in such cases that, as Barthes says quoting Stéphane Mallarmé, "It is language which speaks."[40]

The impact of these flexible relationships between artist and expression are most obvious in terms of critical discourse. On the one hand, there are those who would seem to regard art in terms deriving both from the romantic synonymy between art and artist and from a kind of Platonic idealism about the proper content of art. It often seems in hip-hop that those who admit no distance between art and artist are also those who believe artists should only express positive ideas or images and not delve into the darker aspects of the human experience, while those who admit more distance between artist and image are able to enjoy more complicated kinds of expression and perhaps a more complicated consciousness of the reality it tangles with.

The difference between art and artist becomes particularly problematic in a celebrity culture where popular artists are themselves part of a work of art or their whole lives are considered works of art. When it is not only a singer's songs that define him or her, but also what is printed about them in the tabloids, one has to consider a triple level of existence to the artist—the person represented in the songs, the person present in the public's mind, and the actual singer, who may or may not actually conform to any of these when the microphones are off and the cameras are packed up. Trapped between their status as a living work of art and the nature of their songs as smaller works of art that are understood to be reflective of their lives (even if the celebrity lifestyle is clearly not a gangster's), singers can become an embodiment of cognitive dissonance as contradictory visions of authenticity are written about them without their input.

Rumination 8

Catastrophe of Success: Marshall McLuhan, Gilles Deleuze, and Felix Guattari

The title of the rumination is derived from American playwright Tennessee Williams' *A Catastrophe of Success*. The appropriation of this essay's title reflects the struggle of hip-hop artists to achieve true (sometimes global) celebrity status while apparently remaining uncomfortable with that status. Though often appearing in the media as entitled and shameless about wealth and status, commercially successful rappers and artists in general frequently grapple with the disjuncture between the artist as a gifted individual and the celebrity as an industrially produced commodity. This is particularly clear in the Kanye West track "Pinocchio Story," which from its title down engages with the tension between representation and underlying reality, specifically as regards the experiential and informational economy of modern celebrity. This disjunctive combination suggests what I argue here is West's larger struggle personally and extended to hip-hop in general as an artistic theme: the gap between an artist's experience of individual subjectivity, agency, and creativity, and the way that control of one's art and even very personhood can be usurped by media and technology.[1]

Marshall McLuhan in *The Medium Is the Message* said, "All media work us over completely" (McLuhan, 2006, p. 26). This rumination sets out to present a focused reading on one of the artists that has emerged as a product of that original movement—Kanye West—but with pop music and culture as a general backdrop. This text will explore the reasons behind the presentation of Kanye West's "Pinocchio's Story" as a "catastrophe of success." What does it mean when hip-hop heads claim an artist sold his soul, especially in relation to *Keeping it Real*? If the laboring artist, attempting to break through, is unaware of lacking the "authentic soul" needed to sustain their selves and the work they give birth to, what becomes then of this realization in the lives of influential hip-hop artists such as Jay-Z, Lil Wayne, and Nicki Minaj? Does it overwhelm? Does it force them into an interiorized stance relinquishing or deferring the inauthentic soul they inhabit? And who then represents the Geppetto of the aforementioned cautionary hip-hop tale? The main philosophical issue at stake, however, will only arise after one poses an initial question: Do the celebrity artist's channels of expression consume that very act of expression? And do they allow them, in turn, to be received by an audience only as a constructed object rather than a represented subject? Is their authenticity lost or gained depending on the answer to these questions?

In general, asking about the authenticity of any work of art, without distinction between so-called high or low forms of art, implies questioning in turn the validity of a strong presupposition. Art, as an activity and as a product, stands, or at least should stand, outside of daily life. It must be able to subsist under different conditions, under conditions that are not characterized by the relations of domination that are present in capitalist production. It must do so to breathe life, in the form of taste, value or some other criteria to gain perspective over the reproductive character of capitalist relations where art is seen as nothing more than a commodity whose existence is guided by supply and demand. If art can be said to have some value beyond the economic in modern society, it derives from what it can offer, in a unique sense, to daily life. In order to offer something unique, art as a process of production would have to show that it is essentially different from capitalist production and, hence, not determined by the forces of supply and demand. In modern societies, where capitalist methods imply exactly the opposite—the lack of singularity—artists, it is said, return singularity and uniqueness to human life.[2] The opposition between inside and outside, between an institutionalized form of life and a life dedicated to resistance, serves as the underpinning to the evaluation of any artist whatsoever, along the general lines that originality requires a certain genius that X or Y does not possess;

that being authentic means possessing a vision that goes beyond the boundaries of social life; that art presents us with a vantage point from which we can judge society and its values.

From a philosophical point of view, which can be labeled postmodern or at least nonmodern, the metaphysics of transcendence implied in such assertions are not an analytical option; stating that there is an exteriority poses a space that necessarily escapes our analytical grasp—Kant's conundrum about synthetic knowledge. If, in addition, we hold that artistic movements have a history of their own, then this history will be explained or constructed as part of a reality that is submerged under the interiority presupposed by institutional forms. It is by accepting this interiority as a fact of the social sciences that we are able to say that things, such as lack of opportunities and persistent racism, but also rap, break dance, the boom box, digital recording, and so on, are all pivotal and explanatory of the origins of hip-hop. It is precisely at this point that the question "What can be the marker of authenticity?" must be rekindled. We must first ask: what is it that we make reference to when we wonder about how authentic an artwork really is? And can we assess whether an artist is authentic or not?

The philosophical grasp on authenticity proposed here demands that this inside/outside opposition be left behind and, in turn, that immanence be embraced as the better explanatory tool for analyzing authenticity. We must notice, in consequence, that the artist as an entity becomes problematized once we abandon the inside/outside dichotomy, because the notion of a modern subject itself is based upon the epistemological possibility of dividing between subjects and objects, or between nature and culture. Upholding immanence will mean having to renounce the epistemological authority of the monad-like subject and present in turn a feasible alternative. Why? Because the monad-like subject is what allows activities and their outcomes to be traced back to an origin, or to be reduced to an essence. These essential attributes, it turns out, are arranged around a center, from which they are deployed toward an outside. Authenticity, under this view, comes either in the form that such deployment takes (expressiveness), or in the uniqueness of the attributes themselves (artistic genius).

If we argue that the attributes are unique, then their origin must be traced back and founded upon something else. This something else (a daimon, a holy ghost, a brain-in-a-bucket, etc.)

cannot but appear as external to the phenomenon of human life in general, where those attributes are scarce or entirely nonexistent. If, on the contrary, authenticity is said to inhabit the form of such deployment, then the "how" of that same deployment must be founded on a transcendence or exteriority of sorts. In this latter case, being able to create or produce something unique is assessed according to that which is not unique. In this light the thesis-antithesis figure is fundamental in the construction of a feasible analysis. However, an absolute marker of difference will not suffice, because without it, it is impossible to avoid equating insanity with authenticity. This will mean, therefore, that a dialectical turn must be called upon, so that the form of the deployment will be able to inform the rest of us of something unique and relevant to our human lives, which is precisely what insanity cannot do; Art as an unveiling of truth, for example, is a Heideggerian modernist illustrative of this point.[3]

One quickly realizes that such revealing, which is recognized by the collective and not the individual alone, still has a strong rational component to it (truth and revealing), and presupposes an equally high communicational bond, it must be essentially communicable, for otherwise there is no way of assessing whether it is or is not absurdity or nonsense.

Both aspects, the rational and communicable, romanticize the form of the deployment, because they abstract from what is concrete (Picasso's *Guernica*, Warhol's *Campbell's Soup Cans*, Run D.M.C's "Walk This Way" or Public Enemy's "Fight the Power"), and lead us toward a justification of the value at stake that is based upon the effectiveness of its emancipatory calls, or on the existence of the sublime, the beautiful, or other inherently transcendent notions, which naturally need pay little attention to time, space, history, or geography. The medium itself, in consequence, goes under erasure (to use Derridean terminology). That is, it is taken as a transparent, passive, and purely contingent "thing" in the "real" process at stake, which is delivering an authentic experience to us all.

If we say today that we live in a world where virtual reality, social media, and, in short, mediated relationships populate the social field, then the apparently obvious thing to conclude is that "Art is dead" and all we have is artistic production merely being a repetition of what we've seen before. It is precisely this conclusion that we shall strive to avoid, for it is marked by modern romanticism, prejudice, and a lack of historical perspective.

We therefore approach the issue of authenticity from the perspective of the medium, more concretely, from the viewpoint of modern media. I will begin by following the critical assessment made by McLuhan in order to rethink the effective role of media, which not only allows a better explanation of the medium itself to emerge, but also permits a reassessment of the role and usage of authenticity by way of an immanent approach. Additionally, studying the role of media, or better yet, returning media to its proper role as an effective and transformative means, rather than a transparent one, requires this analysis to also reassess the role of the agencies involved in defining authenticity and producing the authentic. This is made possible by a recourse to Deleuze and to a relational understanding of agency, which may be called a-subjective or, more positively, inter-medial.

The Relevance of Media in Developing a Theory of *Authenticity*

In a traditional and romantic approach, media's role would be characterized by its transparency, the degree to which a medium is able to simply transmit or communicate the message that originated in a human emitter. Such a view, one quickly sees, implies an equally pure instrumental approach to the concrete media at stake from print to TV and the Internet. It is against this instrumentality of the medium that one can locate the motivation of McLuhan's critical assessment: "For the 'message' of any medium or technology is the change of scale or pace or pattern that it introduces into human affairs […] 'the medium is the message' because it is the medium that shapes and controls the scale and form of human association and action."[4] McLuhan acts, through these words, as a warning voice that reminds us that the medium is not innocuous, nor is it a mere extension of natural human abilities. His contention has less to do with the medium per se than a naïve understanding of the consequences that its usage carries. When transparency becomes the most obvious characterization of the medium, then whatever consequences it brings become a byproduct that is essentially distinct from the medium itself. To put it differently, the image makes the icon and the icon does not preexist the image.

The fundamental core of McLuhan's assessment lies precisely in two implicated lessons that he wants us to retain: (1) the medium is transformative of the social reality at stake and (2) the act of transmission cannot be understood separately from the medium. Furthermore, McLuhan does not simply want to denounce the naïve gesture that characterizes our traditional view on the media, but wants to do so because such knowledge can be instrumental in the way the medium transforms reality. In his words:

> Cardinal Newman said of Napoleon, "He understood the grammar of gunpowder." Napoleon had paid some attention to other media as well, especially the semaphore telegraph that gave him a great advantage over his enemies. He is on record for saying that "Three hostile newspapers are more to be feared than a thousand bayonets." Alexis de Tocqueville was the first to master the grammar of print and typography. He was thus able to read off the message of coming change in France and America as if he were reading aloud from a text that had been handed to him. In fact, the nineteenth century in France and in America was just such an open book to de Tocqueville because he had learned the grammar of print.[5]

Understanding the transformative power of the medium means much more than acquiring a theoretical perspective on the role of media in human history. Understanding the medium, as in the cases mentioned by McLuhan illustrate, provides a meta-perspective that can be instrumental. Napoleon truly uses the telegraph once he understands its rules, its inner workings. It is based on an enlightenment perspective, which would grant too much to rationality and consciousness so much that he argues in turn that "the serious artist is the only person able to encounter technology with impunity, just because he is an expert aware of the changes in sense perception."[6]

There is in McLuhan a certain uneasiness that focuses on the purpose rather than on the critical assessment of media. His concern is perhaps more with the *How* rather than the *Why*. It is difficult to follow him on the ability that he ascribes to Napoleon or De Tocqueville, inasmuch as it may be serving as a hyperbolical example of his original assessment in understanding the transformative role of the medium. This is not to say that there are no key elements of McLuhan's position to be retained in assessing authenticity and the role of the medium in conveying or denying it.

The artist's ascribed ability, even if it doesn't reduce the medium to a self-serving instrument, can indeed offer an interesting approximation of how the medium relates to authenticity. In a sense, McLuhan's appraisement of the medium asks that we move the medium from a position at the end of a communication process to the beginning of that same process. The medium does not transmit original intentions, but transforms them so that they can actually reach a greater audience. How great and who are they? The answer to these questions lies in the medium at stake. The extension of the audience differs from one medium to the other and across media, while the implied "Who" depends on the material conditions of the medium. What this means is that the iconic image of the pop star is not transmitted but enabled by the media at stake: TV and radio. It is through the dawn of the TV and radio that the massive number of consumers needed for the pop star to exist—an army of the music industry—became a reality. The kind of audience or following that may arise relates to material conditions such as, for instance, literacy and electric power, both of which are needed in order to become a part of the phenomenon brought forward by a pop star.

Looking at the transformation that a person undergoes through media, one might say that such a process is a sort of personal *becoming*. If we need to say something about authenticity at this point, it may be safe to suggest that it is not so much a process of strictly autistic[7] self-creation as one engaged upon in the hope of acting upon a social world. The particular ways in which any given artist acts upon the social world are only available in and through media, and that media will simultaneously makes possible and constrains the processes of self-creation and self-discovery.

If I dismiss McLuhan's hyperbolic argument about the role of media, it is precisely because whatever media may be at stake, there is simply no way to locate a center of power; that is, there is no way of asserting some original intentions that would be carried through without change. Popular music followers, it is easy to see, are not an army acting in the name of this or that artist, or of the industry as a whole. Their appreciation of the artist, which is at times difficult to comprehend, is better understood along the lines of the relationship between the religious believer and an icon, where the line between fan and fanatic is a difficult one to draw.

Immanence and Subjectivity

The traditional view of the medium is not an accidental construct, but one entirely in line with the monad-like figure that represents the modern view of subjectivity. If one rekindles the medium, then one must reassess subjectivity as well. This can be achieved by following Deleuze and Guattari, who are able to situate subjectivity within a perspective where transcendence is not necessary, and where, in turn, human agency works jointly with the medium rather than simply instrumentalizing the latter for its own interests.

To begin with, society and individual are no longer entities that stand opposed to each other: "The function of the *socius*, of the social machinery, is to 'codify' the flows of desire, to inscribe them, to record them, to see it to it that no flow exists that is not properly dammed up, channeled, regulated."[8] This means, therefore, that "the social axiomatic of modern societies is caught between two poles, and is constantly oscillating from one pole to the other [...] These societies are caught between the urstaat that they would like to resuscitate as an overcoding and reterritorializing unity, and the unfettered flows that carry them toward the absolute threshold. [...] They are torn in two directions: archaism and futurism, neo-archaism and ex-futurism, paranoia and schizophrenia."[9]

The relationship between individual and society is one of codification, where the individual becomes codified at every turn. The purpose of such codification is normalization and, in the worse-case scenario, state control. Society is therefore not artificial in the sense of being simply a set of instruments used for control (Marxist infrastructure), while the individual is also not a naturally endowed being that is churned into a malleable or robotic citizen. There is no individual without society. Without a reified or transcendent Nature or Culture, immanence can set in. This can be defined as needing both the agent and the social structure to construct an understanding of reality at large.[10] A transcendent perspective can never even be thought of, and, hence, authenticity in even its most ideal form still remains anchored within the concrete society/individual that enables it. So, how can we judge or recognize the traces of an authentic life in this view?

A possibility of life is evaluated through itself in the movements it lays out and the intensities it creates on a plane of immanence: what is not laid out or created is rejected. A mode of existence is good or bad, noble or vulgar, complete or empty, independently of Good and Evil or any transcendent value: there are never criteria other than the tenor of existence, the intensification of life.[11]

Deleuze and Guattari argue in favor of seeing the process of self-creation as one that leads to an authentic life (similar to Foucault's view on the same), where experimentation of sense and reflection[12] (intensities) become the central aspects that define the authentic as opposed to the merely repetitive. If we want to discuss the artistic life in particular, then the same intensities must be pursued, while avoiding becoming entirely normalized by the process of codification that characterizes social life. Lyotard's words are, in this case, illustrative of what is at stake:

> The secret of an artistic success, like that of a commercial success, resides in the balance between what is surprising and what is "well-known", between information and code. This is how innovation in art operates: one re-uses formulae confirmed by previous success, one throws them off-balance by combining them with other, in principle incompatible, formulae, by amalgamations, quotations ornamentations, pastiche. One can go as far as kitsch or the grotesque. One flatters the "taste" of a public that can have no taste, and the eclecticism or a sensibility enfeebled by the (multiplication of available forms and objects.[13]

The balance lies, therefore, in a subjectivity that does not surrender to codification. It lies in a subject that does not concede to the prejudices or temptations offered by media that result in the figure of the icon surrounded by fans and fanatics, who, despite the political strength they represent, become entirely domesticated by an industry and an economy that codifies them as product and consumer.

A-Subjectivity: From Conjunctive to Disjunctive Syntheses

To stand beside or against the codification that makes of the artist a subject in the modern sense of the term but also in the sense of being held subject to certain authority, can only be done through the process of experimentation that Deleuze and Guattari have argued for. From an analytical perspective, this means rekindling the way we construct the monad subject that gathers properties or attributes around a core so that it can now allow for connections or relations to emerge and produce new forms of subjectivities. This change of perspective is referred to by Deleuze and Guattari as a passage from a conjunctive synthesis, which gathers and reduces concrete properties and powers, to a disjunctive synthesis that maintains difference while acknowledging the transformations that occur with each connection: "The conjunctive synthesis can therefore be expressed: 'So *I* am the King! So the kingdom belongs to *me!*' But this me is merely the residual subject that sweeps the circle and concludes a self from its oscillations on the Circle."[14] This implies in turn that modern identities, and the emblematic form of the modern monad (the ego), must be revised in their presupposed role. As Deleuze and Guittari affirms, "there is no ego that identifies with races, peoples, and persons in a theater of representation, but proper names that identify races, peoples, and persons with regions, thresholds, or effects in a production of intensive quantities."[15]

Subjectification, one can argue from an immanent perspective, appears as an assemblage. It is the formalization of a particular way of expression, as Althusser says, "Subjectification as a regime of signs or a form of expression is tied to an assemblage, in other words, an organization of power that is already fully functioning in the economy, rather than superimposing itself upon contents or relations between contents determined as real in the last instance. Capital is a point of subjectification par excellence."[16] To rephrase this, subjectification can never occur outside of society, of the economy, or of the process of codification that marks our human lives. Authenticity, therefore, must be searched for in the cracks or fissures of that same process where relationships that challenge the authority and necessity of a code come into play as a sort of nonviolent or nonchalant resistance.

Inter-Mediality and Authenticity

Authenticity, to sum up, is not determined through the involvement, or lack thereof, with modern institutions or even with the social field at large. A perspective that judges human life based on its distance from institutions inevitably constructs an Outside, which however, can be neither conceptualized nor discussed.[17] The relationship with institutions is not to be disregarded as unimportant, for it is indeed one characterized by constant tension and negotiation. For example, as an individual I want to select my own clothes, which is a choice based on criteria such as taste and strategy (what best communicates who I am). Still, this choice, even if one argues it is not coerced, poses an issue of correlation and causation. Perhaps I am using media as a foundation from which to piece together a sense of self, rather than selecting media according to a sense of self I've already achieved. Once again, the presence of the modern subject informing our thought is palpable and almost heavy to lift.

If, as I have begun to argue, it is in the tension between institutions and the body's boundaries that subjectification emerges, then causation and correlation are inaccurate approaches. One must bear in mind the consequences of leaving the modern monad for our understanding of individuality, personal character, and the like: "The end of the bourgeois ego or monad no doubt brings with it the end of the psychopathologies of that ego as well […] But it means the end of much more—the end for example of style, in the sense of the unique and the personal, the end of the distinctive individual brushstroke."[18] Artistic authenticity must be found, therefore, in the way the individual plays, resists, and, in short, constructs the tension between institutions and the self. Controversial rapper, Tyler the Creator, fits in this discussion well as he embraces his position as something larger than human, yet very basically human at the same time. My research assistant, Adam Schueler, reported on a heated discussion he had about with Tyler that his "existential reckonings tell his story of almost instant wealth—he literally, as Drake popularizes, 'started from the bottom'. His authenticity lies in his ability to not embrace fame as an end-all."

The media exemplifies the tangible aspect of such tension, which lies between the instrumental and the transparent. This in-between zone grows in importance for a form of subjectivity that is neither modern nor premodern, neither essential nor socialized. Artistic life can be understood "as a coherent practice of multimedial, interdisciplinary and interactive elements comes to the fore."[19] The authentic lies in the artist embracing inter-mediality and renouncing the egocentric game of the icon. Henk Oosterling says, "in intermedial experiments of avant-garde artists criticism towards society as a given reality becomes explicit as a medium-specific reflectivity."[20]

Whatever the content and form of the criticism made, it is not done in the name of emancipation. It would be hypocritical to do so. Emancipation as a plight from social grasp is but a vague promise in the best of cases, and nothing but an empty threat or a bluff in the worst. Furthermore, where emancipation is not the main goal, authenticity is no longer reduced to a domesticated notion, where it is viewed as a specialized form of expressiveness.[21] Instead of authenticity being reduced to the constant pursuit of the new, of the ever more outrageous, its true being will lie in the ability of the artist to play with the media; to break with stereotypes, with prejudices, and with the "return of the same," an always-present temptation.[22]

So how can we configure this inter-medial subject if all dichotomies seem to be out of place? Inter-mediality does not come void of concepts, but offers a series of underlying concepts: ensemble, composition, assemblages.[23] The use of these will help to regulate the tension that arises between the oppositions that characterizes the authentic: between sense-nonsense/sensation, between active/passive, and between contact/distance. If we now wonder how the tension manifests in the artist, whose popularity forms the temptation to give in to the ego and the promise of happiness in the form of money and fame, it is not surprising that dealing with such tension is not an easy task. It is not something to be expected from all artists. Yet how many artists are really concerned about being authentic?

It is in dealing with this tension that the emotional content of Kanye West's "Pinocchio Story" is so revealing of the social and psychological meanings at stake. The song is filled with regret, with a sorrow that brings to mind the clichéd warning: be careful what you wish for, you just might get it. The opening lyrics of "Pinocchio Story" reflect exactly these thoughts of conflict, the tension arising from a feeling of being in between absorption by something greater that oneself, and being an active part of something bigger and perhaps more meaningful than an individual's life.[24] An artist is concerned with his own reality, with his own feelings and his own uneasiness. A postmodern consciousness compels him to recognize the psychological void, the emptiness, in spite of a culturally coded appearance of fulfillment: "There is no Gucci I can buy / There is no Louis Vuitton to put on."

The celebrity icon emerges into being as an object, which in turn becomes a fragment-ideal in which subjects attempt to overcome the messiness and the limits of being by conforming. In "Pinocchio Story," there is a sense that West is coming to grips with the trappings of fame and wealth. He ends up wishing he was not famous. Everywhere he goes, everyone asks him for an autograph or a picture, unwanted intruders invade his personal space. This experience makes him wonder whether he could find a more authentic sense of self in anonymity (like a "real boy," or a normal, mediocre, average, everyday person). What exactly is he in search of?

His inner search and his outer journey are surely not so different from anyone else's. That is, to find the happiness and joy that no one can take away, that is always already within, is pure bliss, and that lasts. It is not the external materialistic indicators of wealth, power, and success. If we accept that West reveals to us his melancholic and blue feelings in "Pinocchio Story," it is because he has yet to fully abandon his ego, to turn within, and is, in consequence, still experiencing an existential dread and a tangible anxiety or angst.

To be a personally authentic celebrity artist is an impulse, in the form of a strain against postmodern despair and in the hope of transcendence. Many of rap's lyrics and persona permit an exploration of the way West endeavors to invest as much of himself in his image as he can through sincere and even deliberately impulsive action. Through its special treatment of concepts that make up our understanding of our mediated human lives, Kanye's "Pinocchio Story" can be seen as a manifesto, as a creative and philosophical effort. Ultimately, it suggests that the tragedy of the image (of the icon) is the simultaneous necessity and inadequacy of image (of presence) as foundation of those empathic opportunities (those connections) that art serves to form. I will argue, finally, that the journey is indeed a philosophical endeavor in the sense of a revealing and a critique, yet it is also more than that. Oosterling's words are perhaps the best way to summarize my concluding thoughts as he asserts: "Authentic Dasein is an unceasing attempt to give a decisive turn to our state of throwness in the world By moving together to design a society. Dasein, then, equates to making decisions about form in order to liberate ourselves from the arbitrariness of life." Lastly, paraphrasing Nietzsche, we can see this as a throw of the dice on the table of the gods.[25]

Notes

Prologue

1. Francis Bowen, *The Metaphysics of Sir William Hamilton, Collected, Arranged, and Abridged for the Use of Colleges and Private Students* (Cambridge, MA: Sever and Francis, 1863), pp. viii, 40–59, 563. doi: 10.1037/12181-003.
2. See page 7 in Emery Petchauer, *Hip-Hop Culture in College Students' Lives* (New York: Routledge, 2012).
3. This phrase, meaning to elevate ones image to self and others, was made popular by a rapper named Soulja-boy in his single "Turn my Swag on" from the album iSouljaBoyTellem. Interscope Records (2008).

Introduction

1. See W. E. B. DuBois' Forethought in *Souls of Black Folk* (New York: Dover Thrift Editions, 1994 [1903]) where this phrase was borrowed.
2. Benedict Anderson. *Imagined Communities: Reflections on the Origin and Spread of Nationalism* (New York: Verso Books, 2006).
3. Bertrand Russell. *History of Western Philosophy* (London: George Allen & Unwin, 1962), p. 13.
4. I see first-order questions as dealing with the absolutes, as in Plato's Forms in which the observable instance, the empirical phenomenon, is an instance of an abstract concept. These often are metaphysical questions about the existence, the reality, the universe, the reality of life, and of matters related to the mind. While second-order is phenomenological and based on our experiences within the world.
5. C. Janeaway. "Plato," in *Routledge Companion to Aesthetics*, D. Lopes and B. Gaut (eds.) (New York: Routledge, 2000), p. 3.
6. Immanuel Kant. *Fundamental Principles of the Metaphysics of Morals* (Gutenberg Project, 2004), p. 2.

7. Ibid., p. 5.
8. Theodor Adorno. *The Culture Industry: Selected Essays on Mass Culture* (New York: Routledge, 2001).
9. Simon During. "Introduction," in *The Cultural Studies Reader*, 2nd ed., Simon During (ed.) (New York: Routledge, 1999), p. 20.
10. Dick Hebdige. *Subculture: The Meaning of Style* (London: Methuen, 1979).
11. During, "Introduction," p. 25.
12. F. R. Leavis. *The Great Tradition* (New York: George W. Stewart, 1950).
13. bell hooks. "A Revolution of Values," *The Cultural Studies Reader*, 2nd ed., Simon During (ed.) (New York: Routledge, 1999), p. 237.
14. During, "Introduction," p. 26.
15. Jean-Francois Lyotard. *The Postmodern Condition: A Report on Knowledge*, Geoff Bennington and Brian Massumi (trans.) (Minneapolis: University of Minnesota Press, 1984), pp. xxiv–xxv.
16. G. W. F. Hegel. *Introductory Lectures on Aesthetics*, B. Bosanquet (trans.) (New York: Penguin, 2004), p. 3.
17. Slavoj Zizek. *Less Than Nothing: Hegel and the Shadow of Dialectical Materialism* (New York: Verso, 2012), p. 28.
18. Jurgen Habermas. *The Structural Transformation of the Public Sphere: An Enquiry into a Category of Bourgeois Society*, Thomas Burger (trans.) (Cambridge: MIT Press, 1991), p. 87.
19. Akilah N. Folami, "From Habermas to 'Get Rich or Die Trying': Hip Hop, The Telecommunications Act of 1996, and the Black Public Sphere," *Michigan Journey of Race and Law* (June 2007): 240.
20. Guy DeBord. *The Art of The Spectacle* (New York: Zone Books, 1995).
21. There are some signs that conscious hip-hop and radio airwaves are not (or at least don't have to be) diametrically opposed. The recent commercial success of Macklemore and Ryan Lewis's album, *The Heist*, shows that enlightened artists don't have to sacrifice their independence or compromise their principles to find success.
22. Qtd. in David Thorpe. "Chuck D," *Bomb* 68 (Summer 1999), available at: http://bombsite.com/issues/68/articles/2251. Accessed November 15, 2013.
23. Jay-Z. *Decoded* (New York: Spiegel & Grau, 2010), p. 16.
24. Qtd. in Thorpe, "Chuck D."
25. Macklemore and Ryan Lewis. "Same Love," *The Heist* (Seattle: Macklemore, 2012).
26. The tide may slowly be shifting. Pushback from the LGBT community and its sympathizers has brought rivers of red ink for rappers like T.I., 50-Cent, The Game, and, most prominently,

Eminem for their use of homophobic language. Apologies—not defenses—are being issued by many of these artists.

27. R. Niebuhr. *Moral Man and Immoral Society: A Study of Ethics and Politics* (Westminster: John Knox Press, 2002), p. 1.

1 Of the Beauty and Wisdom of Hip-Hop

1. W. E. B. Dubois. "Criteria of Negro Art," *The Crisis* 32 (October 1926): 290–297.

2. See John Lingon's piece "How Nina Simone and James Brown Mourned M.L.K. Onstage," available at: www.theatlantic.com /entertainment/archive/2013/04/how-nina-simone-and-james -brown-mourned-mlk-jr-onstage/274605/.

3. In my edited essays Julius Bailey, ed. *Jay-Z: Essays on Hip Hop's Philosopher-King* (Jefferson, NC: McFarland Press, 2011), G. Jahwara Giddings considers hip-hop as an African extension consisting of "core Africanist values." Surely we recognize the griot tradition and the tradition of dance as consistent with many (West) African and Caribbean roots but the urban-ness of the culture, coupled with the social/political ethos is what, more appropriately, roots it squarely within a Harlem Renaissance tradition.

4. Shamontiel. "Hip-hop Pioneers and the History of Rap Music: The Medias Con on Hip-hop Icons," *Yahoo! Contributor Network.* n.d. available at: http://voices.yahoo.com/hip-hop-pioneers-his-tory-rap-music-26563.html.

5. Interview with an Ohio-based graffiti artist on November 10, 2013.

6. Interview with Dante Ross on November 10, 2013.

7. Jonathan Scott posted on April 16, 2011, "Sublimating Hip Hop: Rap Music in White America," February 4, 2014, available at: http://sdonline.org/36/sublimating-hiphop-rap-music-in-white -america/.

8. A line from "Strange Fruit" by Billie Holliday.

9. For a wonderful discussion of block party tradition, see Nelson George's "Hip Hop Founders Speak the Truth," in Murray Forman and Mark Anthony Neal's *That's the Joint* (New York: Routledge, 2011), pp. 43–56.

10. Herc would often buy two copies of a record and stretch the break parts by housing two turntables and mixing in both records before the break ends.

11. At Isandlwana, in 1879, a force of 20,000 Zulu, armed almost exclusively with traditional spears and shields, crushed a force of 1,800 British soldiers armed with state-of-the-art weaponry. Though the British soon brought in reinforcements and within a year had utterly

defeated the Zulu kingdom, Isandlwana remains a symbol of anti-colonialist resistance. In choosing to name themselves after these ultimate resisters, the Zulu Nation were staking their claim and clearly announcing their position in regards to their oppressors. The Zulu of 1879 had been defending their culture against an oppressive invader; those of 1973 could be seen as conquered by their oppression, but their choice of name stated their intention to push back against that oppression—if need be, with force.

12. The Notorious B.I.G., "Mo Money Mo Problems," *Life After Death* (Bad Boy Records, July 21, 1997).

13. "A Brief History of Hip-hop and Rap," by Henry Adaso, (September 2013), available at: http://rap.about.com/od/rootsofraphiphop/p/RootsOfRap.htm.

14. Murray Forman and Mark Anthony Neal (eds). *That's the Joint* (New York: Routledge, 2011); Bakari Kitwana. *The Hip-Hop Generation: Young Blacks and the Crisis in African-American Culture* (New York: Basic Civitas, 2003); Jeffrey, O. G. Ogbar. *Hip-Hop Revolution: The Culture and Politics of Rap* (Lawrence: University Press of Kansas, 2007).

15. For a fascinating, booze-fuelled ramble through the practices that inspired Elvis's hip thrusts and pelvis swivels, see Levon Helm's discussion in Scorsese's *The Last Waltz*.

16. Bakari Kitwana quoted in "Explaining White Hip-hop Fans" by Michelle Yankson (2008). *The Michigan Daily,* February 6, 2008. William (Billy) Wimsatt's book, *Bomb the Suburbs* (Berkeley, CA: Soft Skull Press, 1999) is a staple in my classroom along with Kitwana's *Why White Kids Love Hip Hop* (New York: Basic Civitas, 2006).

17. As quoted in Bill Dotson's "Expanding the Definition of Hip-hop Culture," *USC News,* 2007, available at: www.usc.edu/uscnews/stories/14379.html.

18. Bakari Kitwana quoted in "Explaining White Hip-hop Fans" by Michelle Yankson in *The Michigan Daily,* February 6, 2008.

19. Movies like *White Boyz* (1999) or the character played by Jamie Kennedy in *Malibu's Most Wanted* (2003) highlight a sort of "Blackface" that to some may be a slap in the face to that ethos that birthed the culture. White suburban housewives taking hip-hop dance classes, putting hip-hop on a par with Jane Fonda workouts also emits that air of misappropriation.

20. See Jeff Chang. *Can't Stop Won't Stop: A History of the Hip Hop Generation* (New York: St. Martin's Press, 2005) and Forman and Neal, *That's the Joint.*

21. Ibid.

22. Forman and Neal, *That's the Joint,* p. 3.

23. Ice Cube is credited for the creation of *The Friday* movies (1995, 2000, 2002), *Dangerous Ground* (1997), *The Players Club* (1998),

All about the Benjamins (2002), *Barbershop* (2004), *Beauty Shop* (2005), *Are We There Yet?* (2005), and *Are We Done Yet?* (2005).

24. Roman Cooper, "DMC Lashes Out at Jay Z & Lil Wayne, Jay Z & Dame Dash Reunite," August 10, 2013, available at: www .hiphopdx.com/index/news/id.24993/title.the-hip-hop-week-in -review-dmc-lashes-out-at-jay-z-lil-wayne-jay-z-dame-dash-reunite.

2 Firebrands and Battle Plans: Jean-Paul Sartre, Friedrich Nietzsche, and G. W. F. Hegel

1. Jean-Paul Sartre. "The Black Orpheus," *The Massachussets Review*, John MacCombie (trans.) 6(1) (1964–1965): 18.
2. Ibid., p. 20.
3. James Spady. "IMA Put My Thing Down: Afro American Expressive Culture and the Hip Hop Community," in *TYANABA: Revue de la Societe d'Anthropologie* (Decembre, 1993): 93–98.
4. Sartre. "The Black Orpheus," p. 53.
5. Ibid., pp. 21–26.
6. Ibid., p. 21.
7. Jean-Paul Sartre. "Preface" by Frantz Fanon. *The Wretched of the Earth*, Richard Philcox (trans.) (New York: Grove, 2004), p. xlviii.
8. Jeff Chang. *Can't Stop Won't Stop: A History of the Hip Hop Generation* (New York: St. Martin's Press, 2005), p. 49.
9. Ibid., p. 73.
10. Peter Shapiro. *Rough Guide to Hip Hop*, 2nd ed. (London: Rough Guides, 2005), p. 401.
11. This idea has been explored by a number of twentieth-century continental philosophers: Wittgenstein, Heidegger, Quine, all of them made entity dependent on identity. An identity is created from the practice of naming, that is, a performative act that reiterates the particular signifiers generating the contextual structure. West African Naming patterns share a similar process by divining the newborn into its essence based on the familial influence and circumstances of the birth.
12. Friedrich Nietzsche. *The Antichrist* (Mineola, NY: Tribeca Books, 2010), p. 18.
13. Friedrich Nietzsche. *The Gay Science* Walter Kaufman (trans.) (New York: Vintage, 1974), p. 87.
14. John P. Pittman. "'Y'all Niggaz Better Recognize': Hip Hop's Dialectical Struggle for Recognition," in *Hip-Hop and Philosophy: Rhyme 2 Reason*, Derrick Darby, Tommie Shelby, and William Irwin (eds.) (Peru, IL: Carus, 2005), p. 47.
15. G. W. F. Hegel. "Lordship and Bondage," *The Phenomenology of Mind* (New York: Dover Books, 2003).

16. Relatively recently, critics have begun to connect this tenet of
    Hegel's philosophy with a coded rejection of theism (God/master
    being entirely dependent on the faith of the believers/slaves). The
    reasons for coding his atheism in this way are obvious enough
    when you consider the treatment religious authorities afforded his
    predecessors, Spinoza and Kant.
17. Jay-Z. "Takeover," *The Blueprint* (Roc-a-Fella Records, released
    September 11, 2001).
18. Lil B. "G.O.R. (God of Rap)."
19. Lou Benny. "Dobar Rep," available at: www.youtube.com/watch?v
    =DHEmQqgojV0.
20. Ibid.
21. Lou Benny. "Neman a cemu."
22. Lou Benny. "Nemoj da stajes," available at: www.youtube.com
    /watch?v=9Uv0_Lt1NqA.
23. Blackalicious. "Searching," *Nia* (released by Quannum, February 8,
    2000).
24. Blackalicious. "Ego Trip by Nikki Giovanni." *Nia* (released by
    Quannum February 8, 2000).
25. Blackalicious. "Searching." *Nia* (released by Quannum, February 8,
    2000).

3 Conscious Hip-Hop versus the Culture Industry

1. Greg Tate. "Hiphop Turns 30: Whacha Celebratin' For?" *The
   New York Village Voice*. December 28, 2004, accessed September
   19, 2013, available at: www.villagevoice.com/2004-12-28/news
   /hiphop-turns-30/.
2. Notwithstanding the fact that, in some respects the term conscious is quite the ambiguous term, this is, of course, only a small
   sampling of conscious hip-hop artists, many of whom have been
   credited with preserving the fiercely independent spirit of hip-hop.
3. "Making it rain" is the throwing of money into the air and onto
   women, an action usually performed in strip clubs. On a limited
   budget and in a more private setting, ejaculate can be substituted
   for cash.
4. For a particularly powerful articulation of the tenets of the philosophy of hip-hop as a lived culture, see: KRS-One. *The Gospel of
   Hip-Hop: The First Instrument* (New York: Powerhouse, 2009).
5. Abe Daudi. "Hip-Hop and the Academic Canon," *Education,
   Citizenship and Social Justice* 263(4), (2009): 268.
6. Carol S. Dweck. "Prejudice: How If Develops and How It Can Be
   Undone." *Human Development* 52 (2009): 371–376.

7. Mohammed Addow. "Nigeria's Dangerous Skin Whitening Obsession." *Al Jazeera*. April 6, 2013, available at: www.aljazeera.com/indepth/features/2013/04/20134514845907984.html.
8. Theodor Adorno and Max Horkeimer. *Dialectic of Enlightenment: Philosophical Fragments*, Edmund Jephcott (trans.) (Stanford, CA: Stanford University Press, 2007), p. 94.
9. Ibid., p. 107.
10. Ibid., p. 99.
11. Ibid., p. 109.
12. Ibid., p. 96.
13. Friedrich Nietzsche, "Twilight of the Idols," in *Portable Nietzsche*, Walter Kaufman (trans.) (New York: Random House, 1966), aph. 24.
14. This is, of course, gangsta rap.
15. "White House Invite of Political Rapper Stirs Controversy." *Fox News*. May 10, 2011, available at: www.foxnews.com/politics/2011/05/10/white-house-invite-political-rapper-stirs-controversy/.
16. Melissa Bell. "Common Putting the Controversy in White House Poetry Night." *The Washington Post*. May 11, 2011, available at: www.washingtonpost.com/blogs/blogpost/post/white-house-poetry-night-whats-your-favorite-poem/2011/05/11/AFmpVUqG_blog.html.
17. *Look to the Stars: The World of Celebrity Giving*. May 15, 2013, available at: www.looktothestars.org/ celebrity/common#charities.
18. John McWhorter. "How Hip-Hop Holds Blacks Back," *The City Journal* (Summer 2003), available at: www.city-journal.org/html/13_3_how_hip_hop.html.
19. Pierre Perrone. "Camouflage: A Gangster Rapper in Search of a 'Universal Language.'" *The Independent*. May 24, 2003 available at: www.independent.co.uk/news/obituaries/camoflauge-730322.html.
20. Ibid.
21. The Hip-hop declaration of Peace, available at: http://www.thetika.com/the-hip-hop-declaration-of-peace/.
22. Ibid.
23. "krs One Speaks about Philosophy and the Origins of Hip-Hop," YouTube video, 1:24:55, posted by Tipman2000 (September 17, 2011), available at: www.youtube.com/watch?v=SBrlvOmxU6g.
24. Anthony Thomas. "The Spirit and Philosophy of Hip-Hop," *The New Statesman*. September 12, 2007, available at: www.newstatesman.com/blogs/the-faith-column/2007/09/hip-hop-movements-thought.

4 Toward a Philosophy of Hip-Hop Education

1. A recent report in *USA Today* found that "just 26% of [American] high school graduates in the class of 2013 met college readiness benchmarks in all four of the subjects its tests cover: English, reading, math and science." Mary Beth Marklein. "Test Scores Flat, Raising Concerns About Students' Readiness." *USA TODAY,* (September 26, 2013), available at: www.usatoday.com /story/news/nation/2013/09/26/high-school-sat-scores-flat -for-college/2873633/.
2. Charles J. Sykes, *Dumbing Down Our Kids: Why America's Children Feel Good about Themselves but Can't Read, Write, or Add* (New York: St. Martin's Griffin, 1995), pp. 143–151.
3. Thanks to Emery Petchauer for his insistence that there is a valid and crucial critique to bare here and this may be too simple of a statement while feeding into various "panic arguments." Further he points to the work of Diane Ravitch, *The Reign of Error* (New York: Knoff, 2013) and *The Death and Life of the Great American School System* (New York: Basic, 2010) who has devastatingly shown all similar comparisons are negligible if they're not based upon the NAEP (National Assessment of Educational Progress) test. Further that this neglect was a big flaw of the movie *Waiting for Superman.*
4. C. Emdin. "Reality Pedagogy: Hip-Hop Culture and the Urban Science Classroom," in *Science Education from People for People: Taking a Standpoint*, W. M. Roth (ed.), (New York: Routledge, 2009), pp. 70–89.
5. John Dewey. *Experience and Education: The 60th Anniversary Edition* (Indianapolis: Kappa Delta Pi, 1998), p. 15.
6. W. E. B. Dubois. *The Souls of Black Folk* (New York: Dover Thrift Editions, 1994), p. 2.
7. Earnest Morrell. "Toward a Critical Pedagogy of Popular Culture," *Journal of Adolescent and Adult Literacy* 46(1) (September 2002): 72–73.
8. Ibid., p. 73.
9. H. S. Alim. "Critical Language Awareness in the United States: Revisiting Issues and Revising Pedagogies in a Resegregated Society," *Educational Researcher* 34(7) (2005): 24–31; H. S. Alim, "Hip Hop Nation Language," in *Linguistic Anthropology: A Reader* A. Duranti (ed.) (Malden, MA: Wiley Blackwell, 2009), pp. 272–289; H. S. Alim and A. Pennycook. "Glocal Linguistic Flows: Hip-Hop Culture(s), Identities, and the Politics of Language Education," *Journal of Language, Identity, and Education* 6(2) (2007): 89–100; E. Richardson, *Hip Hop Literacies* (New York: Routledge, 2006).
10. Vershawn Ashanti Young. "'Nah, We Straight': An Argument Against Code Switching," *JAC* 29(1), (2009): 63–65.

11. Ibid., p. 65.

12. See Elaine Richardson and Samy Alim who are important here as they see hip-hop, especially the freestyle, is instantaneously creative, It is improvised—some instances of this produce remarkable poetry. But we cannot omit the traditionally received methods of instruction, based on memorization and recitation, are also prevalent in the art form (see Ice-T film documentary "Something from Nothing: The Art of Hip Hop" [2012], and Emery Petchauer. *Hip Hop in College Students' Lives.* [New York: Routledge 2011]).

13. Cited from Dead Prez. "They School," *Let's Get Free* (Loud Records, 2000).

14. Allen N. Smith. "No One Has a Right to His Own Language." *CCC* 27(2) (1976): 155.

15. Special thanks to Dr. Bettina Love for pointing this out to me.

16. Allan Bloom. *The Closing of the American Mind* (New York: Simon & Schuster, 1987), p. 75.

17. Noam Chomsky. *Understanding Power,* Peter R. Mitchell and John Schoeffels (ed.) (New York: The New Press, 2002), p. 233.

18. Such critiques are frequent enough to be a commonplace in spite of the fact that statistical evidence shows that violent crime, since its peak in the early 1990s, has been in a pattern of nearly uniform decline in nearly every category. FBI. "Crime in the United States by Volume and Rate per 100,000 Inhabitants, 1993–2012," *Federal Bureau of Investigation,* accessed June 2013, available at: www.fbi.gov/about-us/cjis/ucr/crime-in-the-u.s/2012/crime-in-the-u.s.-2012/tables/1tabledatadecoverviewpdf/table_1_crime_in_the_united_states_by_volume_and_rate_per_100000_inhabitants_1993–2012.xls#overview

19. Henry A. Giroux and Roger I. Simon. "Schooling, Popular Culture, and a Pedagogy of Possibility," *Journal of Education* 170(1) (1988): 11–20.

20. Ibid., p. 20.

21. Iain Chambers. "Popular Culture, Popular Knowledge," *One Two Three Four: A Rock and Roll Quarterly* (1989): 1–8.

22. See Marc L. Hill (2013) and David Stovall. "We Can Relate: Hip-Hop Culture, Critical Pedagogy and the Secondary Classroom." *Urban Education* 41(6), (2006): 585–602. For we educators often use the kind of hip-hop like in the classroom, thus replicating a different kind of canon. We all can re-canonize if we begin to reify our "appreciation" and denigrate, implicitly through omittance, that which speaks to the students.

23. G. Ladson-Billings. "Toward a Theory of Culturally Relevant Pedagogy," *American Educational Research Journal* 32 (1995): 465–491.

24. Carol Lee. *The Role of Culture in Academic Literacies: Conducting Our Blooming in the Midst of the Whirlwind* (New York: Teachers College Press, 2007) Also Carol Lee. "A Culturally Based Cognitive Apprenticeship: Teaching African American High School Students Skills in Literary Interpretation," *Reading Research Quarterly* 30(4) (1995, 2007): 608–631.

25. C. Emdin "Moving Beyond the Boat without a Paddle: Reality Pedagogy, Black Youth, and Urban Science Education," *The Journal of Negro Education* 80(3) (2011): 284–295.

26. Paris Django. "Culturally Sustaining Pedagogy: A Needed Change in Stance, Terminology, and Practice," *Educational Researcher* 41(3) (April 2012): 93–97.

27. Emory Petchauer. "Framing and Reviewing Hip-Hop Educational Research," *Review of Educational Research* 79(2) (2009): 946.

28. Interview with Bettina Love, November 4, 2013. See also R. N. Brown and C. J. Kwakye. *Wish to Live: The Hip-Hop Feminism Pedagogy Reader* (New York: Peter Lang Publishing, 2012); J. A. Cooks, "Writing for Something: Essays, Raps, and Writing Preferences," *English Journal* (2004): 72–76; Emdin, "Moving beyond the Boat," pp. 284–295; C. Emdin and Knee Lee. "Hip-Hop, the 'Obama Effect', and Urban Science Education," *Teachers College Record* 114(2) (2012): 1–24; Shawn Ginwright. *Black in School* (New York: Teachers College Press, 2004); David Kirkland. "'The Rose That Grew from Concrete': Postmodern Blackness and New English Education," *English Journal* 97(5) (2008): 69–75; E. Morrell and J. Duncan-Andrade. "Toward a Critical Classroom Discourse: Promoting Academic Literacy Through Engaging Hip-Hop Culture with Urban Youth." *English Journal* 91(6) (2002): 88–92; E. Richardson. *Hip Hop Literacies* (New York: Routledge, 2006); Stovall, "We Can Relate," pp. 585–602.

29. C. Emdin. "Pursuing the Pedagogical Potential of the Pillars of Hip-Hop through Urban Science Education," *The International Journal of Critical Pedagogy* 4(3) (2013): 83–97.

30. Earnest Morrell. "Toward a Critical Pedagogy of Popular Culture," *Journal of Adolescent and Adult Literacy* 46(1) (2002): 74.

31. A. A. Akom. "Critical Hip Hop Pedagogy as a Form of Liberatory Praxis." *Equity & Excellence in Education* 42(1) (2009): 52–66; Julius Bailey. "Hip Hop's Stronghold on 21st Century Philosophical Analysis," *International Journal of Africana Studies* (Spring 2011); Brown and Kwakye, *Wish to Live*; Cooks, "Writing for Something," pp. 72–76; Marc L. Hill. "Using Jay-Z to Reflect on Post-9/11 Race Relations," *English Journal* (2006): 23–27.

32. B. L. Love. "Urban Storytelling: How Storyboarding, Moviemaking & Hip Hop-Based Education Can Promote Students' Critical Voice." *English Journal* (in Press).

33. Song is from Jay-Z's *The Black Album* (Roc-A-Fella Records, 2003) and features John Legend. The song later received a Grammy Award with its collaboration with pop group, Linkin Park.
34. Malcom X speaking to young students in Selma, Alabama, February 4, 1965, in a speech that is titled "The Klu Klux Klan Are Cowards," available at: http://vimeo.com/58923092 and http://wn.com/malcolm_x_on_klan_cowards.
35. Regina N. Bradley. "Contextualizing Hip Hop Sonic Cool Pose in Late Twentieth – and Twenty-first Century Rap Music," *Current Musicology* 93 (Spring 2013).

5 Lost in the City and Lost in the Self: Sin and Solipsism in Hip-Hop's Dystopia; St. Augustine, Toni Morrison, and Paul Tillich

1. G. Dimitriadis. *Performing Identity/Performing Culture: Hip Hop as Text, Pedagogy, and Lived Practice,* rev. ed. (New York: Peter Lang Publishing, Inc., 2009).
2. Ibid.
3. M. E. Dyson, *Know What I Mean? Reflections on Hip Hop* (Philadelphia: Basic Civitas Books, 2007).
4. W. Urichio. *The Batman's Gotham City (TM): Story, Ideology, Performance*, in *Comics and the City: Urban Space in Print, Picture and Sequence*, Jorn Ahrens and Arno Meteling (eds.) (Maiden Lane, NY: The Continuum International Publishing Group Inc, 2010).
5. Ibid.
6. Ibid.
7. Ibid.
8. For the claim of 'Ad, see Nicholas Clapp. *The Road to Ubar: Finding the Atlantis of the Sands,* (Boston, MA: Houghton Mifflin, 1998). (Though many doubt this is in fact 'Ad, but represents a city buried in the desert.)
9. For eruption in 1628 BCE, see Jan Heinemeier, Walter L. Friedrich, and David Warbuton, eds., *Time's Up: Dating the Minoan Eruption of Santorini. Acts of the Minoan Eruption Chronology Workshop Sandberg November 2007* (Athens: Danish Institute at Athens, 2009).
10. For Thera see: Christos Doumas. *Thera: Pompeii of the Ancient Aegean* (London: Thames and Hudson, 1983).
11. What seems clear to Dr. Brooks Hedstrom is that "Plato, himself, could not have known of this city. The archaeological and geological study of Santorini and the environmental impact of the eruption on the wider Mediterranean world has demonstrated that localized disturbances, such as earthquakes and volcanic eruptions can and did impact communities around the Mediterranean Basin" (written interview notes, July 3, 2013).

12. National Geographic often sponsors documentaries on various expeditions. This is one on the work in Spain, available at: http://channel.nationalgeographic.com/channel/episodes/finding-atlantis/. A news article on the same is available at: http://news.bbc.co.uk/2/hi/science/nature/3766863.stm.

13. Interview notes provided by a colleague of Antiquities, Dr. Darlene Brooks-Hedstrom (July 3, 2013).

14. See Robert Sarmast. *Discovery of Atlantis: The Startling Case for the Island of Cyprus* (San Rafael, CA: Origin Press, 2004); Also refer Martin Bernal. *Black Athena: The Afroasiatic Roots of Classical Civilization* (New Brunswick, NJ: Rutgers University Press, 1987).

15. Darlene Brooks Hedstrom suggests this article is about recent discoveries in Egypt of a port city totally submerged. Available at: www.telegraph.co.uk/earth/environment/archaeology/10022628/Lost-city-of-Heracleion-gives-up-its-secrets.html. Works on environmental history related to antiquity. These are good sources for environmental archaeology. Liba Taub. *Ancient Meterology* (London: Routledge, 2003); Bill McGuire et al. eds., *The Archaeology of Geological Catastrophes* (London: Geological Society, 2000), covers a whole spectrum of sites.

16. Sarmast, *Discovery of Atlantis*. See also Bernal, *Black Athena*.

17. According to Dr. Brooks Hedstrom: "The truth of Atlantis is likely more in the general idea of Mediterranean cities being greatly affected by environmental changes and disappearing either entirely or being abandoned as residents found new homes. This was certainly the case for the inhabitants of Santorini. They had enough time, apparently, to take all their possessions with them and leave the island in 1628 BCE. The inhabitants in Pompeii and Herculaneum in 79 CE were not so fortunate. Despite experiencing earlier earthquakes on the Italian coast, a large portion of the population in both cities was unable to escape the toxic fumes from the volcano and died while running away" (interview notes, July 3, 2013).

18. *Republic* by Plato, trans. G. M. A. Grube (Indianapolis: Hackett Pulishing, 1992).

19. National Geographic often sponsors documentaries on various expeditions. This is one on the work in Spain available at: http://channel.nationalgeographic.com/channel/episodes/finding-atlantis/.

20. One ostensible example of this paradox would be the track's explicit approach to drug culture. While some citizens of Sin City profit immensely (in CyHi's case, drug dealing has provided him with the resources to have a "house as a stash spot" as well as a luxury car, a "Lexus coupe with the rag-top"), others are ravaged

by drug use: Scott's girlfriend, an apparent cocaine addict, "can't eat right," and CyHi notes that many dreams that were born in "glass pots" end in the "state pen."

21. St. Augustine. *The City of God*, Part III, Book IX, G. Walsh, G. Monahan (eds.) (New York: Image Books, 1950), Chapter 1, p. 206.
22. Romans 7:15–19.
23. Augustine, *The City of God*.
24. The Sophists would be exemplary of such epistemological skepticism, which justifies amoral choice.
25. Karl Rahner. *Spiritual Exercises,* Kenneth Baker (trans.) (New York: Herder and Herder, 1965).
26. See various writings by Karl Marx, Sigmeund Freud, Frederick Nietzche, and Jean Paul Sartre.
27. Johannes Baptist Metz and Matthew Ashley James. *a Passion for God: the Mystical-Political Dimension of Christianity* (New York: Paulist Press, 1998).
28. Kanye West. "Jesus Walks," *College Dropout* (Roc-a-Fella, February 10, 2004), CD.
29. James Strong, *The New Strong's Expanded Exhaustive Concordance of the Bible* (Nashville: Thomas Nelson, 2010), p. 16.
30. The verb form of the noun Harmartia.
31. A note for clarification: I realize that the entire world system *(kosmos* in the Greek) is fallen because of sin. Sin brings death. It must be understood that from the Christian perspective, theologically we battle the flesh (or sin nature), and desire to live by the Spirit (spiritual nature); however, this does not mean that Christians, obviously have two natures, since they have been regenerated they claim a new nature (2 Cor 5:17) and merely battle the flesh (Mk 14:38). Furthermore, every human, as a son of Adam, is dead in their sin, which is why a metaphysical rebirth must take place in order for salvation to occur that is imputed from Christ (John 3, 2 Cor 5:21). When that metaphysical rebirth occurs, we no longer are tenants of the earth *(kosmos)*, but are citizens of heaven (Phil 3:20) and are aliens to the world (1 Pt 2:11). With that being said, I'm merely making the physical distinction that everyone living on earth is a resident of Kanye West's "Sin City" inasmuch as the entire world system is fallen (no one has a monopoly on sin, violence, etc.), even though St. Augustine was obviously saved, Kanye West, and the other individuals that we have hitherto discussed, are obviously not.
32. St. Augustine. *Confessions* (Mineola, NY: Dover Publications, 2002), p. 142.
33. St. Augustine. *City of God,* Vol. 1 (London: T&T Clark Publishing, 1888), p. 11.

34. Thanks to Rev. Dr. Charles Montgomery for that clarification as we discussed this matter.
35. Timothy G. McCarthy. *The Catholic Tradition: The Church in the Twentieth Century* (Chicago: Loyola Press, 1998).
36. Paul Tillich. *Love, Power, and Justice: Ontological Analyses and Ethical Applications* (New York: Oxford University Press, 1960), p. 112–113.
37. Nature appears, for Aristotle, as a cause (of movement, and of action in sentient beings) Bertrand Russell. *History of Western Philosophy* (London: George Allen & Unwin, 1962), p. 206.
38. For Socrates, when one insists that humans want simply to do what they please, without necessary moral considerations, his reply would be: based on what does one decides what one should do? It is precisely at this point that Socrates is able to turn the issue into one that cannot but force us to make a reflection on why we want what we want, and whether what we want is, in fact, opinion or knowledge. Heda Segvic. *From Protagoras to Aristotle: Essays in Ancient Moral Philosophy* (Princeton, NJ: Princeton University Press, 2006), p. 174. The *nature* of any activity, furthermore, is qualified by the goals that are desirable and by what is needed to achieve them. H. A. Kamtekar. *Companion to Socrates* (Blackwell Companions to Philosophy). (Hoboken: Wiley-Blackwell, 2006), p. 221.
39. Based, for example, on the natural character of the Polis, Aristotle explains its essence by discussing that good, which is proper to its function in the natural order of things (Aristotle. *Politics*, 1252a1–1252a8 in Ernest Barker, revised by Richard Stalley (Oxford: Oxford University Press, 1995).
40. Allusion to Shakespearian tragedy.
41. An allusion to Shakespeare's *Hamlet*, on moral corruption.

6 Hip-Hop and International Voices of Revolution: Brazil, Cuba, Ghana, and Egypt

1. R. James Ferguson., "Political Realism, Ideology and Power: A Discussion and Critique via Machiavelli, Morgenthau and Sun Tzu," 2004, available at: www.international-relations.com/History/Machiavelli.htm, accessed August 14, 2013.
2. Shawn Carter aka Jay-Z in Michael E. Dyson. *You're Listening to a Sample of the Audible Audio Edition. Learn More Know What i Mean? Reflections on Hip-Hop* (New York: Basic Civitas, 2007)
3. R. Posner "Post-Modernism, Post-Structuralism, Post-Semiotics? Sign Theory at the Fin De Siècle," *Semiotica*. ISSN. 2011 (183) (March 2011): 9–30. doi: 10.1515/semi.2011.002.

4. Consider songs like "So Many Tears" and "Blasphemy" where Tupac challenges religious authority and asks God to take pain away from a rugged condition. There is certainly a spiritual core to Tupac that affects his political views.

5. M. Morgan and D. Bennett. "Hip Hop and the Global Imprint of a Black Cultural Form," *American Academy of Arts & Sciences* (2011): 176–196.

6. D. P. Aldridge. "From Civil Rights to Hip Hop: Toward a Nexus of Ideas," *The Journal of African American History* (2005): 226–252.

7. See Fat Sam interview in Nicholas Mangialardi, "Egyptian Hip Hop and the January 25th Revolution." Thesis. The Ohio State University, 2013.

8. Ibid.

9. See Nicholas Mangialardi, "Egyptian Hip Hop and the January 25th Revolution," Thesis. The Ohio State University, 2013.

10. Hass Re-Volt. "Interview: Rebel through Hip Hop," 2011, available at: http://mashallahnews.com/?p=1640.

11. See Mark LeVine's *Heavy Metal Islam* (New York: Three Rivers Press, 2008) for more on the heavymetal's popularity in the region.

12. Cited in M. Asante. *It's Bigger Than Hip Hop: The Rise of the Post-Hip-Hop Generation* (New York: St. Martin's Press, 2008), p. 110.

13. See Christopher Vourlias' "Pidgin English Helps Rappers' Musical Fly," *Variety*, 422(3) (February 28, 2011): 3.

14. Vanessa Arrington, "Party Or Protest? Cuban Hip-Hop Reaches Crossroads in Its Young History," AP News, 2004, available at: www.latinamericanstudies.org/cuba/hip-hop-04.htm.

15. Ibid.

7 The Artist and the Image: Ervin Goffman, Marshall McLuhan, and Roland Barthes

1. Guy DeBord. *The Art of The Spectacle* (New York: Zone Books, 1995).

2. Benjamin Fink. *The Lacanian Subject.* (New Jersey: Princeton University Press, 1996); Jacques Lacan, *The Seminar of Jacques Lacan: Freud's Papers on Technique.* Vol. Book I (New York: W. W. Norton & Company, 1991).

3. John Durham. *Speaking into the Air: A History of the Idea of Communication* (Chicago: University of Chicago Press, 2001).

4. g. Deleuze and f. Guattari. *Anti-Oedipus: Capitalism and Schizophrenia* Huxley R., Seem M., and Lane H. R. (trans.) (Minneapolis: University of Minnesota Press, 2008).

5. K. McLeod. "Authenticity within Hip-hop and Other Cultures Threatened with Assimilation," *Journal of Communication* 49(4) (1999): 134–150. Accessed June, 2013. doi:10.1111/j.1460-2466.1999.tb02821.x.

6. H. Samy Alim. "On Some Serious Next Millennium Rap Ishhh Pharoahe Monch, Hip Hop Poetics, and the Internal Rhymes of Internal Affairs," *Journal of English Linguistics* 31(1) (March 1, 2003): 60–84. doi:10.1177/0075424202250619; Bradley. *Book of Rhymes: The Poetics of Hip Hop* (New York: Basic Books, 2009); William J Cobb. *To the Break of Dawn: A Freestyle on the Hip Hop Aesthetic* (New York: New York University Press, 2007).

7. As Tricia Rose has pointed out, a comprehensive analysis of hip-hop that *only* focuses on lyricism can in effect denigrate the musical innovations of the form, particularly important for their rootedness in African diasporic traditions of rhythm and repetition (Tricia Rose. *Black Noise: Rap Music and Black Culture in Contemporary America* [Middleton, CT: Wesleyan, 1994], p. 62). It's also notable that strictly lyrical exegetic approaches to hip-hop can lead to significant misinterpretations of the broader meaning of the music as art is also imagination.

8. George Lipsitz. "The Hip Hop Hearings: Censorship, Social Memory, and Intergenerational Tensions Among African Americans," in *Generations of Youth: Youth Cultures and History in Twentieth Century America* (New York: New York University Press, 1998), pp. 395–411; Cheryl L. Keyes. *Rap Music and Street Consciousness* (Champaign: University of Illinois Press, 2004), p 2; Jeanita W. Richardson and Kim A. Scott. "Rap Music and Its Violent Progeny: America's Culture of Violence in Context," *Journal of Negro Education* 71(3) (2002): 175–192. doi:10.2307/3211235.

9. Mickey Hess. "Hip Hop Realness and the White Performer," *Critical Studies in Media Communication* 22(5) (December 1, 2005): 372–389.

10. Keyes, *Rap Music and Street Consciousness*; B. N. Kopano. "Rap Music as an Extension of the Black Rhetorical Tradition: 'Keepin' It Real,'" *Western Journal of Black Studies* 26(4) (2002): 204–214; K. McLeod. "Authenticity Within Hip-hop and Other Cultures Threatened with Assimilation," *Journal of Communication* 49(4) (1999): 134–150. Accessed June 2013. doi:10.1111/j.1460-2466.1999.tb02821.x.

11. Shakur's story is another parable of the complexities of discourses of authenticity. Raised by a politically hyper-engaged mother, and clearly a thoughtful, even introspective person, Shakur was consumed by the performance of a "thug life" that reflected, at best,

only part of his experience and perception; Richard Shusterman. "Rap Aesthetics: Violence and the Art of Keeping It Real," in *Hip-Hop and Philosophy: Rhyme 2 Reason* (Chicago/La Salle: Open Court Publishing, 2005), p. 54.

12. Hess, "Hip Hop Realness and the White Performer," pp. 372–389.
13. The Smoking Gun. "Screw Rick Ross," *The Smoking Gun.* July 21, 2008, available at: www.thesmokinggun.com/documents/crime/screw-rick-ross.
14. Francis Waterhouse. "Romantic 'Originality,'" *The Sewanee Review* 34(1) (January 1926): 40–49; Jessica Millen. "Romantic Creativity and the Ideal of Originality: A Contextual Analysis," *Cross-Sections, The Bruce Hall Academic Journal* VI (2010) 91–105; Forest Pyle. *The Ideology of Imagination: Subject and Society in the Discourse of Romanticism* (California: Stanford University Press, 1995).
15. Aidan Day. *Romanticism* (London and New York: Routledge, 1996), p. 4.
16. In 2008 records were exposed on the Internet that showed William L. Roberts (aka Rick Ross) as a corrections officer and not a historic gangster. This hypocrisy, with his musical lyrics initially led him to deny the charge (for street credibility) but later he had to admit to the truth. See Shaheem Reid, "Rick Ross Reaffirms Gangster Past In New Freestyle, Despite Report That He Worked As Prison Guard," MTV News, July 22, 2008. accessed August 5, 2008.
17. It is particularly interesting how Ross's story parallels that of Vanilla Ice, with investigative journalists digging up evidence to the "falsehood" of their artistic personae.
18. Roland Barthes. *Image-Music-Text,* Stephen Heath (trans.) (New York: Hill and Wang, 1978), p. 144.
19. Michel Foucault. "What Is an Author?" in *Societe Francais de Philosophie* (1969), accessed June, 2013. available at: https://wiki.brown.edu/confluence/download/attachments/74858352/FoucaultWhatIsAnAuthor.pdf.
20. Franz Boas. "On Alternating Sounds," *American Anthropologist* A2(1) (1889): 47–54. doi:10.1525/aa.1889.2.1.02a00040; Edward Sapir. "The Status of Linguistics as a Science," *Language* 5(4) (December 1929): 207–214.
21. Ferdinand de Saussure and Roy Harris. *Course in General Linguistics.* Reprint (LaSalle, IL: Open Court, 1998).
22. Michael Lane. *Introduction to Structuralism* (University of Michigan: Basic Books, 1970).
23. Erving Goffman. *The Presentation of Self in Everyday Life.* 1st ed. (New York: Anchor, 1959); James Trevino, (ed). *Goffman's Legacy*

(Oxford: Rowman and Littlefield, 2003). This line of reasoning would ultimately resurface in the work of Judith Butler, who focused on gender and of course added much depot to Goffman's viewpoint.

24. Here "culture" is used in the limited sense to denote texts.
25. Stuart Hall. "Encoding/Decoding," in *The Cultural Studies Reader*, Simon During (ed.) (London: Routledge, 2007), pp. 93–94.
26. Ibid., p. 100.
27. Jacques Lacan. *Ecrits: The First Complete Edition in English*, Bruce Fink (trans.) (New York: W. W. Norton & Company, 2002), p. 139.
28. "The child latches on to what is indecipherable in what the parent says." B. Fink. *The Lacanian Subject* (New Jersey: Princeton University Press, 1996).
29. Lacan, *Ecrits*, p. 6.
30. John P. Muller and William J. Richardson. *The Purloined Poe: Lacan, Derrida, and Psychoanalytic Reading.* 4th Printing (Baltimore, MD: The Johns Hopkins University Press, 1987), p. 21.
31. Reed Fischer. "Danny Brown's Triple Rock Show Sparks Unseemly Oral Sex Controversy," *Gimme Noise.* Accessed April 30, (2013), available at: http://blogs.citypages.com/gimmenoise/2013/04/danny_browns_triple_rock_show_sparks_oral_sex_controversy.php.
32. Kitty Pryde. "My Thoughts on This Whole Danny Brown Oral Sex Thing | NOISEY." *Noisey.* May 1, 2013. Accessed June, 2013, available at: http://noisey.vice.com/blog/my-thoughts-on-this-whole-danny-brown-oral-sex-thing.
33. Shusterman, "Rap Aesthetics."
34. Kitty Rose. *Black Noise: Rap Music and Black Culture in Contemporary America* (Middleton, CT: Wesleyan, 1994), p. 10.
35. Henry Louis Gates. *The Signifying Monkey: A Theory of African-American Literary Criticism* (Oxford: Oxford University Press, 1989).
36. Cheryl L. Keyes. *Rap Music and Street Consciousness* (Champaign, IL: University of Illinois Press. 2004), p. 4.
37. Adam Krims. *Rap Music and the Poetics of Identity* (Cambridge: Cambridge University Press, 2000).
38. Yvonne Bynoe. "Getting Real about Global Hip-Hop," *Georgetown Journal of International Affairs* 3(1) (2004): 77–84.
39. Cheryl Thompson. "Standing in the Shadows of America: Afro-Diasporic Oral Culture and the Emancipation of Canadian Hip-Hop," *Canadian Theatre Review* (130) (2007): 113–116; Ian Condry. *Hip-Hop Japan: Rap and the Paths of Cultural*

Globalization (Durham, NC: Duke University Press, 2006); Christopher Malone and Martinez George. "The Organic Globalizer: The Political Development of Hip-Hop and the Prospects for Global Transformation," *New Political Science* 32 (4) (December 2010): 531–545. doi:10.1080/07393148.2010.520439.
40. Barthes, *Image-Music-Text.*

8   Catastrophe of Success: Marshall McLuhan, Gilles Deleuze, and Felix Guattari

1. There exists an entire side issue here regarding the album's legacy in hip-hop, which may or may not be relevant to this piece in particular. *808's* set off a wave of introspective hip-hop and R&B that moved away from braggadocio and focus on money, and which also sounded both more overtly electronic and more vulnerable. Examples include Kid Cudi, Drake, The Weeknd, and Frank Ocean (cf. Paine, Jake (November 12, 2011). "Parkbench Studies: Is 808's & Heartbreak Our Chronic?" *HipHopDX*; Greg Kot. "Drake Album Review; Take Care Reviewed," *Chicago Tribune*, November 13, 2011.

2. It is not surprising that artists and their life becomes quickly romanticized. Take for instance some of W. Kandinsky's words in his classic work *Concerning the Spiritual in Art* (Mineola, NY: Dover Publications, 1977), where he says about art: "There is no must in art because art is free." And about the artist: "The artist must train not only his eye but also his soul."

3. The artist, for Heidegger (which in his example is Van Gogh), reveals a truth that is not analytical in form, yet is still meaningful and revealing of the human circumstances of the peasant who labors the nineteenth century fields in Holland.

4. Marshall McLuhan. "The Medium Is the Message," in *Media and Cultural Studies Key Works*, G. Durham and L. M. Kellner (eds.) (London: Blackwell Publishing, 2006), p. 108.

5. Ibid., p. 111.

6. Ibid., p. 114.

7. Autistic in the sense of being a process disconnected from social relations—a process that would take place in isolation from societal rules

8. G. Deleuze and F. Guattari. *Anti-Oedipus: Capitalism and Schizophrenia*, R. Huxley, M. Seem, and H. R. Lane (trans.) (Minneapolis: University of Minnesota Press, 2008), p. 33.

9. Ibid., p. 260.

10. "We will say that THE plane of immanence is, at the same time, that which must be thought and that which cannot be thought. It is the nonthought within thought. It is the base of all planes,

immanent to every thinkable plane that does not succeed in thinking it. […] Perhaps this is the supreme act of philosophy: not so much to think THE plane of immanence as to show that it is there, unthought in every plane […]." G. Deleuze and F. Guattari. *What Is Philosophy*, Hugh Tomlinson and Graham Burchell (trans.) (New York: Columbia University Press, 1994), p. 59.

11. Ibid., p. 74.

12. Deleuze and Guattari say of consciousness, for instance: "Let consciousness cease to be its own double, and passion the double of one person to another. Make consciousness an experimentation in life, and passion a field of continuous intensities, an emission of particles-signs." G. Deleuze and F. Guattari. *A Thousand Plateaus: Capitalism and Schizophrenia*, B. Massumi (trans.) (London and New York: Continuum, 1988), p. 134.

13. J. Lyotard. *The Inhuman: Reflections on Time*, G. Bennington and R. Bowlby (trans.) (Cambridge, UK: Polity Press, 1991), p. 106.

14. Deleuze and Guattari, *"Anti-Oedipus,"* p. 88.

15. Ibid., p. 86.

16. Ibid., p. 130.

17. One of Wittgenstein's maxims in the *Tractatus* illustrates this best: "Whereof one cannot speak, thereof one must be silent."

18. F. Jameson. "Postmodernism, Or the Cultural Logic of Late Capitalism," in *Media and Cultural Studies Key Works*, G. Durham and D. M. Keller (eds.) (London, UK: Blackwell Publishing, 2006), p. 492.

19. Henk Oosterling. "Philosophy, Art, and Politics as Interesse," in *Issues in Contemporary Culture and Aesthetics* (Maastricht: Department of Theory, Jan van Eyck Akademie, 1999), p. 95.

20. Ibid., p. 95.

21. Ibid., p. 101.

22. One of my research assistants, Adam Schueler believes that Tyler the Creator's complete renovation of his style represents his authenticity—not only does he break away from the apparent ever-present temptation to return to his previous material, which largely represents his alternate persona, "Wolf Haley." In this light, Tyler takes pride in constructing his own identity outside of the traditional "rap game"—"These fucking rappers got stylist, it's cause they can't think for themselves / See, they don't have an identity, so they needed some help."

23. Oosterling, "Philosophy, Art, and Politics as Interesse," p. 36.

24. See Tyler the Creator's Adam Schueler who points out, in a written communication to me on August 20, 2013, that "as the speaking introduction, perceivably by one of Tyler's fans, to Rusty relays, the artist is undeniably much more than an individual making

choices for themselves." This can be highlighted as he iterates, "You go from being a kid, just doing your thing, hanging out with your friends/months later you're world famous/ You're a gay rights activist, and you don't even know it."

25. Henk Oosterling. "Dasein as Design Or: Must Design Save the World?" in Premsla lecture, translated by L. Martz (Spring/ Summer 2009).

Bibliography

Abbas, Basel. "An Analysis of Arabic Hip Hop." Thesis. SAE London, 2005. Accessed September 2013. Available at: http://profheitner-racemediaculture.files.wordpress.com/2009/08/arabic-hip-hop-see-palestinian-chapter.pdf.

Adaso, Henry. "A Brief History of Hip-Hop and Rap." n.d. Accessed September 2013. Available at: http://rap.about.com/od/rootsofrap hiphop/p/RootsOfRap.htm.

Addow, Mohammed. "Nigeria's Dangerous Skin Whitening Obsession." *Al Jazeera.* April 6, 2013. Available at: www.aljazeera.com/indepth/features/2013/04/20134514845907984.html.

Adorno, Theodor. *The Culture Industry: Selected Essays on Mass Culture.* New York: Routledge, 2001.

Adorno, Theodor and Max Horkeimer. *Dialectic of Enlightenment: Philosophical Fragments.* Translated by Edmund Jephcott. Stanford, CA: Stanford University Press, 2007.

Akom, A. A. "Critical Hip-Hop Pedagogy as a Form of Liberatory Praxis." *Equity & Excellence in Education* 42(1) (2009): 52–66.

Aldridge, D. P. "From Civil Rights to Hip Hop: Toward a Nexus of Ideas." *The Journal of African American History* (2005): 226–252.

Alim, H. S. "Critical Language Awareness in the United States: Revisiting Issues and Revising Pedagogies in a Resegregated Society." *Educational Researcher* 34(7) (n.d): 24–31.

———. "Hip Hop Nation Language." In *Linguistic Anthropology: A Reader.* Edited by A. Duranti. Malden, MA: Wiley Blackwell, 2009, pp. 272–289.

———. "On Some Serious Next Millennium Rap Ishhh Pharoahe Monch, Hip Hop Poetics, and the Internal Rhymes of Internal Affairs." *Journal of English Linguistics* 31(1) (March 1, 2003): 60–84. doi:10.1177/0075424202250619.

Alim, H. S., A. Ibrahim, and A. Pennycook. *Global Linguistic Flows: Hip Hop Cultures, Youth Identities, and the Politics of Language.* New York: Routledge, 2009.

Alim, H. S. and A. Pennycook. "Global Linguistic Flows: Hip-Hop Culture(s), Identities, and the Politics of Language Education." *Journal of Language, Identity, and Education* 6(2) 2007: 89–100.

Alonzo, P. *Exhibit: Os Gemeos. Institute of Contemporary Art/Boston. 2012.* Accessed September 28, 2013. Available at: www.icaboston.org /exhibitions/exhibit/os_gemeos.

Alves, L. "Racism and Language." In *The Student Writing Anthology.* Edited by P. Zukowski. Boston, MA: Custom Publishing, 2009.

Anderson, Benedict. *Imagined Communities: Reflections on the Origin and Spread of Nationalism.* New York: Verso Books, 2006.

Arrington Vanessa. "Party or protest? Cuban hip-hop reaches crossroads in its young history *AP News.* 2004. Available at: www.latinamerican-studies.org/cuba/hip-hop-04.htm.

Asante, M. *It's Bigger Than Hip Hop: The Rise of the Post-Hip-Hop Generation.* New York: St. Martin's Press, 2008.

Bailey, Julius. "Hip Hop's Stronghold on 21st Century Philosophical Analysis." *Internation Journal of Africana Studies* Spring (2011): 77–101.

———, ed. *Jay-Z: Essays on Hip Hop's Philosopher-King.* Jefferson, NC: McFarland Press, 2011.

Baker, G. !Hip Hop, Revolución! Nationalizing Rap in Cuba. *Ethnomusicology* 49(3) (2005): 369–402.

Ball, J. "Free Mix Radio: The Original Mixtape Radio Show: A Case Study in Mixtape 'Radio' and Emancipatory Journalism." *Journal of Black Studies* 39(4) (2009): 614–634.

Barker, Earnest. *Politics.* By Aristotle. Revised by Richard Stalley. Oxford: Oxford University Press, 1995, pp. 1252a1–1252a8.

Barthes, Roland. *Image-Music-Text.* Translated by Stephen Heath. New York: Hill and Wang, 1978.

Bell, Melissa. "Common Putting the Controversy in White House Poetry Night." *The Washington Post.* May 11, 2011. Accessed June 2013. Available at: www.washingtonpost.com/blogs/blogpost/post /white-house-poetry-night-whats-your-favorite-poem/2011/05/11 /AFmpVUqG_blog.html.

Benny, Lou. "Dobar Rep." Accessed September 20, 2013. Available at: www.youtube.com/watch?v=DHEmQqgojV0.

———. "Nemoj da stajes." Accessed September 20, 2013. Available at: www.youtube.com/watch?v=9Uv0_Lt1NqA.

Bernal, Martin. *Black Athena: The Afroasiatic Roots of Classical Civilization.* New Brunswick, NJ: Rutgers University Press, 1987.

Bhabha, H. K. "Postcolonial Authority and Postmodern Guilt." In *Cultural Studies.* Edited by L. Glossberg, C. Nelson, and P. Treichler. London: Routledge,1992, pp. 56–68.

Blackalicious. "Ego Trip by Nikki Giovanni." *Nia*. Released by Quannum. February 8, 2000.

———. "Finding." *Nia*. Released by Quannum Projects. February 8, 2000.

———. "Searching." *Nia*. Released by Quannum. February 8, 2000.

Blauner, R. "Internal Colonialism and Ghetto Revolt." *Social Problems* 16 (1969): 393–408.

———. *Racial Oppression in America*. New York: Harper & Row, 1972.

Bloom, Allan. *The Closing of the American Mind*. New York: Simon & Schuster, 1987.

Boas, Franz. "On Alternating Sounds." *American Anthropologist* A2 (1) (1889): 47–54. doi:10.1525/aa.1889.2.1.02a00040.

Bohmer, P. "African-Americans as an Internal Colony: The Theory of Internal Colonialism." In *Readings in Black Political Economy*. Edited by John Whitehead and Cobie Kwasi Harris. Dubuque, IA: Kendall/Hunt, 1999.

Bradley, A. *Book of Rhymes: The Poetics of Hip Hop*. New York: Basic Books, 2009.

Bradley, R. N. "Contextualizing Hip Hop Sonic Cool Pose in Late Twentieth- and Twenty-First Century Rap Music." *Current Musicology* 93 (Spring 2013).

Brown, A. "Drive Slow: Rehearsing Hip Hop Automotivity." *Journal of Popular Music Studies* 24(3) (2012): 265–275. doi:10.1111/j.1533–1598.2012.01333.x.

Brown R. N. and C. J. Kwakye. *Wish to Live: The Hip-Hop Feminism Pedagogy Reader*. New York: Peter Lang Publishing, 2012.

Brown v. Board of Education, 347 U.S. 483.1954. (*Brown et al. v. Board of Education* of Topeka et al. Appeal from the United States District Court for the District of Kansas.) Accessed June 20, 2013. Available at: http://caselaw.lp.findlaw.com/scripts/getcase.pl?court=US&vol=347&invol=483.

Bynoe, Y. "Getting Real about Global Hip-Hop." *Georgetown Journal of International Affairs* 3 (1) (2004): 77–84.

Carmichael, S. and C. V. Hamilton. *Black Power: The Politics of Liberation in America*. New York: Vintage Books, 1967.

Chambers, Iain. "Popular Culture, Popular Knowledge." *One Two Three Four: A Rock and Roll Quarterly* (1989): 1–8.

Chang, Jeff. *Can't Stop Won't Stop: A History of the Hip Hop Generation*. New York: St. Martin's Press, 2005.

———. *Total Chaos: The Art and Aesthetics of Hip-Hop*. New York: Basic Civitas, 2006.

Chomsky, Noam. *Understanding Power*. Edited by Peter R. Mitchell and John Schoeffels. New York: The New Press, 2002.

Clark B. K. and P. M. Clark. "Racial Identification and Preference in Negro Children." In *Readings in Social Psychology*. Edited by T. Newcomb and E. Hartley. New York: Holt, Rinehart & Winston, 1947.

Clapp, N. *The Road to Ubar: Finding the Atlantis of the Sands*. Boston, MA: Houghton Mifflin, 1998.

Cobb, W. *To the Break of Dawn: A Freestyle on the Hip Hop Aesthetic*. New York: NYU Press, 2007.

Condry, I. *Hip-Hop Japan: Rap and the Paths of Cultural Globalization*. Durham, NC: Duke University Press, 2006.

Cooks, J. A. "Writing for Something: Essays, Raps, and Writing Preferences." *English Journal* (2004): 72–76.

Cooper, R. "The Hip Hop Week in Review: DMC Lashes Out at Jay Z & Lil Wyane, Jay Z & Dame Dash Reunite." *HipHop DX*. August 10, 2013. Available at: http://hiphopdx.com/index/news/id.24993/title.the-hip-hop-week-in-review-dmc-lashes-out-at-jay-z-lil-wayne-jay-z-dame-dash-reunite.

Curry, Tommy. *I'm Too Real For Yah: Krumpin' as a Culturalogical Exploration of Black Aesthetic Submergence*. *Radical Philosophy Review* 12 (1–2) (2009): 61–77.

Darby, P. *Africa, Football, and FIFA: Politics, Colonialism, and Resistance*. London, UK: Frank Cass, 2002.

Daudi, Abe. "Hip-hop and the Academic Canon." *Education, Citizenship and Social Justice* 263(4) (2009): 268.

Day, Aidan. *Romanticism*. London and New York: Routledge, 1996.

Dead Prez. "They School." *Let's Get Free*. Released by Loud Records. February 8, 2000.

Debord, Guy. *The Art of The Spectacle*. New York: Zone Books, 1995.

Deleuze, G. and F. Guattari. *Anti-Oedipus: Capitalism and Schizophrenia*. Translated by R. Huxley, M. Seem, and H. R. Lane. Minneapolis: University of Minnesota Press, 2008.

———. *A Thousand Plateaus: Capitalism and Schizophrenia*. Translated by B. Massumi. London and New York: Continuum, 1988.

———. *What Is Philosophy*. Translated by Hugh Tomlinson and Graham Burchell. New York: Columbia University Press, 1994.

Dewey, J. *Experience and Education: The 60th Anniversary Edition*. Indianapolis: Kappa Delta Pi, 1998.

Dimitriadis, G. *Performing Identity/Performing Culture: Hip Hop as Text, Pedagogy, and Lived Practice, Revised Edition*. New York: Peter Lang Publishing Inc., 2009.

Django Paris. "Culturally Sustaining Pedagogy: A Needed Change in Stance, Terminology, and Practice." *Educational Researcher* 41(3) (April 2012): 93–97.

Dolemite. Directed by D'Urville Martin. USA release. July 1, 1975.

Dotson, B. "Expanding the Definition of Hip-Hop Culture." *USC News.* 2007. Accessed June 2013. Available at: www.usc.edu/uscnews/stories /14379.html.

Doumas, C. *Thera: Pompeii of the Ancient Aegean.* London: Thames and Hudson, 1983.

Dubois, W. E. B. "Criteria of Negro Art." *The Crisis* 32 (1926): 290–297.

———. *The Souls of Black Folk.* New York: Dover Thrift Editions, 1994.

During, S. Introduction to *The Cultural Studies Reader, 2nd Edition.* Edited by Simon During. New York: Routledge, 1999, pp. 1–28.

Dweck Carol, S. "Prejudice: How If Develops and How It Can Be Undone." *Human Development* 52 (2009): 371–376.

Dyson, M. E. *Know What I Mean? Reflections on Hip Hop.* Philadelphia, PA: Basic Civitas Books, 2007.

Egyptian Underground. Directed by Nicholas Mangialardi. Accessed June 2013. Available at: www.youtube.com/watch?v=z3dyWczTkSo.

Emdin, C. "Droppin' Science and Dropping Science: African American Males and Urban Science Education." *Journal of African American Males in Education* 2 (2011): 66–80.

———. "Moving beyond the Boat without a Paddle: Reality Pedagogy, Black Youth, and Urban Science Education." *The Journal of Negro Education* 80(3) (2011): 284–295.

———. "Pursuing the Pedagogical Potential of the Pillars of Hip-Hop through Urban Science Education." *The International Journal of Critical Pedagogy* 4(3) (2013): 83–97.

———. "Reality Pedagogy: Hip-Hop Culture and the Urban Science Classroom." In *Science Education from People for People: Taking a Standpoint.* by W. M. Roth. New York: Routledge, 2009, pp. 70–89.

Emdin, C. and Knee Lee. "Hip-Hop, the 'Obama Effect,' and Urban Science Education." *Teachers College Record* 114(2) (2012): 47–68.

Fanon, F. *The Wretched of the Earth.* Translated by Richard Philcox. New York: Grove, 2004.

FBI. "Crime in the United States by Volume and Rate per 100,000 Inhabitants, 1993–2012." *Federal Bureau of Investigations.* Accessed June 2013. Available at: www.fbi.gov/about-us/cjis/ucr/crime-in-the -u.s/2012/crime-in-the-u.s.-2012/tables/1tabledatadecoverviewpdf /table_1_crime_in_the_united_states_by_volume_and_rate _per_100000_inhabitants_1993–2012.xls#overview.

Ferguson, R. James. " Political Realism, Ideology and Power." In *Essays in History, Politics and Culture.* Accessed August 14, 2013. Available at: www.international-relations.com/History/Machiavelli.htm.

Fernandes, S. "Fear of a Black Nation: Local Rappers, Transnational Crossings, and State Power in Contemporary Cuba." *Anthropological Quarterly* 76(4) (2003): 575–608.

Fernandez, A. SBS. "¿Timba con Rap? El hip hop de la polémica." *Revista Salsa Cubana* 5(17) (2002): 43–45.

Fink, B. *The Lacanian Subject*. New Jersey: Princeton University Press, 1996.

Fischer, R. "Danny Brown's Triple Rock Show Sparks Unseemly Oral Sex Controversy." *Gimme Noise*. Accessed April 30, 2013. Available at: http://blogs.citypages.com/gimmenoise/2013/04/danny_browns _triple_rock_show_sparks_oral_sex_controversy.php.

Folami, Akilah, N. "From Habermas to 'Get Rich or Die Trying': Hip Hop, The Telecommunications Act of 1996, and the Black Public Sphere." *Michigan Journal of Race and Law* (2007): 235.

Foucault, M. "What Is an Author?" In *Societe Francais de Philosophie* (1969). Accessed June, 2013. Available at: https://wiki.brown .edu/confluence/download/attachments/74858352/Foucault WhatIsAnAuthor.pdf.

Fox News. "White House Invite of Political Rapper Stirs Controversy." May 10, 2011. Accessed May 11, 2011. Available at: www.foxnews .com/politics/2011/05/10/white-house-invite-political-rapper-stirs -controversy/.

Gallagher, Eugene V. and W. Michael Ashcroft. *History and Controversies: Introduction to New and Alternative Religions in America*. Westport: Praegar Publishing, 2006.

Gana, N. "Rap Rage Revolt." *Jadaliyya*. August 5, 2011. Accessed January 27, 2013. Available at: www.jadaliyya.com/pages/index/2320 /rap-rage-revolt.

Gates, Henry Louis. *The Signifying Monkey: A Theory of African-American Literary Criticism*. Oxford: Oxford University Press, 1989.

Gee, J. P. *Social Linguistics and Literacies: Ideology in Discourses*, 2nd ed. London: Taylor & Francis, (1996).

George, Nelson. *Hip Hop America*. New York: Penguin, 2005.

———. "Hip Hop Founders Speak the Truth." In *That's the Joint*. Edited by Mark Anthony Neal and Murray Forman. New York: Routledge, 2011, pp. 43–56.

Ginwright, Shawn. *Black in School*. New York: Teachers College Press. 2004.

Kandinsky, W. *Concerning the Spiritual in Art*. Mineola, NY: Dover Publications, 1977.

Kirkland, David. "'The Rose That Grew from Concrete': Postmodern Blackness and New English Education." *English Journal* 97(5) (2008): 69–75.

Giroux, Henry, A. and Roger I. Simon. "Schooling, Popular Culture, and a Pedagogy of Possibility." *Journal of Education* 170(1) (1988): 11.

Goffman, Erving. *The Presentation of Self in Everyday Life*. 1st ed. New York: Anchor, 1959.

Habermas, Jurgen. *The Structural Transformation of the Public Sphere: An Enquiry into a Category of Bourgeois Society*. Translated by Thomas Burger. Cambridge: MIT Press, 1991.

Hall, Stuart. "Encoding/Decoding." In *The Cultural Studies Reader*. Edited by Simon during 90–104. London: Routledge, 2007.

Hass Re-Volt. "Interview: Rebel Through Hip Hop" (2011). Accessed June 20, 2013. Available at: http://mashallahnews.com/?p=1640.

Hebdige, Dick. *Subculture: The Meaning of Style*. London: Methuen and Co., 1979.

Hegel, G. W. F. *Introductory Lectures on Aesthetics*. Translated by B. Bosanquet. New York: Penguin, 2004.

———. "Lordship and Bondage." *The Phenomenology of Mind*. Translated by J. B. Baillie. New York: Dover Books, 2003.

Heidegger, Martin. "Nietzsche's Fundamental Metaphysical Position." Translated by David Farrell Krell *Nietzsche*, Vol. 2, Chap. 26, pp. 198–208.

Heinemeier, J., Walter L. Friedrich, and David Warburton, eds., *Time's Up: Dating the Minoan Eruption of Santorini*. Acts of the Minoan Eruption Chronology Workshop, Sandjberg. November 2007. Athens: Danish Institute at Athens, 2009.

Hess, Mickey. "Hip Hop Realness and the White Performer." *Critical Studies in Media Communication* 22(5) (December 1, 2005): 372–389.

Heywood, Linda, and John Tornton. *Central Africans, Atlantic Creoles and the Foundation of the Americas, 1585–1660*. Cambridge: Cambridge University Press, 2007.

Hill, Marc L. "Using Jay-Z to Reflect on Post-9/11 Race Relations." *English Journal* (2006): 23–27.

Hill, Marc L. and Emery Petchauer. *Schooling Hip-Hop: Expanding Hip-Hop Based Education across the Curriculum*. New York: Teachers College Press, 2013.

hooks, bell. "A Revolution of Value." In *The Cultural Studies Reader*, 2nd ed. Edited by Simon During. New York: Routledge, 1999, p. 237.

Ice T. *Something from Nothing: The Art of Hip Hop*. Film documentary. USA release: June 15, 2012.

I Love Hip Hop in Morocco. Directed by Joshua Asen and Jennifer Needleman. 2007.

James, J. "F**k tha Police [State]: Rap, Welfare, and the Leviathan." In *Hip Hop and Philosophy: Rhyme 2 Reason, Popular Culture and Philosophy*, Vol. 16. Edited by Derrick Darby and Tommie Shelby. Illinois: Carus, 2005, 71–76.

Jameson, Frederick. "Postmodernism, or the Cultural Logic of Late Capitalism." In *Media and Cultural Studies Key Works*. Edited by G. Durham and D. M. Kellner. London: Blackwell Publishing, 2006.

Janeaway, C. "Plato." In *Routledge Companion to Aesthetics*. Edited by D. Lopes and B. Gaut. New York: Routledge, 2000.

Jay-Z. *The Black Album*. Roc-a-Fella Records. Released November 14, 2003.

———. (Shawn Carter) *Decoded*. London: Random House, 2010.

———. "Takeover." *The Blueprint*. Roc-a-Fella Records. Released September 11, 2001.

Kahf, Usama. "Arabic Hip Hop: Claims of Authenticity and Identity of a New Genre." *Journal of Popular Music Studies* 19(4) (2007): 359–85.

Kamtekar, H. A. *Companion to Socrates* (Blackwell Companions to Philosophy). Hoboken: Wiley-Blackwell, 2006.

Kant, Immanuel. *Fundamental Principles of the Metaphysics of Morals*. Gutenberg Project, 2004. Accessed June 2013. Available at: www.gutenberg.org/ebooks/5682.

West, Kanye. "Jesus Walks." *College Dropout*. Roc-a-Fella/Def Jam Recordings. February 10, 2004.

———. "Sin City." *Cruel Summer*. Good Music/Def Jam Recordings. September 14, 2012.

Keyes, Cheryl, L. *Rap Music and Street Consciousness*. Champaign, IL: University of Illinois Press, 2004.

Khu, D. "How Os Gêmeos Legitimized Street Art in Brazil." *Understanding the Urban Visual Landscape: The Everywhere Everyday*. December 2010. Accessed June 2013. Available at: http://streetartscene.wordpress.com/2010/12/15/how-os-gemeos-legitimized-street-art-in-brazil/.

Kirkland, David. "'The Rose That Grew from Concrete': Postmodern Blackness and New English Education." *English Journal* 97(5) (2008): 69–75.

Kitwana, Bakari. *The Hip-Hop Generation: Young Blacks and the Crisis in African-American Culture*. New York: Basic Civitas, 2003.

———. *Why White Kids Love Hip Hop: Wankstas, Wiggers, Wannabes, and the New Reality of Race in America*. New York: Basic Civitas, 2006.

K'naan. *The Dusty Foot Philosopher*. Interdependent Media Sony/BMG CD. 2008.

Kopano, B. N. "Rap Music as an Extension of the Black Rhetorical Tradition: 'Keepin' It Real." *Western Journal of Black Studies* 26(4) (2002): 204–214.

Kot, Greg. "Drake Album Review: Take Care Reviewed." *Chicago Tribune*. November 13, 2011.

Krims, Adam. *Rap Music and the Poetics of Identity*. Cambridge: Cambridge University Press, 2000.

"krs One Speaks about Philosophy and the Origins of Hip-Hop." YouTube video, Accessed September 17, 2011. Available at: www.youtube.com/watch?v=SBrlvOmxU6g.

KRS-One. *The Gospel of Hip-hop: The First Instrument.* New York: Powerhouse, 2009.

Lacan, Jacques. *Ecrits: The First Complete Edition in English.* Translated by Bruce Fink. New York: W. W. Norton & Company, 2002.

———. *The Seminar of Jacques Lacan: Freud's Papers on Technique.* Vol. Book I. New York: W. W. Norton & Company, 1991.

Ladson-Billings, G. "Toward a Theory of Culturally Relevant Pedagogy." *American Educational Research Journal* 32 (1995): 465–491.

Lane, Michael. *Introduction to Structuralism.* University of Michigan: Basic Books, 1970.

Leavis, F. R. *The Great Tradition.* New York: George W. Stewart, 1950.

Lee, Carol. "A Culturally Based Cognitive Apprenticeship: Teaching African American High School Students Skills in Literary Interpretation." *Reading Research Quarterly* 30(4) (1995, 2007): 608–631.

———. *The Role of Culture in Academic Literacies: Conducting Our Blooming in the Midst of the Whirlwind.* New York: Teachers College Press, 2007.

LeVine, Mark. *Heavy Metal Islam.* New York: Three Rivers Press, 2008.

Lewis, David, L. *W.E.B. DuBois: A Reader.* New York: Henry Holt & Company, 1995.

Lingon, John. "How Nina Simone and James Brown Mourned MLK Onstage." *The Atlantic.* April 4, 2013. Accessed June, 2013. Available at: www.theatlantic.com/entertainment/archive/2013/04/how-nina-simone-and-james-brown-mourned-mlk-jr-onstage/274605.

Lipsitz, George. "The Hip Hop Hearings: Censorship, Social Memory, and Intergenerational Tensions Among African Americans." In *Generations of Youth: Youth Cultures and History in Twentieth Century America.* New York: New York University Press, 1998, pp. 395–411.

Look to the Stars: The World of Celebrity Giving. Accessed May 15, 2013. Available at: www.looktothestars.org/.

Love, B. L. "Urban Storytelling: How Storyboarding, Moviemaking & Hip Hop-based Education Can Promote Students' Critical Voice." *English Journal* (In Press).

Lusane, C. "Rhapsodic Aspirations: Rap, Race and Power Politics." *The Black Scholar* 23 (1993): 37–51.

Lyotard, Jean-François. *The Inhuman: Reflections on Time.* Translated by Geoffrey Bennington and Rachel Bowlby. Cambridge, UK: Polity Press, 1991.

———. *The Postmodern Condition: A Report on Knowledge.* Translated by Geoff Bennington and Brian Massumi. Minneapolis: University of Minnesota, 1984.

Macklemore and Ryan Lewis. "Same Love." *The Heist.* Seattle: Macklemore LLC, 2012.

Malone, Christopher, and George Martinez. "The Organic Globalizer: The Political Development of Hip-Hop and the Prospects for Global Transformation." *New Political Science* 32 (4) (December 2010): 531–545. doi:10.1080/07393148.2010.520439.

Mangialardi, Nicholas. "Egyptian Hip Hop and the January 25th Revolution." Thesis. The Ohio State University, 2013.

Marklein, Mary Beth. "Test Scores Flat, Raising Concerns About Students' Readiness." *USA Today*. September 26, 2013. Accessed September 2013. Available at: www.usatoday.com/story/news/nation/2013/09/26/high-school-sat-scores-flat-for-college/2873633.

Marrati, Paola. *Gilles Deleuze: Cinema and Philosophy*. Translated by Alisa Hartz. Baltimore, MD: The John Hopkins University Press, 2003.

McCarthy, Timothy, G. *The Catholic Tradition: The Church in the Twentieth Century*. Chicago, IL: Loyola Press, 1998.

McLeod, K. "Authenticity Within Hip-hop and Other Cultures Threatened with Assimilation." *Journal of Communication* 49 (4) (1999): 134–150.

McLuhan, Marshall. "The Medium Is the Message." In *Media and Cultural Studies Key Works*. Edited by G. Durham and L. M. Kellner. London: Blackwell Publishing, 2006.

McGuire W. J., D. B. Griffiths, P. L. Hancock, and I. S. Stewart. eds., *The Archaeology of Geological Catastrophes*. London: Geological Society, 2000

McWhorter, John. "How Hip-hop Holds Blacks Back." *The City Journal*. Summer 2003. Accessed June 2013. Available at: www.city-journal.org/html/13_3_how_hip_hop.html.

Metz, Johannes, Baptist and James Matthew Ashley. *A Passion for God: The Mystical-Political Dimension of Christianity*. New York: Paulist Press, 1989. Available at: http://books.google.com/books?id=C7lqBAqnQHcC&pg=PA8.

Microphone. Directed by Ahmad Abdalla. Released September 14, 2010.

Millen, Jessica. "Romantic Creativity and the Ideal of Originality: A Contextual Analysis." *Cross-Sections, The Bruce Hall Academic Journal* VI (2010): 91–104.

Mitchell, A. and A. Pennycook. *Hip Hop as Dusty Foot Philosophy: Engaging Locality*. New York: Routledge, 2009.

Morgan, M. and D. Bennett. "Hip Hop and the Global Imprint of a Black Cultural Form." *American Academy of Arts & Sciences* (2011): 176–196.

Morrell, E. "Toward a Critical Pedagogy of Popular Culture." *Journal of Adolescent and Adult Literacy* 46(1) (2002): 72–73.

Morrell, E. and J. Duncan-Andrade. "Toward a Critical Classroom Discourse: Promoting Academic Literacy Through Engaging Hip-Hop Culture with Urban Youth." *English Journal* 91(6) (2002): 88–92.

Morris, David. "The Sakura of Madness: Japanese Right-Wing Hip Hop and the Parallax of Global Identity Politics." *Communication, Culture & Critique,* 6 (3) (2013): 459–480..

Muller, John P. and William J. Richardson. *The Purloined Poe: Lacan, Derrida, and Psychoanalytic Reading. 4th Printing.* Baltimore, MD: The Johns Hopkins University Press, 1987.

Murrell, M. "This Is Real Hip Hop: Hip Hop's Rejection of Paul Butler's Theory of Justice in Let's Get Free." *The Georgetown Law Journal* (2011): 1179–1225.

Niebuhr, R. *Moral man and Immoral Society: A Study of Ethics and Politics.* Westminster: John Knox Press, 2002.

Nietzsche, Friedrich. *The Antichrist.* Mineola: NY. Tribeca Books, 2010.

———. *The Gay Science.* Translated by Walter Kaufman. New York: Vintage, 1974.

———. "Twilight of the Idols," in *Portable Nietzsche.* Translated by Walter Kaufman. New York: Random House, 1966, aph. 24.

Nkrumah, K. *Neo-Colonialism: The Last Stage of Imperialism.* New York: International Publishers, 1965.

Ntangwari, M. *East African Hip Hop: Youth Culture and Globalization.* Champaign: University of Illinois Press, 2009.

N.W.A. "Express Yourself." *Straight Outta Compton.* Priority/Ruthless. Released October 7,1988.

Ogbar, Jeffrey, O. G. *Hip-Hop Revolution: The Culture and Politics of Rap.* Lawrence: University Press of Kansas, 2007.

Oosterling, Henk. "Dasein as Design Or: Must Design Save the World?" In Premsela lecture. Translated by Laura Martz (Spring/Summer, 2009).

———. "Philosophy, Art, and Politics as Interesse." In *Issues in Contemporary Culture and Aesthetics.* Maastricht: Department of Theory, Jan van Eyck Akademie, 1999.

———. "Sens(a)bleIntermediality and Inter-esse: Towards an Ontology of the In-Between." In *Intermedialities* Number 1. Montreal: Montreal University, 1999.

Palast, G. *The Best Democracy Money Can Buy: An Investigative Reporter Exposes the Truth about Globalization, Corporate Cons, and High-Finance Fraudsters.* Sterling, VA: Pluto Press, 2002.

Parmar, Priya. *Knowledge Reigns Supreme: The Critical Pedagogy of Hip-Hop Artist Krs-One.* Rotterdam, The Netherlands: Sense Publishers, 2009.

"Party Or Protest? Cuban Hip-Hop at Crossroads." *NBC News.* October 4, 2004. Accessed May 2013. Available at: www.today.com/id/6173947 /ns/today-today_entertainment/t/party-or-protest-cuban -hip-hop-crossroads/#.Ujvn5cYkJ8E.

Peters, J. D. *Speaking into the Air: A History of the Idea of Communication.* Chicago: University of Chicago Press. 2001

Perrone, Pierre. "Camouflage: A Gangster Rapper in Search of a 'Universal Language.'" *The Independent.* May 24, 2003. Available at: www.independent.co.uk/news/obituaries/camoflauge-730322.html.

Perry, Imani. *Prophets of the Hood: Politics and Poetics in Hip Hop.* Durham, NC: Duke University Press, 2004.

Perry, M. "Global Black Self Fashionings: Hip Hop as Diasporic Space." *Identities: Global Studies in Culture and Power* 15(6) (2008): 635–664.

Perullo, A. "Hooligans and Heroes: Youth Identity and Hip-Hop in Dar es Salaam, Tanzania," *AfricaToday* 51(4) (2005): 75–101.

Petchauer, Emery. "Framing and Reviewing Hip-Hop Educational Research." Review of Educational Research 79(2) (2009): 946–970.

———. *Hip Hop in College Students' Lives.* New York: Routledge, 2012.

Pittman, John P. "Y'all Niggaz Better Recognize: Hip Hop's Dialectical Struggle for Recognition." In *Hip-Hop and Philosophy: Rhyme 2 Reason.* Edited by Derrick Darby, Tommie Shelby, and William Irwin. Peru, IL: Carus, 2005, 41–54.

Posner, R. "Post-Modernism, Post-Structuralism, Post-Semiotics? Sign Theory at the Fin De Siècle" *Semiotica* 183 (March 2011): 9–30. Accessed June 2013. doi: 10.1515/semi.2011.002.

Pritchard, G. "Cultural Imperialism, Americanization and Cape Town Hip-Hop Culture: A Discussion Piece." *Social Dynamics: A Journal of African Studies* 35(1) (2009): 51–55.

Pyle, Forest. *The Ideology of Imagination: Subject and Society in the Discourse of Romanticism.* Stanford, CA: Stanford University Press, 1995.

Pryde, Kitty. "My Thoughts on This Whole Danny Brown Oral Sex Thing | NOISEY." May 1, 2013. Accessed June 2013. Available at: http://noisey.vice.com/blog/my-thoughts-on-this-whole-danny-brown-oral-sex-thing.

Rahner, Karl. *Spiritual Exercises.* Translated by Kenneth Baker. New York: Herder and Herder, 1965.

Ravitch Diane. *The Death and Life of the Great American School System.* New York: Basic, 2010.

———. *The Reign of Error.* New York: Knoff, 2013.

Reid, Shaheem. "Rick Ross Reaffirms Gangster Past in New Freestyle, Despite Report That He Worked as Prison Guard." *MTV News.* July 22, 2008. Accessed August 5, 2008. Available at: www.mtv.com/news/articles/1591284/rick-ross-denies-reports-prison-guard-past.jhtml.

Reid, Shaheem and Jayson Rodriguez. "Donda West, Noted Scholar and Kanye's Mother, Dies at 58—Music, Celebrity, Artist News | MTV.com." *MTV News.* November 12, 2007. Accessed June 2, 2013.

Available at: www.mtv.com/news/articles/1573999/donda-west -noted-scholar-kanyes-mother-dies.jhtml.

Richardson, E. *Hip Hop Literacies*. New York: Routledge, 2006.

Richardson, Jeanita W. and Kim A. Scott. "Rap Music and Its Violent Progeny: America's Culture of Violence in Context." *Journal of Negro Education* 71(3) (2002): 175–192. doi:10.2307/3211235.

Rose, Tricia. *Black Noise: Rap Music and Black Culture in Contemporary America*. Middleton, CT: Wesleyan, 1994.

Roth W. M., ed. *Science Education from People for People: Taking a Standpoint*. New York: Routledge, 2009.

Russell, Bertrand. *History of Western Philosophy*. London: George Allen & Unwin, 1962.

Sapir, Edward. "The Status of Linguistics as a Science." *Language* 5(4) (December) (1929): 207–214.

San Roman, G. "I MiX What I Like! An Interview with Jared Ball (Parts I-II)." *OC Weekly*. June 2011. Accessed August 2011. Available at: http://blogs.ocweekly.com/heardmentality/2011/06/i_mix_what _i_like_an_interview.php.

Sarmast, Robert. *Discovery of Atlantis: The Startling Case for the Island of Cyprus*. San Rafael, CA: Origin Press, 2004.

Sartre, Jean Paul. "The Black Orpheus." Translated by John MacCombie. *The Massachussets Review* 6(1) (1965).

Saussure, Ferdinand de and Roy Harris. *Course in General Linguistics*. Reprint. LaSalle, IL: Open Court. 1998.

Scott, Jonathan. "Sublimating Hiphop: Rap Music in White America." *Socialism & Democracy* 18(2) (2004): 135–155. Academic Search Complete. Accessed December 4, 2012. Available at: http://blog .richmond.edu/rapmusic/2012/12/04/white-vs-hip-hop/.

"Screw Rick Ross." *The Smoking Gun*. July 21, 2008. Available at: www .thesmokinggun.com/documents/crime/screw-rick-ross.

Segvic, Heda. *From Protagoras to Aristotle: Essays in Ancient Moral Philosophy*. Princeton, NJ: Princeton University Press, 2006.

Shamontiel. "Hip-Hop Pioneers and the History of Rap Music: The Medias Con on Hip-Hop Icons." *Yahoo! Contributor Network*. n.d. Available at: http://the-spinzone.blogspot.com/2007/08/hip-hop -pioneers-history-of-rap-music.html Accessed on February 10, 2014.

Shapiro, Peter. *Rough Guide to Hip Hop*. 2nd ed. London: Rough Guides, 2005.

Shusterman, Richard. "Rap Aesthetics: Violence and the Art of Keeping It Real." In *Hip-Hop and Philosophy: Rhyme 2 Reason*. Chicago/La Salle: Open Court Publishing, 2005.

Slingshot Hip Hop. Directed by Jackie Salloum. Released January 18, 2008.

Smith, Allen, N. "No One Has a Right to His Own Language." *CCC* 27(2) (1976): 155.

Smitherman, Geneva. *Talkin That Talk: Language, Culture, and Education in African America*. London: Routledge, 2001.

Sorett, Josef. "Singing in My Soul: Black Gospel Music in a Secular Age; the Holy Profane: Religion in Black Popular Music." *Pneuma* 29 (1) (2007): 164–166.

Sorett, J. "Hip-Hop Religion and Spiritual Sampling in a 'Post-Racial' Age." *Religion Dispatches* March 24, 2010.

Southern, Eileen. *The Music of Black Americans* 2nd ed. New York: WW Norton & Company, 1997.

St. Augustine. *The City of God*. Edited by G. Walsh and G. Monahan. New York: Image Books, 1950.

———. *City of God*. London: T&T Clark Publishing Co., 1888.

———. *Confessions*. Mineola, NY: Dover Publications Inc., 2002.

Stovall, David. "We Can Relate: Hip-Hop Culture, Critical Pedagogy and the Secondary Classroom." *Urban Education* 41(6) (2006): 585–602.

Strong, James. *The New Strong's Expanded Exhaustive Concordance of the Bible*. Nashville, TN: Thomas Nelson, 2010.

Sykes, Charles, J. *Dumbing Down Our Kids: Why America's Children Feel Good about Themselves But Can't Read, Write, Or Add*. New York: St. Martin's Griffin, 1995.

Taub, Liba. *Ancient Meterology*. London: Routledge, 2003.

Tate, Greg. "Hiphop Turns 30: Whacha Celebratin' For?" *The New York Village Voice*. December 28, 2004. Accessed September 19, 2013. Available at: www.villagevoice.com/2004–12–28/news/hiphop -turns-30/.

Terkourafi, Marina. *The Languages of Global Hip-hop*. London: Continuum, 2010.

The Notorious B.I.G. "Mo Money Mo Problems." *Life after Death*. Bad Boy Records. July 21,1997.

Thomas, Anthony. "The Spirit and Philosophy of Hip-hop." *The New Statesman*. September 12, 2007. Available at: www.newstatesman .com/blogs/the-faith-column/2007/09/hip-hop-movements -thought.

Thompson, Cheryl. "Standing in the Shadows of America: Afro-Diasporic Oral Culture and the Emancipation of Canadian Hip-Hop." *Canadian Theatre Review* (130) (2007): 113–116.

Thorpe, David. "Chuck D." *Bomb* 68 (Summer 1999). Accessed November 15, 2013. Available at: http://bombsite.com/issues/68 /articles/2251.

Tickner, A. B. "Aquí en el Ghetto: Hip-Hop in Colombia, Cuba, and Mexico." *Latin American Politics and Society* 50(3) (2008): 121–146.

Tillich, Paul. *Love, Power, and Justice: Ontological Analyses and Ethical Applications*. New York: Oxford University Press, 1960.

Trevino, James, ed. *Goffman's Legacy*. Oxford: Rowman and Littlefield, 2003.

Urichio, W. "The Batman's Gotham City (TM): Story, Ideology, Performance." In *Comics and the City: Urban Space in Print, Picture and Sequence*. Edited by Jorn Ahrens and Arno Meteling. Maiden Lane, NY: The Continuum International Publishing Group Inc., 2010.

Utley, E. A. *Rap and Religion: Understanding the Gangsta's God*. Santa Barbara: Praeger, 2012.

Vourlias, Christopher. "Pidgin English Helps Rappers' Musical Fly." *Variety* 422(3) (February 28, 2011): 3.

Waterhouse, Francis. "Romantic 'Originality.'" *The Sewanee Review* 34(1) (January) (1926): 40–49.

Watkins-Owens, Irma. *Blood Relations: Caribbean Immigrants and the Harlem Community, 1900–1930*. Bloomington: Indiana University Press, 1996.

Wimsatt, William. *Bomb the Suburbs*. Berkely, CA: Soft Skull Press, 1999.

Wilkerson, Isabel. *The Warmth of Other Suns: The Epic Story of America's Great Migration*. Brilliance Audio on CD Unabridged edition, August 20, 2013.

Williams, Raymond. *Keywords: A Vocabulary of Culture and Society*. New York: Oxford University Press, 1976.

Yankson, Michelle. "Interview with Bakari Kitwana: Explaining White Hip-Hop Fans." *The Michigan Daily*. February 6, 2008.

Young, Vershawn Ashanti. "Nah, We Straight: An Argument against Code Switching." *JAC* 29(1) (2009): 63–65.

Zizek, Slavoj. *Less than Nothing: Hegel and the Shadow of Dialectical Materialism*. New York: Verso, 2012.

Index

CPSIA information can be obtained
at www.ICGtesting.com
Printed in the USA
LVHW081744310721
694234LV00023B/2271